HOW YOUR GUITAR WORKS

This work is dedicated to everyone who loves guitars.

How Your Guitar Works

An Introduction to Music Instrument Science

Bill Foley

c 2023 Bill Foley
All rights reserved
ISBN: 979-8-35092-236-3
First Edition, First Printing,
Library of Congress Control Number: 2023914068
Book Design by Varin Acevedo
Illustrations by Varin Acevedo and Brad Lewis

GVM Publishing
Columbus, Ohio

INTRODUCTION

"Study hard what interests you the most in the most undisciplined, irreverent and original manner possible."

Richard Feynman

Sometime in 1984, my beautiful wife informed me she was carrying our second child. It was right about then I realized the world was probably ready for a how-to guide for do-it-yourself guitar assembly.

I had been contemplating such a project for a few years. The early '80s had seen guitar necks and bodies, pickups and bridges, and everything needed to build a guitar enter the marketplace. It was finally becoming possible to build your own electric guitar. Then the book's title occurred to me. Build Your Own Electric Guitar, ISBN 0-9618361-0-5, was published in 1986, and by 1990, I was thinking about a second edition with updates, but I had another idea. And another child.

What if luthiery were to become a branch of science? Music instrument science? String division? What if someone who wanted to learn to service and build guitars could go to a university and study the physics, history, and technique of this craft and earn an accredited degree in this field? Wouldn't that be fun!

I couldn't and still can't start a university program, but I could and still can write a book and hopefully get a conversation started in that direction. The historic record shows luthiery being treated as a serious academic subject from the time of Pythagoras up to the dawn of the dark ages. Maybe it's time to catch up with the rest of the scientific community. So began a thirty-plus-year project to bring this work to completion.

There is a lot of applied science in use in contemporary instrument manufacture and repair, but for the field as a whole there is barely a name, let alone any unification. Music instrument science, as a general term, says it all: the science of musical instruments. But it could use a little hype.

I made an acronym, the ALE (Analyze Listen Experiment) standard, to serve as a theme song of sorts for the practice of music instrument science. It's not a standard in the scientific sense, but it does contain the signature parameter that sets this branch of study apart from everything else.

The scientific method most commonly begins with an observation of some sort of phenomena. The observer makes a hypothesis about the phenomena and performs some tests to validate and refine the hypothesis. Then the observer shares this information with a peer group, who examines and performs its own tests to prove, disprove, or improve the hypothesis. The common body of knowledge advances in this manner.

Music instrument science should be conducted similarly, but in the field of music the end results must make some sort of difference that can be heard. If we can't hear it, it's not music, right? This sets some conditions on the equations.

I have some suggestions:

1. The final form of the hypothesis should be expressed mathematically. Math speaks across generations. Words are great, but their meanings shift with ideologies, cultures, political trends, and old age. Numbers aren't as susceptible to semantic skewing. This is the A, or Analysis, part of the ALE standard.
2. The end product of the range and domain of these equations must fall within the

human audible frequency spectrum. We can't hear magnetic flux pushing free electrons through a wire, but we can hear that phenomenon after it is amplified. This kind of data fits in music instrument science. The universe is full of activities that have no demonstrable effect on anything we can hear, such as the velocity of light or water pressure. While scientific knowledge about these events is valuable, these phenomena fall outside our immediate range of interest until they are demonstrated to be useful in a musical instrument. This is the L, or Listening, part of the ALE standard, which determines the boundary conditions, so to speak, for our work.

3. After a hypothesis is formatted into an equation, a bench test, or Experiment, should be performed. This is the E, or Experiment, part of the ALE standard.

The ALE standard isn't anything novel to scientific method, but it can serve as a helpful focal point.

Creating and working with musical string instruments in this manner requires a working knowledge of wave behavior.

Paraphrasing Newton's observations from 1687, we can infer this: (1) forces are always in motion, and (2) they only react to other forces. The interacting forces in a string instrument that give rise to the sounds we can hear operate as waves. These interacting forces make for a good platform for building observations, and the wave function makes for a good perspective for hypothesis creation.

This book, then, begins with a look at the rudiments of wave motion. A vibrating string, conveniently enough, provides a great mechanical study of both transverse and longitudinal wave behavior.

Next, a brief evolutionary history of the guitar spanning from roughly fifteen thousand years ago to the present is presented, with emphasis on the development of the key components found in contemporary instruments.

The focus then moves to the two primary force exchange structures of the guitar: the nut and the bridge, and their associated substructures, the headstock, neck, and body.

The mechanical wave motion is converted into an electrical signal at some point, which is detailed in magnetism, electricity, pickup design, and circuit components. This is followed by a wiring diagram section featuring an easy-to-understand coding system that will help in the visualization of most guitar circuits.

There's also a reference section at the end of the book that includes a math review area with systems of units in scientific and engineering notation, tips for faster calculations, tables of symbols and abbreviations, conversion tables, and test results from some of my own research.

If you're ready, I hope you'll join this nonfiction adventure with me. You can be the protagonist with endless guitars in need of improvement, the universe will be the antagonist doing everything possible to stop you, and the stakes are higher than just bad sounding guitars. We, as a species, must ultimately outsmart the universe if we are to avoid extinction, and this means we need to advance our knowledge base and standards in all areas including my favorite, music instrument science.

I think the process will go better if there are lots of great guitars available to everyone. And there is our challenge.

BF 2023

Table of Contents

Introduction..IV

CHAPTER ONE..1
INTRODUCTION TO WAVE MOTION

CHAPTER TWO..14
THE DEVELOPMENT OF THE GUITAR

CHAPTER THREE..22
GUITARS PARTS AND THEIR FUNCTIONS
    The Nut and Headstock..23
    The Neck and Fingerboard..37
    Musical Considerations..38
    Structural Considerations...42
    The Bridge Assembly...45
    The Body..47

CHAPTER FOUR..51
MAGNETISM
    The History and Discovery of Use...................................51
    Part I 600 BCE to 1900 CE..51
    Part II The Quantum Era 1900 CE to Present...................51
    Basic Magnet Characteristics...53
    Demagnetization...58
    Demagnetizing Effects on Pickups..................................60
    Magnet Stability..61
    Magnetic Circuits..61
    Magnetic Fields and String Movement...........................63

CHAPTER FIVE..67
ELECTRICITY
    The History of Discovery:
    The Quest for the Electron...67
    Basic Conceps..69
    Resistance..71

Table of Contents

    Resistance Combinations 72
    DC and AC 73
    DC and AC Combintions 73
    Capacitance, Inductance, and Impedance 74
    Capacitance 74
    Capacitive Current 77
    Capacitors in Series and Parallel 78
    Inductors 78
    Resonance 80

CHAPTER SIX 83
PICKUP DESIGN
    The Early Designs 1931-1942 85
    The Golden Age 1950-1970 90
    The 70's, 80's and 90's 103

CHAPTER SEVEN 112
GUITAR CIRCUIT COMPONENTS
    Switches 112
    Potentiometers 113
    Resistors 114
    Capacitors 116
    Inductors 117
    Connectors 118
    Wire 120

CHAPTER EIGHT 122
CIRCUIT DIAGRAMS AND ORGANIZATION

EPILOGUE 130

APPENDIX 132

INDEX 145

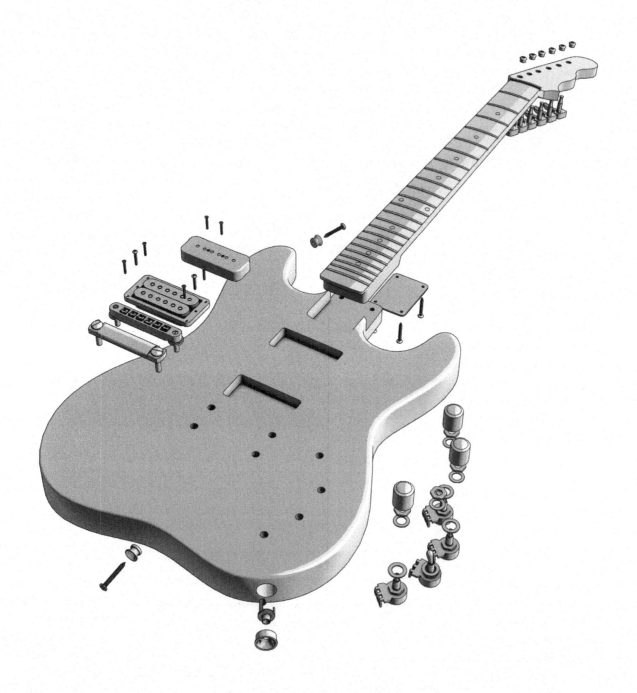

Chapter One
Introduction to Wave Motion

We are all familiar with wave motion to some extent. Waves can be detected in just about every aspect of the universe we examine, from quantum to galactic levels. Wave function relevant to the propagation of sound should be of particular interest to us.

Looking at a wave in water tells us visually that there is a repeating or oscillating motion associated with this phenomenon. If you have ever been upended by a large wave at the beach, then you will know firsthand that the wave also transports energy through a medium. Let's look at the features of a wave.

Over three centuries ago, on July 5, 1687, Isaac Newton's fundamental observations on interacting forces were first published. In his *Philosophiae Naturalis Principia Mathematica* (Mathematical Principles of Natural Philosophy), now commonly referred to as the Principia, Newton introduced his three laws of motion. The three laws, which became the foundation for classical mechanics, describe the relationships between an object in motion and its associated interacting forces.

From Cohen and Whitman's 1999 translation of the Principia's original Latin:

Law 1.) Every body perseveres in its state of being at rest or of moving uniformly straight forward, except insofar as it is compelled to change its state by force impressed. In today's language, the first law states that an object at rest stays at rest and an object in motion stays in an unchanging state of motion unless it is acted upon by an external force. This law is also known as the *law of inertia*.

From Motte's 1729 translation of the Principia:

Law 2.) The alteration of motion is ever proportional to the motive force impressed and is made in the direction of the right line in which that force is impressed.

Newton's concept of *motion* is read to be momentum, or mass times velocity, and *motive force* is read as impulse, or the intensity of force applied over a period of time. Thus, a contemporary reading of the second law states that an object's rate of change of momentum is proportional to the interfering force and is in the same direction as the impulse.

The differential expression of this concept becomes

$$F = d(mv)/dt$$

or force equals the change of momentum with the change of time.
When the mass becomes a constant, this relationship becomes the more commonly found

$$F = ma$$

or force equals mass times acceleration. Note that the acceleration of an object is proportional to the interfering force, and inversely proportional to the mass of the object, and in the same direction as the interfering force.
The second law can be called the *law of force proportional acceleration*.
Law 3.) To every action there is always opposed an equal reaction: or the mutual actions of two bodies upon each other are always equal and directed to contrary parts. This is commonly read as, for every interfering force, there is an equal, opposing reaction force.
The third law can be called the *law of reciprocal forces*.

If we transpose Newton's observations into guitarspeak, we can say that forces in the universe, which includes our guitars, only react to other forces. The tone of a guitar is therefore a function of all the interacting forces at play in the instrument. And these forces propagate in waveform.

The fundamental wave is characterized by an oscillation around a reference point and a transfer of energy. Let's look at this integral phenomenon in the context of the production of a note on a guitar string.

Imagine an idealized form of a string, one that has a uniform density all along its length, one that can only move in one dimension (like across the surface of a flat piece of paper), and one that is stretched taut by a force that pulls equally from either end. We can start the string motion by plucking it gently. A segment of the string will become stretched away from its stationary position by the displacing force of your finger or pick. As you remove the starting force, the original tension on the string will begin working to restore the string to its original state. The segment you stretched will begin pulling itself back to its original position, but as it does so, it will develop inertia, overshoot the starting position, and travel to a point in space approximately opposite the point where you released the starting force. This interaction between displacing and restoring forces will not only continue at this point for a while, but it will begin to travel, or propagate, along the length of the string on either side of the initial disturbance.

If we slow down time and look at this disturbance, we will observe a pattern consisting of a rounded top rising to a peak followed by a rounded bottom dropping to a symmetrically matched valley. This pattern will repeat itself and travel away in either direction from the point of origin. This elementary *transverse wave*, whose constituent particle motion is perpendicular to the direction of wave travel, is said to be *oscillating*. The time, t, it takes for the wave to complete one full cycle of the up and down motion is called a *period*. This time property is described in *frequency*, which is the number of periods the wave completes in one second.

$$f = 1/t \qquad (1.1)$$

Frequency, then, can be expressed mathematically as the reciprocal of time, or the period. The unit of measurement of frequency, or cycles of oscillation per second, is called *hertz* and is abbreviated to *Hz*.

The maximum displacement the oscillation achieves is called the *amplitude*. This is the farthest distance the string gets away from its original, undisturbed position. This is a measurement of vertical displacement on the y axis of a typical graph.

A *wavelength* is a measurement of one complete cycle of the wave, gauged from any two matching points on the waveform. The two matching points are said to be in *phase* with each other when they are exactly one wavelength apart. Wavelength is a measurement of horizontal displacement on the x axis of a typical graph.

The speed that the wave maintains across one wavelength in one period of time can be represented as

$$v = f\lambda \qquad (1.2)$$

or, since $f = 1/t$, then $v = \lambda (1/t)$, or

$$v = \lambda/t \qquad (1.3)$$

where v is wave velocity and λ is wavelength.

At this point, we have some terminology to describe this elementary *traveling wave*. So, instead of saying there's a curly q hightailing it into eternity, we can somewhat more accurately say there's a transverse wave propagating along the length of string. We can refine our description, however. We now have synonyms for the wave unit, period, and cycle. We also have terminology for the wave unit's vertical and horizontal dimensions, amplitude, and wavelength. We have a time measurement called frequency whose unit is the hertz. We've even organized a relationship describing the velocity of the traveling wave as a function of frequency and wavelength.

Let's take another string in conditions identical to the previous one, except this time the string will not extend into the nether regions of infinity. This string will have a specific length, and both ends of the string will be secured to fixed, unmoving points. Although not as idealized as the first, this example will begin to resemble the conditions existing on guitars, basses, and most common string instruments.

This time, when the string is plucked, waves propagate to the left and right of the starting point. These transverse waves travel along the length of the string to the fixed positions at either end, where they reflect at the *boundary points*. The reflected waves then travel back along the string length until they meet and interact, where a realignment of the waveforms occurs. The passing wavelengths that are close to or completely out of phase with one another cancel each other. This is called *destructive interference*. The passing waveforms that are close to or completely in phase with one another reinforce each other. This is called *constructive interference*. The wavelengths that fall between the extremes are subject to *intermediate interference* and are pushed either into

THE GREEK ALPHABET

A	α	Alpha	N	ν	Nu
B	β	Beta	Ξ	ξ	Xi
Γ	γ	Gamma	O	o	Omicron
Δ	δ	Delta	Π	π	Pi
E	ε	Epsilon	P	ρ	Rho
Z	ζ	Zeta	Σ	σ	Sigma
H	η	Eta	T	τ	Tau
Θ	θ	Theta	Y	υ	Upsilon
I	ι	Iota	Φ	φ	Phi
K	κ	Kappa	X	χ	Chi
Λ	λ	Lambda	Ψ	ψ	Psi
M	μ	Mu	Ω	ω	Omega

Figure 1.1 Greek Alphabet

cancellation or reinforcement. The waveforms that develop from the interactions of these traveling waves are called *standing waves*, and these form the basic elements of tone.

Let's look more closely at these standing waves.

Standing waves on a bounded idealized string will always organize themselves into a symmetrical grouping of half-wavelengths. It may seem counterintuitive to regard all the wavelengths as a bunch of halves, but let's look at them from a perspective of *nodes* and *antinodes*. A node is a point of no transverse motion; an antinode is a point of maximum transverse motion. Each complete wavelength, then, will have a node at either end and one at its center, for a total of three, and an antinode at its most extreme distance above and below the plane of the nodes, for a total of two. The longest possible standing wave on a string will be one that has a node at each bounded end and an antinode at the center of its length. Since this movement forms only half of a complete wavelength, the actual wavelength is equal to twice the length of the string. This relationship can be summarized by

$$\lambda = 2l/h_n \qquad (1.4)$$

where λ is the wavelength, l is the vibrating length of string, and h_n is the harmonic. This primary wavelength has two commonly used names: the fundamental tone, and the first harmonic. The fundamental tone, or first harmonic, thus becomes

$$\lambda = 2l/h_1 \qquad (1.4a)$$

or, for h_1, $\lambda = 2l/1 = 2l$ and $l = \lambda/2$.

The second longest standing wave on this same string will be shaped by a node at either boundary and a node at its mid-length and two mirroring antinodes. The horizontal S shape of this standing wave is the classic symbol used to describe wave motion in general and is also known as a *sinusoidal wave*. This motion's wavelength is the same as the string's vibrating length and can be represented by

$$\lambda = 2l/h_2 \qquad (1.4b)$$

or, for h_2, $\lambda = 2l/2 = l$ and $l = \lambda$.

This is called the first overtone or second harmonic.

The third longest standing wave is formed from three half-wavelengths, which will have four points of no motion and three points of maximum motion. Thus,

$$\lambda = 2l/h_3 \qquad (1.4c)$$

or, for h_3, $\lambda = 2l/3$ and $l = 3\lambda/2$.

This is called the second overtone or third harmonic.

The fourth longest standing wave is one of four half-wavelengths on this same string, which becomes

$$\lambda = 2l/h_4 \qquad (1.4d)$$

or, for h_4, $\lambda = 2l/4 = l/2$ and $l = 2\lambda$.

This is called the third overtone or fourth harmonic.

This overtone, or harmonic series, will continue this sequence of divisions all the way down to quantum levels on an idealized string. On a real string, the divisions will be limited by the physical parameters of the mechanical construction and the extent of the elasticity of the mechanical construction of the string. The ALE standard will limit the number of divisions to those we can audibly perceive.

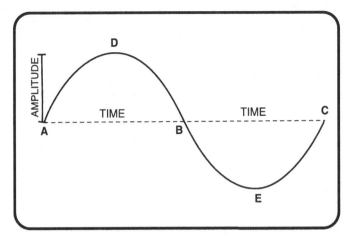

Figure 1.2 Sine Wave

Distances AB and BC are half Wavelengths
Distance AC is a whole Wavelength
Points A, B, C are Nodes
Points D, E are Antinodes
Antinode D is a Crest
Antinode E is a Trough

I've used both overtone and harmonic series terminologies to illustrate this aspect of wave composition. The overtone series perspective has traditionally been used in a musical context, whereas the harmonic series is more commonly found in analytical treatments. Both terminologies are describing the same phenomena, and either may be used, but it's like using metric and SAE measurements. Always be sure your conversions are accurate.

Up to this point, we have a good generalization of the order in which transverse waves establish themselves on a tensioned string with two fixed position ends, such as we'd find on a typical string instrument. Now let's refine our look at string motion a bit further to include the three factors that determine the actual pitch at which a string will vibrate.

The first of these factors is the averaged density of the string or mass per unit of length, m/l. This is commonly referred to as the linear mass density, μ.

The second of these factors is the vibrating string length, l. On a guitar the bounded string length could be between the nut and the saddle or between the fret and the saddle.

The third factor is the force, or tension, T, applied across the length of the string. The wave velocity, v, is related to the tension and linear mass density, μ, by

$$v = (T/\mu)^{1/2} \qquad (1.5)$$

Recalling Equation 1.2, $v = f\lambda$, we can see that frequency is equal to the wave velocity per wavelength, or,

$$f = v/\lambda \qquad (1.2)$$

The frequency, then, for any overtone/harmonic can be determined by

$$f_n = n/2l \, (T/\mu)^{1/2} = nv/2l \qquad (1.6)$$

For a fun exercise, grab a calculator and some scratch paper, and let's plug some numbers into Equation 1.6. Keep the value of n at 1 to arrive at the fundamental/first harmonic, and keep the l value at some constant, such as 5. In the first group of exercises, keep the μ value constant as well, and start it at 4. Start the value of the tension, T, at 100, and solve. Increase the value of T by double and solve again, then repeat this process a few times. You will notice the value of the frequency increases as the value of the tension increases.

Next, hold the first group of variables to a constant again, except this time hold the tension, T, constant, and increase the value of the mass density, μ. Double the value of μ and solve, and repeat this process a few times. You will notice that the frequency decreases as the value of the mass density increases.

This equation provides some insights into the nature of string behavior. The first solution illustrates something we all become familiar with the first time we tune a guitar: as the tension on the string increases, the pitch of the string increases. The second solution illustrates a characteristic equally familiar: as strings become progressively thicker, the pitches they can produce will become progressively lower.

At this point we have assimilated the information that describes the elemental framework of the tone that a vibrating string can produce. The specific voicing, or overtone arrangement, a string ultimately achieves upon this framework is primarily determined by four factors:
- the mechanical arrangement of the linear mass density,
- the sum resonant contribution of the instrument's parts,
- the nature of the string's starting motion, and,
- the nature of any magnetizing forces.

We will first look at the topic of the mechanical arrangement of the linear mass density, and then we will examine the issue of the sum resonant contribution of the parts of the instrument. The third factor, the nature of the string's starting motion, will be addressed in the section on damping, and the final factor of magnetizing influences will be covered in the Magnetics chapter of this book.

The mechanical arrangement, or physical manifestation, of the mass density will vary according to the parameters of the string's construction. On plain strings, for example, there is little variation in the mechanical arrangement, except for plain strings with external plating or coating. The mass per unit length on this type of construction is rather uniform for each diameter and type of material. On wound strings, however, there is much more variation in construction.

A wound string typically will have an internal core element with one or more wraps of a secondary element around the core. On an electric guitar string, for example, the core may be made of a steel alloy, which can be round or hexagonal, and can vary in diameter as well. The outer wrap can be made of different materials, such as nickel or steel or nickel-plated steel, and can vary in thickness. Additionally, the outer wrap may be processed further by pressing, grinding, polishing, etc. or made of a flat ribbon wire. This winding could also be plated or covered in a synthetic sealant. The mass density thus becomes an averaged figure of several different materials, each having their own distinct wave velocity.

So, what does this mean for Equation 1.6? It is realistic to have two different wound strings both made of steel, both with the same outer diameter, both with the same averaged mass density, but one with a round wound outer wrap and the other with a ribbon wound flat wrap. Even with the same averaged mass per unit length, the two will sound dramatically different!

Equation 1.6 predicts where the fundamental and all the overtone frequencies will appear on a string of certain length under certain tension and having a certain mass density; however, it doesn't predict the *strength* of the harmonic se-

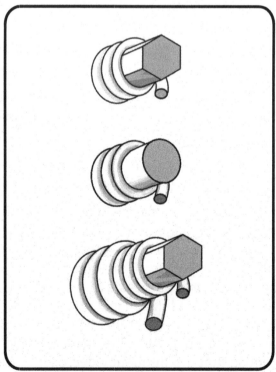

Figure 1.3
Wound Strings with different cores

ries. The table can be set for a certain number of places, but not everyone may show up, and those that do may take very different helpings. So, Equation 1.6 remains unchanged. I would recommend, however, if you're doing weight testing on wound strings, use a subscript with your mass density results, such as μ_w, to differentiate wound from plain strings.

The strength of the fundamental and overtone series is determined in large part, in addition to the nature of the string composition, by the sum of the resonant contribution from all the parts of the instrument. This occurs through a secondary wave process known as *longitudinal motion*.

Imagine a spring, instead of a string, stretched a bit and then plucked with a pick as though it were a guitar string. A group of areas of *compression* and *rarefaction* will develop as the spring works to restore itself to its original, undisturbed condition. The energy transfer will form areas called compressions, which are more densely populated with coils of spring, followed by areas called rarefactions, which are thinly populated with coils of spring.

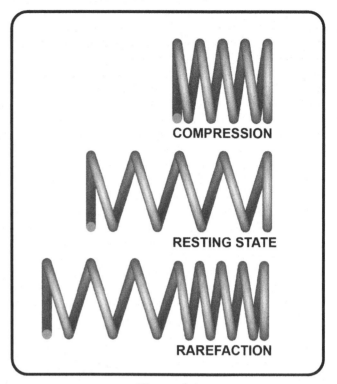

Figure 1.4
Rarefaction and Compression

The molecular bonds that hold matter together behave very much like springs. Some of the bonds are very rigid; others are very flexible. Those in the materials that are suitable for string manufacture must be rigid enough to prevent deformation, yet flexible enough to allow musical tones to establish. All the rest of the parts of the instrument will have similar requirements, depending on their applications. This quantum level spring-like behavior is the mechanism by which the longitudinal waveform propagates.

The longitudinal wave motion develops in accordance with the string's elasticity, density, and length and carries initially the same information as the transverse waveform. The longitudinal wave velocity is represented by

$$vl = (Y/\rho)^{1/2} \tag{1.7}$$

where v is the wave velocity, Y is Young's modulus for the string's material, and ρ is the density of the material.

Young's modulus is a proportionality constant for the elasticity of a material.

$$Y = \sigma/\epsilon = (F/A)/(\Delta l/l) \tag{1.8}$$

Young's modulus is defined by stress, σ, divided by strain, ϵ. The stress, σ, on the string is described by the force, F, (tension) per cross section unit of area, A. The strain, ϵ, is described by the change in length, Δl, divided by the original length, l.

The frequency relationship for longitudinal wave motion can be derived from the basic wave velocity, frequency, and wavelength equation,

$$v = f\lambda \tag{1.2}$$

Inserting the longitudinal value for wave velocity,

$$(Y/\rho)^{1/2} = f\lambda \tag{1.9}$$

And solving for frequency, becomes, like Equation 1.6,

$$f_n = n\,[(Y/\rho)/2l]^{1/2} \tag{1.10}$$

The energy driving the longitudinal wave motion, however, does not reflect at the bridge or nut or fret boundary as does the transverse form. At the saddle boundary point of the bridge, for example, a large portion of the longitudinal wave energy flows from the string into the saddle, following what I like to think of as a mechanical *line of force*. This mechanical line of force, which is traditionally described as potential energy, is directed perpendicular to the plane of the vibrating string length, with intensity proportional to the degree of incline of the string from the saddle down to the string's termination point.

The longitudinal motion can only follow this line of force, however, from one medium to the next, by means of *coupling*. The molecules transmitting the motion must have other molecules to bump into for the wave to propagate. Thus, as the area of contact between the string and the saddle surface increases, the impedance to the flow of longitudinal wave motion decreases. Something very interesting happens, however, as the wave motion moves along the line of force from the string into the saddle. Even though the line of force is directing the flow downward, the wave motion has now found itself in the saddle, which is a resonant entity independent of the string. The motion is now also free to bump into all the molecules comprising this new bit of matter. The saddle will have its own unique resonant function, consisting of a fundamental frequency and associated overtones, which will oscillate when the saddle is disturbed. If this disturbance, which is also known in resonant terms as the *forcing function*, and in our example consists of the wave information from the string motion, matches the natural frequencies of the saddle, *resonance* occurs. The wave motion from the string adds energy at the right moment during the saddle's oscillation cycle so that the saddle's cycle is reinforced, thus building the amplitude of the oscillation.

The resonant function of the saddle will join with the *primary longitudinal motion* from the string, and following the line of force, will move into the next component by way of the most expedient coupling path. In this example, the saddle couples with an adjusting screw, the bottoms of the saddle head, and the bottom and sides of the saddle to move into the bridge chassis.

It would be simpler to illustrate this motion with just a bone saddle on an acoustic guitar, but I've chosen a commonplace metal adjustable bridge so that you may have a better insight into the convoluted movement the waveform must often take inside many instruments.

As with the saddle, if the screw and the chassis happen to have matching frequencies with the forcing motion moving into them, they, too, will contribute some of their resonance. From the chassis the motion is forced to move into the height adjuster wheels and the wheel screw threads looking for resonance, so to speak, before finally coupling into the wood of the guitar's body. This same process spreads throughout the wood and into any other parts of the instrument, where they ultimately either reflect back up into the string via their original path or continue on to and into the opposite end of the string.

Bear in mind, however, that this same process will be transpiring through the frets, nut, retainers, tuners, tailpiece, and any other line of force pathways into the instrument and back out. The waves propagating through these multiple entrance/exit points all will join *superimposed*, carrying the resonant information from all the parts back into the string. This, then, is the mechanism for the voicing of an instrument by the unique resonant contributions of all its parts.

Up to this point we've looked at the general aspects of wave behavior in a musical instrument as the string motion is started and fully developed. For a moment, at the height of this activity, we will have what could be described as a smooth-running machine, depending on the nature and condition of all its parts. But this is only a temporary status, and, in the final part of this chapter, we'll look at the factors that bring this activity to a halt.

From Newton's first law, we know that an object in motion tends to stay in motion with a constant velocity in the absence of interacting forces. In our case, the moving object is the guitar string with its associated wave motion, and the interacting forces are the *damping factors*. To the physicist, damping is a process that removes mechanical energy by converting it to heat. To the musician, damping is any process that chokes the movement of the string. Since both the physicist and the musician seem to be describing the same phenomenon, let's see if we can devise a definition that is compatible with both perspectives. Thus, any action, whether internal or external to the propagating medium, that dissipates wave energy may be regarded as damping.

To better appreciate the function of damping, let's revisit the topic of resonance, and consider what happens without damping. As resonance occurs, the cycle of the driving oscillation matches the cycle of the resonating object, reinforcing the oscillation. The oscillation, without damping, grows larger and larger, approaching infinity. The resonating object, however, can only contain so much energy before its molecular bonds begin to separate. If there is a line of force through the resonating object, the initial bond separation will begin at the point of the highest energy concentration. A chain reaction of separation will follow, and the object will break, in the terminology of the woodworker.

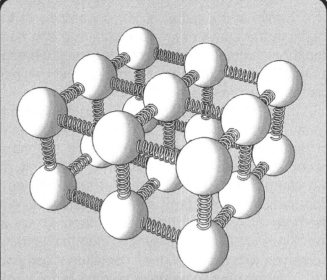

Figure 1.5 Matter Model

Imagine a big three-dimensional elongated version of this. The balls can represent a basic unit of mass, such as a molecule. The springs connecting the balls represent the forces holding the matter together. This will be an idealized homogenous material, such as a plain guitar string, where all the balls are equal in mass and all the springs are equal in force. If you bump one part of this substance, the disturbance will propagate proportionately throughout the material in accordance with the incoming line of force.

The disturbance will travel to the boundary conditions of the material, then reflect back and forth until the energy is dispersed. The velocity of the traveling wave in this material will be uniform.

In an inhomogeneous material, such as a piece of wood, the balls of mass can vary in size and the strength of the springs can vary from one area of the material to the next. The wave velocity will change with each variation in density.

An everyday example of infinity-bound resonance can occur when the octave g string of a twelve-string guitar is left undamped in the presence of the same note played very loudly in the same room. The octave g can oscillate wildly and break. What if, though, we could build a guitar that had no damping whatsoever, and the first note played would sound a beautiful, sustaining tone, which would begin to howl louder and louder until ultimately the instrument exploded?

So, we can see that some degree of damping is useful, and necessary, in many situations. To get the octave g string back under control, all that is required is a simple palm mute, or resting the hand somewhere along the vibrating string's length. The flesh of the hand becomes an elastic boundary, which not only prevents breakage but also effectively stops the string motion completely. But how can we prevent our beautiful sounding theoretical, non-damping guitar from exploding after one note? If we apply too much damping, we lose the note altogether. If there's no damping, we lose the string and possibly the instrument, too. Since we have already identified the limitations of the damping function, let's familiarize ourselves with the individual, constituent components.

In the playing mode of a string instrument, in any resonant situation, the wave energy is dissipated over a period of time. This wave energy dissipation can be attributed to several factors, some affecting the transverse motion and others affecting the longitudinal motion. The total damping effect can be a function of one or several of these factors.

The first of the transverse damping effects establishes itself at the onset of string motion at the point of contact between the applied force and the string. A point of no transverse motion, or a *node*, is created. A node, of course, establishes itself in accordance with the half-wavelength points along the string, which we have seen are determined by the string's mass density, tension, and vibrating length. However, the node that is introduced by the applied force, which could be transmitted by your finger or your pick, will generally not coincide with a natural, lower-order node due to the positioning of your picking hand. I prefer to call this type of node a *forced node*.

You will also recall the transverse wave's inclination for reflection at boundary conditions. The higher energy conditions of a forced node create a *filtering boundary* condition at that point. The lower order harmonics, which are more powerful, push through the forced node with negligible reflection. As the harmonics progress sequentially upward, with less and less energy, they are progressively filtered and reflected. Above a certain point, virtually all the upper partials will be reflected. All this reflected energy will establish two secondary notes, which will be described by the same mass density of the string, having the same tension, but with two new vibrating lengths: one will be defined by the point of the forced node to the front of the saddle, and the other will be defined by the point of the forced node to the opposite boundary (front edge of nut or fret top). As these two new harmonic functions superimpose upon the original harmonic function, there will be multiple points of harmonic cancellation or transverse damping.

The severity of this type of damping will increase proportionally with the concentration of force at the forced node. Thus, an aggressive attack with a stiff, pointed pick will produce more damping than a comparable attack with the softer, wider area of the flesh of your thumb or finger.

It should also be noted that as the string is played into the upper register, more energy of the lower order harmonics will filter across the forced node. This initial damping effect, by the way, is the third of the four primary factors affecting overtone arrangement mentioned earlier in this chapter.

After the wave motion has been established on the string, the next and key overall damping effect is the longitudinal transfer of energy into heat and sound. As the longitudinal wave motion works its way through the instrument, its energy is gradually expended. More energy is also used to propagate through more convoluted pathways, such as the adjustable bridge we referenced earlier. Some materials, such as higher water content woods and more elastic plastics, also require more energy to propagate waves. Some of the energy may also be lost as sound. The string motion itself will disturb a tiny bit of surrounding air, but the coupling with the air molecules is minute. Only a tiny amount of energy is used. Longitudinal coupling with any chamber or cavity inside the instrument is greater, and in the case of an archtop or an acoustic guitar, longitudinal coupling between the larger surface area of the instrument's top and the air expends a tremendous amount of energy.

Most of the rest of the damping factors will affect the transverse domain and will appear as a function of playing wear and humidity changes.

The most common of these are *discontinuities* along the vibrating string length. A discontinuity is any irregularity affecting the uniformity of the mass density along the working string length. Worn spots, dents, bulges, foreign matter and oxidation all are examples of discontinuities.

Oxidation is the most common discontinuity. When the wave encounters oxidation, which has a different density than the original string, it treats it as a boundary. This situation is similar to that of the forced node condition; part of the wave is reflected, and part of the wave continues through the different material. Since the oxide has a different mass density, it also will have different wave velocity conditions than the non-oxidized material. Here we have two different waveforms establishing on the same length of string with the subsequent phase cancellations. First to go are the weakest, higher frequency upper partials, which we perceive as a loss of presence. As the oxide grows, more of the upper harmonics are damped, and we notice a progressive darkening of the tone. As the oxide begins to dominate parts of the string material, the intonation will begin to shift. Most people change their strings before they get this far gone, however.

After extended playing, all guitars experience some degree of *scale shifting*, another transverse damping effect. Scale shifting is produced by the vibrating string length changing its length as it vibrates. This can be caused by a worn or damaged nut slot or a worn fret. Many new guitars and basses have rounded top saddles which create this condition as well.

On a properly adjusted instrument, the boundary conditions defining the vibrating string length are precisely defined. By precisely defined, we mean the working string length begins and ends at as close to one point as possible. For an open note, that will define the beginning length of string at the front edge of the nut slot, and the ending length of string at the front edge of the saddle slot. For a fretted note, the beginning length of string is at the center of the top of the fret.

In a scale shifting situation, the nut slot may have worn inward, or the saddle slot may have worn backward, or most commonly, the top of the fret wears down to a flattened surface. When this happens, the string length will begin and/or end along several different points, effectively shifting the scale as the string vibrates. This is roughly equivalent to repositioning the saddle to a slightly different location with each oscillation of the string. The net tonal effect of this type of transverse damping is harmonic cancellation.

Another type of transverse damping occurs when one or more of the string boundaries become elastic. The most common elastic boundary is a loose fret. An elastic boundary can change its position during a wave cycle, generating multiple time-altered waveforms, which are highly disruptive. Other elastic boundaries can form from overly elastic nut and saddle materials or soft coatings on under-saddle pickups.

Inappropriate fret noise is another source of transverse damping. This is produced when parts of the vibrating string come in contact with one or more frets. Light contact between the string and the frets will disrupt the upper partials. Heavier contact will not only cause wider spread harmonic disruption, but also start to dominate as the primary, dissonant sound instead of the intended note. The primary causes range from worn frets, or other out-of-plane frets due to humidity related swollen or shrunken fingerboards, excessively low string height, insufficient string mass for desired tuning, and excessive starting motion forces.

Loose parts on the guitar are a source of longitudinal damping. There is no middle ground regarding the rigidity of instrument components; they are either securely mounted and contributing to the total resonant function, or they are loosely mounted and damping the resonant function. This applies to everything from strap buttons, pickups, knobs, pickguards, and tuner parts to untrimmed string ends, plus essentially anything on the instrument that can work itself loose. Routine maintenance should include securing all parts to eliminate or minimize all these elastic boundary conditions. There is also the phenomenon I call *ghost waves*, which are a source of transverse damping, but we will wait until the topic of magnetism is covered later in this book for a fuller examination.

Our consideration of all interfering forces would not be complete without a mention of gravity. Newton's law of universal gravitation states that any two bodies in the universe attract one another with a force that is proportional to the masses of each and varies inversely as the square of the distance between them. It can be written as

$$F = G\,(m_1 m_2 / r^2) \tag{1.11}$$

This is known as the *universal gravitational constant* and is also found in Einstein's theory of general relativity.

Our vibrating strings have a force tugging at them with the *gravitational constant*, in SI units, of

$$6.67 \times 10^{-11}\ \text{Newton-m}^2/\text{kg}^2 \tag{1.11a}$$

This is sometimes found expressed in the older CGS units of

$$6.67 \times 10^{-8}\ \text{dyne-cm}^2/\text{g}^2 \tag{1.11b}$$

Since virtually none of us have any experience playing guitar in a low gravity environment, we treat the damping influence of gravity on our string motion as entirely normal, to the extent that we do not realize the strings are being damped by gravity. From the ALE standard perspective, if we cannot hear the difference gravity is making, even though it can be demonstrated analytically and experimentally, then it is not a valid point. This holds true here on planet Earth; but in a low gravity situation, such as would be experienced during space travel, Earth's gravitational damping would be diminished to the point where the guitar's strings would vibrate longer. In this situation, all three conditions of the ALE standard would be met.

Finally, after some combination of all these damping factors have interfered with the string motion, at the moment the energy of the applied force is completely dissipated, the length of string will resume its original, tensioned state. It will remain in this state until acted upon by new forces.

In this chapter we have looked at the fundamental features of wave motion in the context of string vibration and tone production, from the first application of the starting force to the full development of the instrument's resonance to the complete damping of the system.

In order to understand how a guitar works, we need to understand how wave motion works in all the composite components that constitute a guitar. The next chapter will identify those components and their history.

CITATIONS AND REFERENCES

Isaac Newton Dec 25,1642–Mar 29, 1726/27.

The Principia Philosophiae Naturalis Principia Mathematica, (Mathematical Principles of Natural Philosophy), 1687, The Principia, third edition, 1729, translated by Andrew Motte, The Principia, 1999, translation from the original Latin by Cohen and Whitman.

Wave Motion in Strings Physics of Waves, Wm Elmore and Mark Heald, 1985, Chap. 1, Chap 4.4–4.7. Transverse Waves on a String, pp. 2–45, Chap. 3, Theory of Elasticity, pp. 71–91, Chap. 4, One-Dimensional Elastic Waves, pp. 93–131. A Treatise on the Mathematical Theory of Elasticity, A. E. H. Love, First edition, 1893, First American printing 1944. Wave Motion in Elastic Solids, Karl Graff, 1991, Chap.1, Waves and Vibrations in Strings, pp. 9–72, Chap. 2, Longitudinal Waves in Thin Rods, pp. 75–136, Appendix A, The Elasticity Equations, pp. 582–601. Physics Problem Solver, M. Fogiel, Chief Editor, 1995, Elastic Deformation

Damping Physics problem Solver, M. Fogiel, Chief Editor, 1995, Damping factor, p. 394 Physics for Scientists and Engineers with Modern Physics, third edition, 2000, Daniel Giancolli,
An Introduction to Mechanical Vibrations, Steidel, John Wiley and Sons, 1971.

The Development of Mathematics, E. T. Bell, 1992 p. 50, pp. 161–2, pp. 517, 531, p. 520

Chapter Two
The Development of the Guitar

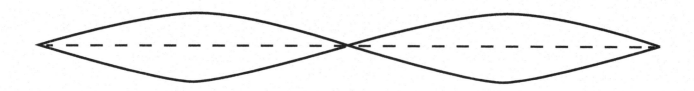

    A guitar, in its most rudimentary form, can be defined as a portable, multi-string instrument with a working register that parallels the fundamental frequency range of the human voice. The manifestations that this instrument can assume are limitless, but they all will have several features in common. These features are an outgrowth of, at the very least, fifty centuries of development.

    The most recent part of this timeline, the twentieth century, has the most abundant and easily researched bodies of information. Databases, books, and instruments are in great supply. As we move back into the nineteenth century, however, the resources shrink dramatically. Print sources are available but surviving examples of the instruments are scarce and not readily available for examination. Original documentation of many string instruments dating from the seventeen hundreds and earlier exists, but the manuscripts are not in great supply, and the instruments themselves are even harder to find. Information from the earliest segment of this timeline, from 700 CE to 3000 BCE, must be gleaned from a diverse body of evidence ranging from illustrations on clay tablets and pottery to stone reliefs, frescos and wall paintings in tombs and excavations, and a few of the actual surviving instruments.

    Intuition would suggest that people have been making music with tensioned strings much earlier than 3000 BCE, and in all likelihood, humankind has probably been monkeying with plucked strings for many millennia. To date, there is no evidence to indicate at what point in history the first dedicated musical string instrument was developed.

    The most logical first musical string instrument would have been the musical bow, a flexed wooden shaft with one or more cords attached to either end. This instrument may have predated the hunting bow or vice versa; there is no evidence to support either supposition. Although there are no surviving specimens or prehistoric depictions that show, unambiguously, an example of a musical bow, there is an image of a bow harp shown in bas relief in the tomb of Ny-kheft-Ka of the V Dynasty, 2498–2345 BCE, in the Necropolis at Saqqara.

    In the Caverne des Trois Freres, or the Three Brothers' Cave, located in Montesquieu- Avantes, Ariege, in southwestern France, there are 280 engraved figures dating from

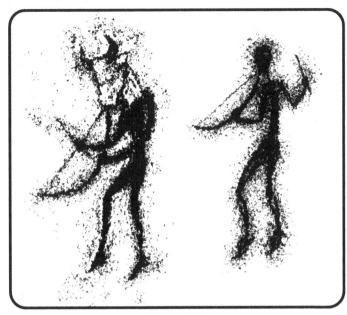

Figure 2.1
Recreation of the Three Brothers Cave Drawings

the Mid-Magdalenian period, roughly fourteen thousand years ago. One of the drawings looks like a man who could be dancing, wearing an animal skin and holding a musical bow in the playing position. However, this is not the only way this art can be interpreted. The most common view among scholars of cave art is that this is another example of a depiction of a shaman. A shaman, of course, was a person who claimed to have a special affinity with the spirit world and could dispense advice, for a consideration, to those in need. But was that the intent of the original artist? Had the artist seen a half man/half beast playing a musical bow? Could that be a rendition of a Neanderthal? Or did the artist want to mark a point in history where we were transcending the common beast and using tools to advance our survival? My first hunch was this was a depiction of a hunting decoy: the resonant chamber of the animal head coupled with the moving string of the hunting bow could have produced a lowing sound similar to the calls of the game being hunted. The body language, though, is not that of a stealthy hunter; the guy clearly appears to be dancing. I think this drawing is the oldest preserved evidence of a musical string instrument in use.

Lending credence to this supposition of the early musical bow is the adaption of the hunting bow for musical purposes in relatively modern times. This has been evidenced in Australia, Africa, India, and South America. Because the vibrating bow has very little coupling area with the air, it produces hardly any volume. But by holding the bow against any resonant chamber, such as the mouth, a hollowed log, gourd, tortoise shell, etc., the coupling area is increased to affect a working volume, and thus a working musical instrument is created. The South American berimbau, with a gourd affixed to the bow, is one example.

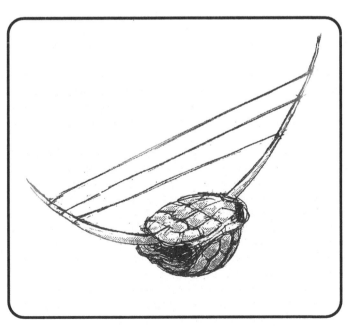

Figure 2.2   The Chelys

The very first dedicated musical string instrument may have been a similar musical bow. A bow would have been inserted through opposing holes of a tortoise shell, which would then have been restrung with one or more tensioned strings. Flexing the bow would have changed the pitch of the plucked strings, which would have sounded through the resonator tortoise shell. Legend has it (Homeric Hymn to Hermes, c. seventh and sixth century BCE) that Hermes invented an instrument, called the *chelys*, after finding a tortoise shell with dried tendons stretched across its insides. I have not seen any surviving examples of this instrument.

The *lyra*, however, of ancient and classical Greece, c. 800–500 BCE, shows modifications of this basic design. This musical instrument was commonly depicted with a tortoise shell resonator with an insert bow member very similar to the musical bow. In order to enlarge the musical register, a crossbar was added, connecting the bow ends. Five to twelve strings were then tensioned between the crossbar and the tortoise shell resonator.

Variations of this basic design are seen in the many popular instruments of antiquity, which include the *barbitos*, the *phorminx*, and the *cithara*. These all have dual arms connected by a crossbar from which multiple strings extend downward to connect to a sound chamber or resonator. This sound chamber part of the instrument has come to be known as, appropriately, the body.

Apollo plays the phorminx at the end of the first Book of the Iliad. It is also shown

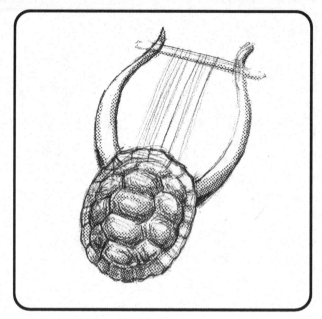

Figure 2.3   The Lyra

being played in the Odyssey. The *barbiton* was the preferred instrument of Sappho, a popular Greek lyric poet of the sixth century BCE. She is shown holding one on one of the Brygos Painter's vase paintings.

The musical limitations of the lyra family, however, were defined by each instrument's number of strings, their thicknesses, tensioning and lengths, of course, and their resultant harmonic combinations. The register could be expanded by increasing the number of strings, which necessitated a sturdier and larger housing, as seen on the epigonions, harps, and angle harps from this same era. As these instruments became larger and more complimentary to the voice, though, they also became less portable and required more skill to play. They also lacked continuously variable pitch capability.

Imagine, then, taking the dual arms of the lyra and joining them together to form one shaft, sized to fit the hand. Attach this shaft to a resonator body and stretch one or more strings across its entire length, and, by stopping the string at any point along the shaft, you'd

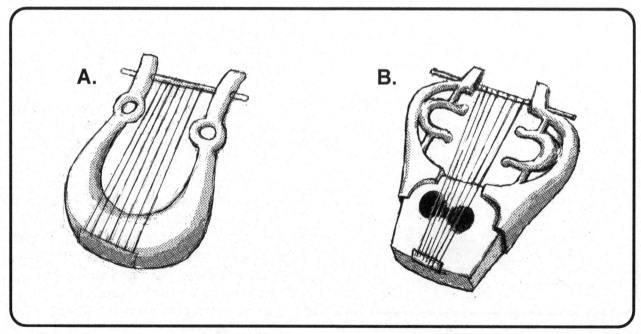

Figure 2.4   The Phorminx(A) and Cithara (B)

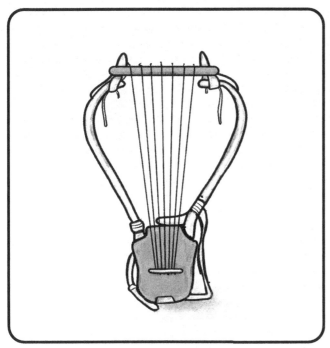

Figure 2.5 The Barbitos

have continuously variable pitch. This innovative shaft that permitted continuously variable pitch change became known as the *neck*.

Depictions of such an instrument, which came to be known as the *lute*, began to appear during the second millennium BCE. A complete instrument belonging to a musician named Har-Mose, who was employed during the reign of Queen Hapshepsut, was excavated with its three original strings still intact. This instrument, dating from c. 1500 BCE, had a cedar wood body with a rawhide head fitted across the top. The head had six symmetrically placed holes in the top, either for resonant tuning or increased coupling or both.

It was, and still is expedient, however, to have some predetermined stops at points beneath the working lengths of the strings. By wrapping and tying strips of cord or gut around the neck, the musicians were able to have, in addition to more accurate pitch stops, the ability to change interval groupings at will. These movable boundaries, or *frets*, were known to have been in use by c. 1450 BCE (wall painting in the Tomb of Nakht, pictured in Subira's History of Music, Vol. 1, pg. 65) and became a standard feature on string instrument necks for the next three millennia. Movable gut frets began to be replaced by glued-in strips of bone, ivory, horn, and metal during the sixteenth century and progressively fell out of favor over the following two hundred years.

From its origins in Mesopotamia c. 2500 BCE, the progenitor of the lute, shown in terracotta plaques from the Old Babylonian Period (British Museum, London, England) as well as other members of the string instrument family, including harps, lyres, and citharas, spread to neighboring regions. As these instruments made their way along trade routes into Mongolia, Russia, China, Persia, Greece, Egypt, and the rest of the emerging civilizations, diversification began to occur.

Figure 2.6 The Lute

The earliest lute-style instruments, notably, had little or no means for adjusting the string tension after the string had been mounted onto the instrument. Har-Mose's pre-lute, for example, could only have its string pitch changed by moving the position of the bridge.

In India, possibly as early as c. 1000 BCE, a variation of a lute-style instrument called a *ravanastron* appeared. This instrument featured two turning pegs with handles, which were fitted through the end of the neck so that the strings could be attached and turned to change tension.

By sizing the holes and pegs appropriately, friction would wedge the wooden pegs in place once the desired pitch was achieved. These pegs came to be known as *tuners*.

In nearby Turkestan, c. 500 BCE, a separate housing for the tuning pegs was developed. This pegbox, which was affixed to the end of the pre-lute's neck, was called the *headstock*. The headstock necessitated the use of a string guide, called a nut, to direct the strings from the pegbox onto the playing surface of the neck. At the opposite end of the instrument, a string seating device also began to be used. This guide, which let the voice (longitudinal wave motion) of the strings cross over into the body, was called the *bridge*.

Over the next few hundred years, the top of the body would more commonly be made from wood instead of skin and was called the *soundboard*. *Sound holes* placed individually or in decorative multiples, under the strings or to either side of the string course, would become a common feature. With the onset of Islamic expansionism in the seventh century CE, a four-string variation of this instrument the Arabs called *al'ud* was carried into North Africa, southern Europe, and the Iberian Peninsula. This Arabic expression, al'ud, which translated literally to "the wood," turned into *laud* in Spanish, *luth* in French, and *lute* in English. The word *luthier*, meaning one who works on string instruments, is a derivative, of course, of the French luth.

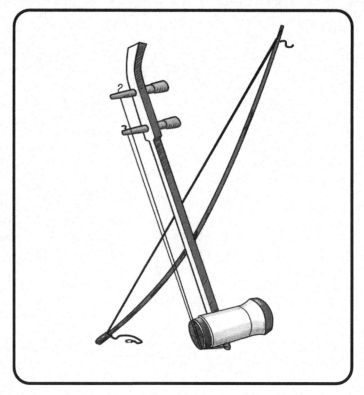

Figure 2.7
The Ravanastron with friction tuners

Before the word al'ud became popular, the prelute was known by many different names. In India, it was the ravanastron; in Turkestan, the *qopuz* and the *dutar*; in China, the *san hsien*; in Japan, the *gekkin*; and in Egypt, the *nefer*. The names associated with the prelutes shown on the earliest clay tablets remain unknown.

Islamic philosopher al-Kindi, 801–873 CE, wrote seven books on music and gives possibly the earliest mention and description of al'ud. In addition to his writings on music, he included some timely advice for the generations: "We ought not to be embarrassed about appreciating the truth and obtaining it wherever it comes from, even if it comes from races distant and nations different from us. Nothing should be dearer to the seeker of the truth than the truth itself, and there is no deterioration of the truth, nor belittling of one who speaks or conveys it."

The lute seemed to blossom in Spain over the next several centuries. Although both long and short neck lutes had been built in Egypt earlier, many different sizes were produced in Spain. Many combinations of different sized bowl-shaped bodies with varying sound hole placements were mixed with different neck lengths. Illustrations in the hymnbooks, psalters, and Gospels of the eighth, ninth, and tenth centuries show these instruments, some with strings attached to the base of the body with a *tailpiece*.

These instruments spread across Europe and into Italy and were adapted and modified by different populations. Of particular interest, however, are drawings found in Spanish king Alfonso X's hymnbook, "Cantigas de Santa Maria," c. 1275 CE. Interspersed through-

Figure 2.8
The Quitarra with *Head*stock

out this book of 420 poems are illustrations of every popular musical instrument of the period, including one with a neck, headstock, tuning pegs, frets, and a box-shaped body with a bridge and sound holes, including one beneath the four strings. This instrument was called the *quitarra Latina*. Although box-shaped bodies had been in use before, such as those on Egyptian Coptic lutes from the fifth century CE, this entry in the Cantigas may be the earliest known reference to an instrument with all the rudimentary components, including the name of the guitar.

The origins of the word *quitarra* are unknown, but it may be a hybrid construction of the Old Persian (Mesopotamian) word for string, tar, plus a stylized form of Spanish for four, quarto. Other instruments with curiously similar nomenclature include the Persian dotar (two-string), the Afghan *panchtar* (five-string), and the Indian *sitar* (many strings). The level of sophistication inherent in the construction of this word certainly suggests a pedigree slightly higher than street level, unlike the word al'ud. Someone in one of the Spanish monasteries prior to or during Alfonso's reign may have been the engineer, but for now, the facts are hidden in the past.

One popular hypothesis about the etymology of the word quitarra ascribes its origin, as well as that of the instruments', to the old Greek cithara. The cithara, with its two arms and string-bearing crossbar, is clearly several rungs down the evolutionary ladder from the quitarra. The cithara does not look like or, except for the fact that it has strings and a resonant chamber, function like the quitarra. The only similarities between the two words are in the pronunciations, and this, I believe, may be a key clue to the actual coining of quitarra. I am inclined to believe that the word quitarra was not only a proper modifier for the four-string instrument but also a clever and catchy play on words on the then-archaic cithara.

I would also venture a guess that, if there are no records of the quitarra earlier than the Cantigas' drawings, the instrument must have been developed as early as the eighth century CE and certainly no later than the early thirteenth century CE.

The quitarra came to be known by many other names during the Middle Ages in Europe. In Spain it was also known as the *vihuela de penola*; in Italy, the *chitarra battente*; in Germany, it was called the *quinterna*. Other names included the *ghiterna lutina, chitarra spagnola, cyntharae hispaniae, quintarra*, and the *guisterne.*

In the early fifteen hundreds, the four-string and four-course tunings began to be replaced by four-course plus one stringing systems, similar to that of lutes, and five-course systems. In Spain and Portugal, the figure-of-eight body shape, with the familiar *upper and lower body bouts*, became the predominant body choice. Soprano, alto, tenor, and bass quitarras were built, with the bass size being closest to that of the contemporary classical guitar.

In England and France in the seventeen hundreds, the five courses were changed to five single strings. A sixth string was added, and standard tuning became E-A-d-g-b-e'. Twelve frets became more common, and a *fretboard* was glued onto the neck's superstructure. Metal frets, driven into the fingerboard, began to replace gut and bone frets. By the end of the eighteenth century, the quitarra had evolved into an instrument easily recognizable as a modern guitar. As its popularity spread across Europe, luthiers from Italy, Spain and Portugal, France, Germany and Austria, and England added the *guitar* to their inventory of offerings.

The first double and triple neck guitars were built in France just prior to and after their Revolution. The *bissex*, a doubleneck, was built in Paris in 1770; a triple neck lyre-guitar was shown in Paris in 1829. There is no evidence, however, that the French invented the headless guitar during that turbulent epoch.

The overall physical dimensions of the guitar changed very little during the eighteen hundreds, but greater use of metal and wire wound strings, with their accompanying higher tensions, led to redesigns and improvements in internal bracing. Geared tuners began to replace friction pegs, with Stauffer of Austria and Martin of the US among the first users in the 1830s. Bridges with string-anchoring bridge pins began to be used more frequently as an alternative to the traditional bridge and tailpiece combinations.

The *truss rod*, a mechanism for adjusting the changing flex of the neck, was developed early in the twentieth century. This device was integral to the widespread use of louder steel strings. Patented in 1923 to Thaddeus McHugh and assigned to the Gibson Mandolin-Guitar Company, it became a standard feature in guitar, bass, mandolin, banjo, and many other instruments using higher tension strings.

The twentieth century also saw a movement toward larger body sizes, with several new styles and many variations on each of the styles. The popular nineteenth century narrow-shouldered guitar came to be known as a *parlor* model. The slightly larger gut/nylon string guitar is called the *classical* model. The most popular model, a larger and louder instrument, is called the *dreadnought*. A smaller bodied steel-string version, closer in size to the classical, is known as the *folk* guitar. The largest of this period's group is called the *jumbo*. The many variations of all these models include such alterations as single and double upper bout cutaways, thinner bodied versions, ¾ and ½ sized models, compact travel guitars, and reduced-dimension children's guitars. The *archtop* guitar, a roughly dreadnought-sized, violin-family inspired instrument, also achieved popularity in the 1920s.

Advancements in the field of electronics dramatically expanded the guitar family in this same century. Even though guitar pickups were being developed in the 1920s, they would not be used commercially on guitars until the 1930s, when amplifiers became available. The ability to amplify wave motion meant that not only could contemporary instruments be outfitted with pickups, but virtually any new design with playable strings could be amplified. First to emerge from this new generation of de-

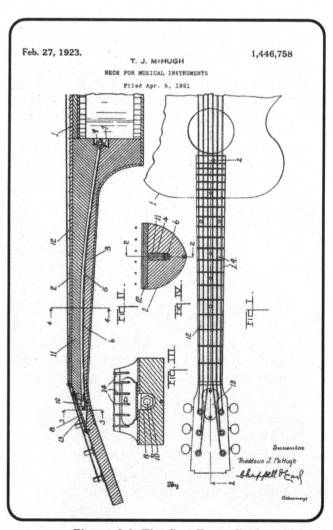

Figure 2.9 The first Truss Rod

signs, in the 1930s, were the *lap steels*. Archtops began to be retrofitted with pickups in the same decade, and, in the late 1940s, Leo Fender and company introduced the first solid-body "electric" guitars. An explosion of electric guitar and bass designs followed over the next several decades.

By the mid-1970s, individual replacement and upgrade guitar parts—such as pickups, necks, bodies, bridges, and tuners—began to join the marketplace, and the level of personalization available to players took a historic step forward.

By the end of the twentieth century there were three primary guitar designs: (1) the acoustic, (2) the solid body, and (3) the hybrid of the first two, the chambered hollow body. The quality of these instruments along with the upgrade and custom parts available for them increased substantially in the 1990s with the advent of the computer age.

The guitar of the early twentieth century, after five thousand years of evolution, is still fundamentally a portable multi-string instrument with a working register that parallels the fundamental frequency range of the human voice. The designs have broadened markedly, and the sophistication of the components has increased exponentially since the instrument's origin.

The next chapter will look at the parts of the guitar and their relevance to the function of the instrument.

CITATIONS AND REFERENCES

The Three Brothers' Cave The Caverne des Trois Freres is located in Montesquieu-Avantes, Ariege, in southwestern France. There are 280 engraved figures dating from the Mid-Magdalelenian Period, or roughly fourteen thousand years ago. Most of the images are found on the interior chamber known as the Sanctuary.

Chelys The chelys is referenced in the Homeric Hymn to Hermes, c. seventh and sixth century BCE. There is a rendering of one on a piece of pottery from the fifth century BCE in the Delphi Archaeological Museum. There is also a wall painting of one at Herculaneum dating to the first century CE.

Lyra The lyra was a very common instrument in ancient Greece, c. 800 BCE–500 BCE. It is referenced in Greek mythology, created by Apollo, and in writings from Ptolemy to Aristoxenus. The Harmonics of Aristoxenus, translation by H. S. Macran, 1902.

Barbitos, Phorminx, Cithara The barbiton was the preferred instrument of Sappho, a popular Greek lyric poet of the sixth century BCE. She is shown holding one on one of the Brygos Painter's vase paintings. Apollo plays the phorminx at the end of the first Book of the Iliad. Iliad and the Odyssey, Homer, c. ninth and eighth centuries BCE. The cithara was the professional version of the lyre, having more strings.

Har-mose, c. 1500 BCE, musician of Senmut, architect of Queen Hapshepsut, entombed with his lute, which still had its strings intact when excavated.

Tomb of Nakht, c. 1450 BCE, has wall paintings showing frets. Subira's History of Music, Vol. 1, p. 65.

Pre-lutes shown on terracotta plaques from the Old Babylonian Period, Mesopotamia c. 2500 BCE, British Museum, London, England.

Cantigas de Santa Maria, c. 1275 CE, has the earliest known drawings of a string instrument with all the features of a modern guitar. There are four surviving manuscripts.

Manual of Guitar Technology, Franz Jahnel, 1981 English edition, Historical Review of the Development of the Lute, Guitar, and Cittern, pp. 15–42.

Chapter Three
Guitar Parts and Their Functions

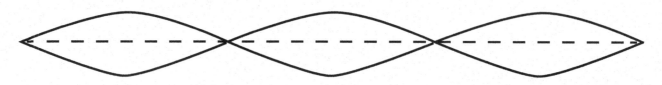

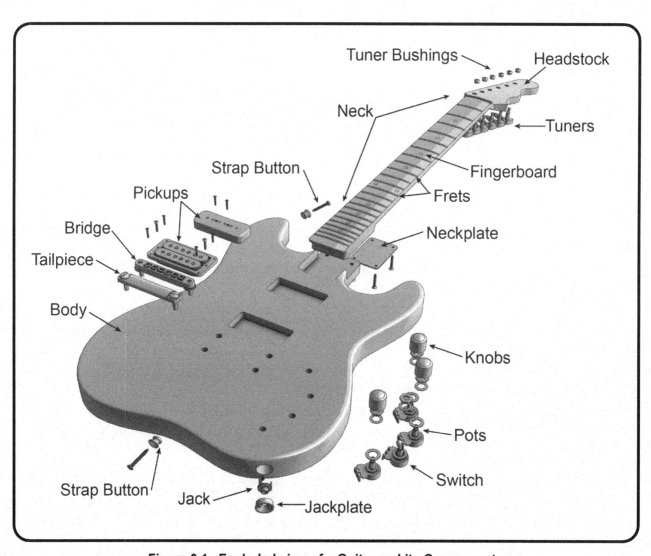

Figure 3.1   Exploded view of a Guitar and its Components

Everyone should be familiar with the names of all the parts and their rudimentary functions on a guitar at this point. Let's organize them from the perspective of energy flow.

The two primary components then become the nut and the saddle/bridge system. The headstock becomes the substructure of the nut, and the body, likewise, becomes the substructure of the bridge. The neck, fretted or fretless, even though it shapes the nature of the energy flow, is a secondary component of the force system.

The electronics, which include the pickups and controls, contribute little to nothing positive to the mechanical voice of the instrument, but they are symbiotic and sophisticated hitchhikers on the body and key to a panorama of voicings. There would be no electric guitar without them.

The rest of the guitar parts, such as the tuners on the headstock and the pickguards and knobs on the body, may be considered components of the substructures. Let's look first at the function of the nut and its substructure, the headstock.

THE NUT AND THE HEADSTOCK

Although the headstock arose early in string instrument history, c. 500 BCE, purely as a mounting station for the tuners, its functionality quickly became infused with style. A review of the historic record of headstock designs reveals a spectrum of creativity ranging from the mundane, sticklike extensions of the fingerboard of the Egyptian nefer to the elegantly carved animal heads of the Iberian quitarra. The mechanical duties of the headstock have been limited to hosting the tuners, determining the angle the strings take at the nut for seating and tonal contribution, aligning the strings in the nut for tuning stability, and occasionally helping adjust the balance of the instrument. The headstock design, over the centuries, has actually had no guiding standards for style or function besides what was popular with the users. Some very functionally efficient designs have appeared and vanished, as much victims of the whims of history as the marginally usable instruments.

One feature that has become a standard in recent history, however, is the assignment of trade dress to the headstock. The use of distinctively designed headstocks as commercial branding began to gain popularity among manufacturers in the nineteenth century. This practice gradually supplanted the use of builder's labels glued inside the body as the primary means of product identification. Commercial trade dress has now become the overriding feature of guitar, bass, and many other string instrument headstocks.

This development bears the hallmark of the advancement of an organized civilization, which is wonderful, except for one significant detail: there is no direct correlation between trade dress and musical func-

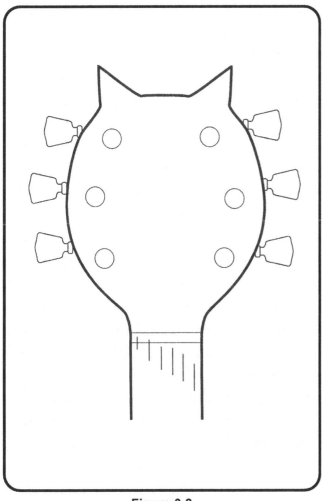

Figure 3.2
Cat Head Headstock

tion. A distinctively designed headstock does not mean that the instrument will tune smoothly, or stay in tune after extended playing, or balance when held, or even contribute constructively to the tone.

We could have, as an example, a headstock that is carved into the shape of a cat's head, with ears and eyes and nose and perhaps a Maine Coon bit of a mane, with tuners mounted in a three-to-a-side pattern. It would be instantly recognizable as a product of the (imaginary) Cat Head Guitar Company, and cat owner guitar players would be good with owning and playing one of these guitars. The size of the headstock, however, would make the guitar top heavy and difficult to hold, and the amount of friction between the strings and the nut, due to the severe angling of the strings, would also make the guitar go out of tune easily. The company would sell many of these models at first, but because of the headstock issues, the buyers would progressively stop playing them, and sales would begin to falter. How could this situation be resolved?

The most obvious solution would be a makeover of the headstock with the goal of improving the balance and tuning stability of the instrument without sacrificing the appeal of the cat head design. The makeover could be attempted with a little trial-and-error style experimentation, but this approach is time consuming and may not produce the most desirable results. A better solution would involve utilizing an understanding of the musical function of the headstock so that the design and commercial styling can fit around the components that contribute to the musical function.

Let's look, then, at how the headstock works.

It is easier to understand the musical function of a headstock if we look at the subject from the perspective of the forces acting on the strings in the nut slots. The primary force of interest is the line of force through the string into the nut slot. The secondary force of interest is the friction, at this same intersection, between the string and the nut slot. These two forces are key influences on both the tone and the tuning stability of an instrument. Brokering these two forces, therefore, becomes critical in fostering an instrument's highest degree of performance.

As we have seen in Chapter 1, longitudinal wave motion tends to propagate more aggressively through regions containing higher levels of stored, or potential, energy. Thus, the greater the force the strings exert in the nut slot, the easier it is for the movement of the longitudinal wave motion. The line of force, also known as the *normal* force, directed into the nut slot can be calculated as a function of an intersected tensioned string. This function, with its *domain*, can be expressed as

$$(F_r) = T_s \sin\theta \quad (0 < \theta \leq 90) \qquad (3.1)$$

This can be read as the resultant line of force directed into the nut is a function of the tension in the string multiplied by

VECTORS

Intersecting forces can be represented by vectors. A vector has magnitude and direction, represented by a line with an arrowhead.

$$a = \overline{AB}$$
$$A \longrightarrow B$$
(Foil) (Head)

A vector's magnitude can be calculated using the Pythagorean theorem.

$$|a| = \sqrt{(x^2 + y^2)}$$

If a vector's magnitude is known, its x and y components can be calculated using polar or cortesian coordinates.

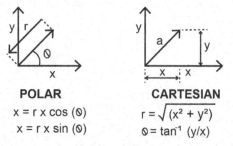

POLAR
$x = r \times \cos(\theta)$
$x = r \times \sin(\theta)$

CARTESIAN
$r = \sqrt{(x^2 + y^2)}$
$\theta = \tan^{-1}(y/x)$

Figure 3.3 Vectors

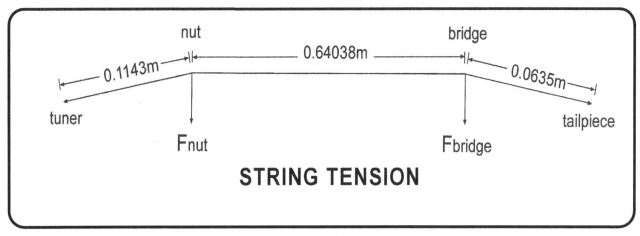

Figure 3.4 String Tension

the sine of the angle of interest, θ, which is the angle of string descent (behind the nut) away from the plane of the playing length of the string. The domain in which this function operates will be anywhere that θ is greater than zero and less than or equal to ninety.

Imagine a single string tensioned across a hypothetical one-string guitar that has a headstock tilted so that when the string is wound to the lowest point on the tuning post, an angle of ten degrees away from the plane of the fingerboard is created.

Since the force in this tensioned string has the qualities of both magnitude and direction, it is simpler to represent it in terms of vector quantities. Also, since vector quantities combine algebraically, calculating the resultant quantities becomes much easier.

The forces in the single tensioned string can be drawn as two equal length opposing vectors, with one angled ten degrees away from the other and the force directed into the nut becoming the resultant vector.

The force in the length of string between the tuner and the nut and the force in the length of string between the nut and the bridge can be shown mathematically, audibly, and experimentally to be equal.

Newton's third law says that for every force, there is an equal and opposite reaction force. We can say then that the sum of these interacting forces equals zero, which can be written as

$$\sum F = 0 \tag{3.2}$$

This is also known as the *first condition of translational equilibrium.*

If we apply this concept to a tensioned string on a guitar, we will see that the force at any point on the string pulling toward the tuner equals the force at that same point pulling toward the tailpiece.

If the string tension in F2 in Illustration 3.5 is 6.499 kgf, and

$$\sum F = F2 - F1 = 0 \tag{3.3}$$

then F1 becomes 6.499 kgf.

Furthermore, let's let the string in Illustration 3.4 be a plain .016 in. steel string tuned to a standard G3 on an instrument with a 25 in. scale. The mass density, μ, derived from the averaged weight from several samples, is .0101159 g/cm, or .00101159 kg/m. Dividing the tension, T, 6.499 kgf, or 63.745 Newtons, by the mass density, μ, .00101159 kg/m, and taking the square root, as in Equation 1.5,

$$v = (T/\mu)^{1/2}$$

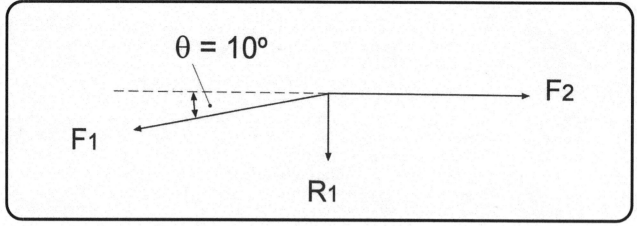

Figure 3.5 Vector Diagram for Nut Slot Line of Force

will give us the wave velocity, v, 251.0267 m/s. If we divide the velocity, v, 251.0267 m/s by the wavelength, λ, 1.28076 m (which is twice, 2l, the intonated string length, .64038 m) we get the frequency, f, 195.998 hz, which is the note G3.

The length of string between the tuner and the back of the nut on this same instrument is 11.43 cm, or .1143 m. Dividing the velocity, v, 251.0267 m/s by the wavelength, λ, of 2l = 2(.1143 m), or .2286 m, gives a frequency, f, of 1098.1045 hz, which falls between C6, 1046.502 hz and C#6, 1108.731 hz.

We can give this result an auditory test by plucking the section of string between the tuner and the nut and comparing that pitch with the pitch we get when we pluck the high E string at the twentieth fret and bend it slightly sharp.

Thus, the statement that the *tension, or force, in the string between the tuner and the nut, and between the nut and the bridge, and by extension, between the bridge and the tailpiece, is equal* is ALE compliant since it can be demonstrated mathematically, aurally, and experimentally.

With this information, calculating the line of force directed into the nut slot becomes very easy. Looking at our vector diagram in Illustration 3.5 we can name the angle between F1 and R1, Φ, and use the trigonometric function

$$F_1 \cos\Phi = R_1 \tag{3.4}$$

to solve for the line of force, Fr.

F_1, 6.499 kgf, multiplied by cosΦ, 80, or .174 equals 1.130826 kgf.

Depending on your method of measuring, it may be easier to obtain the θ angle, in

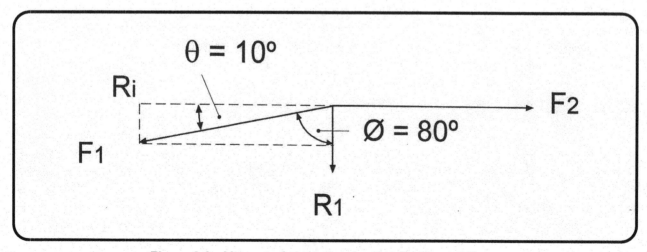

Figure 3.6 Alternate Calculation for Nut Slot line of Force

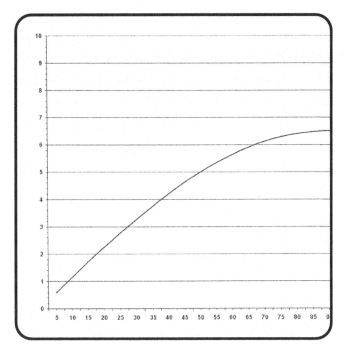

Figure 3.7 Curve of the Line of Force

which case the calculation becomes

$$F_1 \sin\theta = R_i = R_1 = F_r \quad (3.5)$$

F_1, 6.499 kgf multiplied by $\sin\theta$, 10, or .174, equals 1.130826 kgf, which is the imaginary R_i on the adjacent triangle, which has identical leg values.

It's interesting, at this point, to look at the change of intensity of the line of force, ΔF_r, into the nut slot as the values of θ move from the minimum to the maximum range of its operating domain. The minimum value can be anywhere just above zero degrees but never at zero. At zero degrees, the string would lie in the nut slot in a plane parallel to the fingerboard, and the nut junction would cease to be a boundary. The boundary would move back to the tuner, and the nut slot would become a discontinuity, and the musical function of the string would diminish nearly to the point of uselessness.

At any point above zero degrees, force begins to load in the nut slot. At one, using the string tension value, F_2, of 6.499 kgf, from our previous example, the line of force, R_1, becomes a meager .110483 kgf. At five, the value is still only .565413 kgf, and at ten, it passes 1 kgf to 1.130826 kgf. For values higher than ten, the force begins to grow at a higher rate, and by thirty, which is only roughly one third of the total available radial distance, the force loads at 3.2495 kgf, which is half of the total value of the string tension, F_2. At sixty, the value becomes 5.628134 kgf, which is close to the full value of F_2. At eighty-six, R_1 becomes 6.486002 kgf, and at eighty-nine, with a sine value of 1.000, $R_1 = F_2$, or 6.499 kgf. At ninety, the maximum sine value, the line of force, R_1, is at unity with the string tension, F_2.

The value of θ could continue beyond ninety, as found in other instruments such as mountain dulcimers, but the value of R1, the component of force perpendicular to F_2, will remain fixed at the ninety-sine value. Since the ninety value is rarely seen in guitars, the ninety measurement can be used as an arbitrary maximum limit in the range of the function's domain.

As you have probably noticed, the sequence of values of R_1 does not progress in a linear fashion. If the resultants are calculated for all the values of θ in its operating domain, from just above zero to ninety, and plotted on a graph, a familiar form materializes. It is the shape of the first quadrant of a sinusoidal waveform!

This means, then, that the values of R_1 can also be represented by the equation for a repeating waveform,

$$y = \sin(x) \quad (3.6)$$

This is the most rudimentary form of the *wave equation*.

Now, with operating values such as mass density, wave velocity, etc., of the specific strings we are using and Equation 2.5, we can calculate the amount of force pushing into the nut slot. This function is also used as a component in the calculation of the force of *friction*, the secondary force of interest in the examination of the headstock.

The concept of friction can be described as a *mechanically induced, electromagnetically based resistance to a change in motion*. It is best understood from a quantum perspective.

When any two materials are pushed into an interactive proximity (nothing ever actually touches at quantum level) by any type of force(s), some degree of electromagnetic bonding will occur. At quantum level, the surfaces of the two materials, even when polished, may appear as jagged, irregularly shaped protrusions and depressions. These quantum hills and valleys are called *asperities*. The random areas where these opposing surfaces come in close proximity may share electrons or even atoms. The aggregate of this informal bonding is known as the force of friction.

At lower pressures, the force of friction is directly proportional to the force between the interacting surfaces. As the pressure increases, the friction increases at a slightly higher rate. At higher pressures, as the interacting surfaces approach what is known as *saturation*, the force of friction quickly increases to seizing.

Any process that interrupts the electromagnetic interaction will diminish the force of friction. Placing a lubricant between the conjoining surfaces is the most commonly used method to lower friction. Wave motion in the interacting materials will also interrupt the quantum bonding and, thus, lower the force of friction.

Any two materials will have an innate potential for some degree of bonding with each other. The ratio of this bonding, or friction, to the force(s) pushing the two materials together is known as the *coefficient of friction*, fr_{co}. Typically, the designation is μ, which is also used to represent mass density, but in this book, I try to use only one designation per symbol. I prefer μ for mass density and fr_{co} for coefficient of friction.

Since the fr_{co} is simply a ratio, it is expressed as a dimensionless value, always above zero, and usually, but not always, not above one. Common fr_{co} values range between 0.3 and 0.6. In tests I've conducted on polished bone and steel, for example, the average fr_{co} value has been .384. It is important to note that fr_{co} results are empirical; that is, the coefficient cannot be precalculated. It can only be derived from experimentation and observation. As such, test results will be influenced by not only the molecular composition of the two interacting materials but also other factors including atmospheric dust, temperature, gases, vibration, and humidity. In metals, the oxide density and distribution, which is always increasing, adds another variable. The net result is that no two fr_{co} tests will be 100 percent identical when taken in environments similar to those where guitars are used. Although it is not the norm, it would be more accurate if frco values were written as approximations, such as ≈ 0.4. In tests I've conducted, the results ranged up to 30 percent from the averaged values. The fr_{co} could also be written with a ± designation, such as, for polished bone and steel, 0.4 ±30%.

To calculate the force of friction, one must have coefficient of friction values derived for sets of interacting materials that will be found on, for our purposes, guitars and other string instruments. Common materials will include plain steel strings interacting with bone and various branded synthetics, wound steel and nickel strings vs. bone and synthetics, as well as various

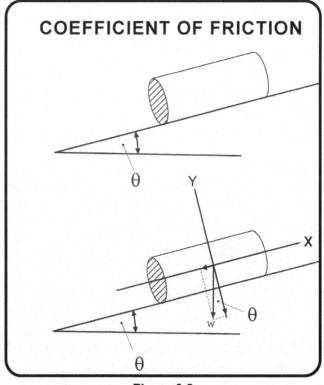

Figure 3.8
Calculating the Coefficient of Friction

bronze alloys and nylon vs. bone and synthetics. Any construction of string should not be neglected, which would include flatwound, groundwound, pressurewound, coated, and any other unique variety you might encounter. The same applies for nut material, whether it's bone, brass, synthetic, horn, wood, ceramic, aluminum, steel, nickel-silver, or any other identifiable, usable material. You should get in the habit of testing as many materials as possible for your own data set. I suspect everyone's test results will be similar to within some reasonable margin, but when it comes to fr_{co} results, don't rely on anyone else's figures until you have compared them with your own.

Determining the coefficient of friction results is actually very easy. To derive an equation for calculating the fr_{co}, set an imaginary object, such as a section of plain steel string, on an imaginary incline made of polished bone and gradually increase the angle of incline, θ, to the point where the piece of string begins to slide.

To determine the ratio between the tangential force acting on the piece of string and the normal, N, force acting between the two surfaces, we must first analyze the forces acting on the piece of string.

We can resolve the forces acting on the section of string into x and y components. The x-component of force is acting in a line parallel to the plane of the incline, and the y-component of force is acting perpendicular to the plane of the incline.

The x-component of force will consist of the normal force, N, which in this case is simply the weight of the string, and the force of friction, which is derived by

$$F_{fr} = fr_{co}N \tag{3.7}$$

So, the x-component becomes

$$Fr_{co}N = w(\sin \theta)$$

The y-component is simply the N force, or,

$$N = w(\cos \theta)$$

To derive our ratio, we divide the x-component by the y-component, which becomes

$$Fr_{co} = \tan \theta \tag{3.8}$$

Thus, to calculate the coefficient of friction for any two materials, all you need to do is measure the angle of incline where the material, such as the string segment in the previous example, begins to slip, and take the tangent of that angle.
Having the coefficient of friction, we can now calculate the approximate friction force in the nut slot. Thus,

$$F_{fr} \leq fr_{co}R1 \tag{3.9}$$

Or, using our calculations for the force perpendicular to the nut slot

$$F_{fr} \leq fr_{co}F1\sin\theta \tag{3.9a}$$

We can expand this description of the force of friction in the nut slot by including the actions of gravity on the mass of the string. Since gravity affects the mass of the string directionally, its frictional influence will be dictated by the way the guitar is held. In other words, when the guitar is held by a player in a prone position, the gravitationally effected force of friction will occur against the side wall of the nut slot. If the guitar is placed on its back, the way a lap steel is held, the additional friction will occur in the bottom of the nut slot. When the alignment of the gravitational force is in tandem with the resultant force, their vector representations are additive and Equation 2.9 becomes

$$F_{fr} \leq fr_{co} [\sin\theta (F_1 + mg)] \qquad (3.9b)$$

The combined function of the resultant force and the force of gravity in Equation 2.9b is referred to as the *Normal* force and is written as

$$F_{fr} \leq fr_{co} N \qquad (3.10)$$

This equation is the general description of the force of friction, which is also known as *Coulomb friction.* This is named after French physicist Charles-Augustin de Coulomb, 1736–1806.

Using Equation 2.9, we can now insert the quantities already derived for a plain .016" steel string tuned to G3 with a θ measure of ten degrees, loaded in a polished bone nut slot with an averaged fr_{co} ratio of .384, to obtain a friction value of

$$.384(1.130826 \text{ kgf}) = .434237 \text{ kgf}$$

This represents the averaged coefficient value, however. The fr_{co} tests did return results as low as .268, which would produce a friction force result of .303061 kgf, and as high as .510, which would show friction of .576721 kgf.

The gravitationally effected friction in the sides of the nut wall in this example is so minute that it may be considered negligible and is not entered into the calculation here. Gravitationally effected friction is proportional to the area of contact between the string and the nut slot and will be at a maximum when the force of gravity and the line of force, R1, are in direct alignment. When the two forces are in direct alignment, the gravitational effect, mg, will couple with the friction force derived from Equation 3.9 and follow the form of Equation 3.9b.

To calculate the gravitational force on the string in the nut slot, we can use torque equations to find its effect both in the nut and in the saddle. We first need to know the length and the weight of the string. Using the previous example, the length from tuner to nut is 0.1143 m; the length from nut to saddle (intonated length) is 0.64038 m; and the length from saddle to tailpiece will be 0.0635 m, for a total length of 0.81818 m. The averaged weight of the .016 in. string is 0.00101159 kg/m. Multiplying this by the length, 0.81818 m, equals .000827662 kg.

Applying the first condition of equilibrium, from Equation 3.2

$$\sum F = F_{nut} + F_{bridge} - 0.000827662 \text{ kg} = 0 \qquad (3.2a)$$

Using a torque equation to solve for F_{nut}

$$0.000827662 \text{kg} (0.34559\text{m}) - F_{nut}(0.64038\text{m}) = 0, F_{nut} = 0.0004466593436 \text{ kg}$$

Multiplying this by the gravitational constant

$$0.0004466593436 \text{ kg} (9.8 \text{m/s}^2) = 0.004377261567 \text{N}$$

Converting Newtons back to kilograms shows a gravitational force at the nut of .0004464806798 kg.

Solving for the force at the bridge, F_{bridge} -0.000827662kg(0.29479m)+ $_{bridge}$(0.64038) = 0, F_{bridge} = 0.000381002656 kg

$$0.000381002656 \text{ kg} + 0.0004466593436 \text{kg} = 0.000827661999 \text{ kg}$$

Including the gravitational force at the nut and recalculating the force of friction according to Equation 3.9b

.384 (1.130826 kg + 0.000446 kg) = 0.434408 kgf

The result for a string of this weight is only slightly higher than the value without the gravitational force and in a low friction nut would probably be insignificant. For a string of greater weight, such as a bass string, or in a higher friction nut in one of the instances when the friction is above its norm, however, the gravitational force could contribute to seizing and the associated tuning problems. Keep in mind that the results of Equation 3.9b will apply when the instrument is held so that the line of force in the nut slot and the force of gravity are in direct alignment. When the instrument is held in any other position, the gravitational force shifts away from the line of force, R1, and, depending on the area of contact between the string and the nut wall, the frictional effects may shift from the maximum predicted by Equation 3.9b to a significantly lower value.

Friction is sometimes discussed in terms of static or kinetic states. The type of friction where the conjoined surfaces of the tensioned string and the nut slot are stationary, such as what we have discussed up to this point, is known as static friction. This describes the state of friction that exists between the string and the nut slot up to the moment when motion occurs. This stationary condition encompasses the lack of movement of the string as well as the absence of any wave motion; this is the state of the instrument when it is not being played. In other words, static friction is a close estimate of the friction value before motion occurs.

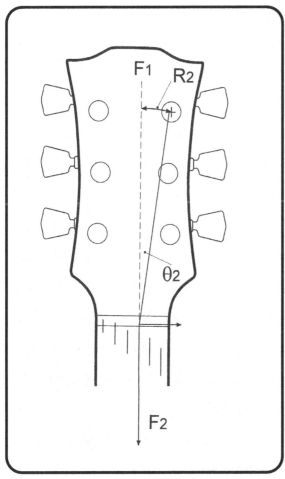

Figure 3.9
Dual Friction Component Headstock

When motion occurs the friction value changes. This type of friction is called kinetic friction and usually has a lower value than its static counterpart. The calculations used for deriving approximate values for kinetic friction are the same as those used for static friction.

The test used to derive the coefficient of kinetic friction is set up like the test for the coefficient of static friction, except instead of finding the angle where the string begins to slide, we find the angle where the string slides with constant speed. Instead of letting gravity start the string movement, we apply a light force, such as a tap, to the assembly. If the string starts and is stopped by the force of friction, we increase the angle of incline and bump it again until the string slides down the test medium. Then, using equation 3.8, we solve for the coefficient of kinetic friction.

The example used thus far in this examination of friction is representative of a headstock whose individual strings would have, neglecting the ranging effect of gravity, only one component of friction. On this type of headstock, the lengths of string between the nut and the tuners lie in the same plane as the lengths of string between the nut and the bridge. The only component of friction is formed by the severity of the angle θ pushing the string into the nut slot. From the friction perspective, this design may be regarded as a one-component headstock.

A more common example is the headstock whose string lengths between the nut and the tuners lie in a plane that intersects the plane occupied by the string lengths between the nut and the bridge. One component of force will be pushing into the bottom of the nut slot as a secondary component of force is pushing, simultaneously, into the wall of the nut slot. The components of these two forces will combine to form a new resultant force, from which the friction force can then be calculated.

This design may be regarded as a dual-component headstock.

Many one-component and dual-component headstocks have one or more string retainers. The string retainer is commonly used to pull the string(s) down securely in the nut slots to prevent the strings from rolling out of the nut. In addition to determining the primary θ angle, the retainer also becomes a secondary wave transit point with its own group of force functions. The friction associated with the retainer, of course, will couple with the friction in the nut slot. Any one or dual component with one or more string retainers may be regarded as a compound-component headstock.

For a dual-component headstock, the F_{fr} is described by the master equation of friction, 3.10, but will follow a variation of Equation 3.9a, which must now allow for the inclusion of the force acting against the side of the nut wall.

The angle formed between the side of the nut slot and the tuner will become the secondary angle of interest, $\theta 2$, and using the form of Equation 3.5

$$F1(\sin\theta 2) = R2 \tag{3.5a}$$

F1 is the same value we used in the previous calculations, $\sin\theta 2$ is the new angle between the side of the nut wall and the tuner, and R2 becomes the new resultant force from which the friction force is calculated. The secondary component force, R2, will increase proportionally with the increase in the angle $\theta 2$ at the side of the nut slot in the same manner as the force R1 increases in the bottom of the nut slot. The force of friction will also increase as R2 increases.

Treating the two resultant forces, R1 and R2, as vector quantities will allow us to combine them algebraically to create their resultant force, R3. This resultant force, R3, can be used to determine the combined effects of friction in the nut slot by revising Equation 3.9 to become

$$F_{fr} \leq fr_{co}\, 3 \tag{3.11}$$

where 3, by the Pythagorean Theorem, is determined by $3^2 = 1^2 + 2^2$.

Let's imagine the angle $\theta 2$, between the nut slot and the tuner post, measures fifteen degrees, and this is on the headstock that is on the guitar used in our previous calculations.

Then, from Equation 3.5a

$$6.499 \text{ kgf } (\sin 15) = R_2$$
$$6.499 \text{ kgf } (.259) = 1.683241 \text{ kgf}$$

Inserting the values of R_1 and R_2 into the Pythagorean Theorem,

$$(1.130826)^2 + (1.683241)^2 = R_3^2$$
$$1.278767442 + 2.833300264 = 4.112067706$$
$$R_3^2 = 4.112067706 \quad R_3 = 2.027823 \text{ kgf}$$

Putting the R3 and our previously determined coefficient of friction values into equation 3.11,

$$F_{fr} \leq .384\, (2.027823391)$$
$$F_{fr} \leq 0.778684182 \text{ kgf}$$

We can see from this example that as the components of friction increase, there is a corresponding increase in the total force of friction in the nut slot.

In summary, then, the musical function of a headstock arises from the interplay between the lines of force between the strings and the nut slots and the associated friction at those points. Any increase in the string-loaded force in the bottom of the nut slot will produce a proportional increase in the potential energy distributed in the immediate region of the nut. The increase in potential energy facilitates longitudinal wave motion, which subsequently improves the communication between the instrument and the strings. This is commonly regarded as an improvement in the tone of the instrument. As the string-loaded force increases, however, the force of friction also increases in all headstocks, regardless of single, dual, or compound component designs. Friction in the nut slot, however, is a source of both tuning problems and lower register intonation difficulties and needs to be minimized.

With this information, let's reassess the problem headstock at the hypothetical Cat Head Guitar Company.

The two head luthiers, Tom and Robert (don't call him Bob!), have decided to analyze their headstock for string force loading and friction qualities using the methodology we have just outlined. Taking some measurements, they note that their headstock tilts away from the plane of the fingerboard at a θ_1 angle of ten degrees, all six strings veer away from the nut slots at a θ_2 angle of twenty degrees, and since there are no string retainers, the force of friction will be calculated as a dual-component design.

They next take tension measurements of the actual strings that are shipped with the guitars. Like most other manufacturers, they use a common set of plain steel trebles and nickel-plated steel round wound basses with diameters of .009 in. to .042 in. Using a force gauge and a monochord, they arrive at the following values after multiple tests:

.009 in. at E4 329.628 Hz	55.573 N or 5.67 kg
.011 in. at B3 246.942 Hz	47.0736 N or 4.8 kg
.016 in. at G3 195.998 Hz	63.745 N or 6.499 kg
.024 in. at D3 146.832 Hz	67.6683 N or 6.9 kg
.032 in. at A2 110.000 Hz	70.6104 N or 7.2 kg
.042 in. at E2 82.407 Hz	66.688 N or 6.8 kg

They next must calculate the total force loading into the nut slot for each of the strings using the two-step process for determining the resultant, R_3, of a dual-component headstock.

The vertical component of force, R_1, will be calculated according to Equation 3.5 using the tension value of each string and the sine value for ten degrees.

E4	5.67 kg (.174) = 0.98658 kg
B3	4.8 kg (.174) = 0.8352 kg
G3	6.499 kg (.174) = 1.130826 kg
D3	6.9 kg (.174) = 1.2006 kg
A2	7.2 kg (.174) = 1.2528 kg
E2	6.8 kg (.174) = 1.1832 kg

The horizontal component of force, R_2, will be calculated according to Equation 3.5a using the same tension value for each string and the sine value for twenty. The Cat (same last name as their guitar company) brothers had used this angle between the nut slot and the tuning post for all six strings to allow for a big-sized cat head that would be easily recognizable from a distance.

E4	5.67 kg (.342) = 1.93914 kg
B3	4.8 kg (.342) = 1.6416 kg
G3	6.499 kg (.342) = 2.22265 kg
D3	6.9 kg (.342) = 2.3598 kg
A2	7.2 kg (.342) = 2.4624 kg
E2	6.8 kg (.342) = 2.3256 kg

Combining R_1 and R_2 for each string via the Pythagorean Theorem will produce its R_3 value.

E4	$(0.98658 \text{ kg})^2 + (1.93914 \text{ kg})^2 = 4.733604035$ $R^3 = 2.1756847$ kg
B3	$(0.8352 \text{ kg})^2 + (1.6416 \text{ kg})^2 = 3.3924096$ $R^3 = 1.8418495$ kg
G3	$(1.130826 \text{ kg})^2 + (2.222658 \text{ kg})^2 = 6.21897602$ $R^3 = 2.4937874$ kg
D3	$(1.2006 \text{ kg})^2 + (2.3598 \text{ kg})^2 = 7.0100964$ $R^3 = 2.6476586$ kg
A2	$(1.2528 \text{ kg})^2 + (2.4624 \text{ kg})^2 = 7.6329216$ $R^3 = 2.7627742$ kg
E2	$(1.1832 \text{ kg})^2 + (2.3256 \text{ kg})^2 = 6.8083776$ $R^3 = 2.6092868$ kg

The total force, then, that is exerted by the three plain steel strings into the nut is 6.5113189 kg. The total force exerted by the three nickel plated steel wound strings into the nut is 8.0197196 kg. The total force exerted by all six strings into the nut is 14.5310385 kg.

With these values Tom and Robert can calculate the amount of friction present in the nut. To help minimize manufacturing costs, they had used a low-cost molded plastic nut on their original headstock, and now they find it has a rather high coefficient of friction. Using the general Equation 3.10 for estimating the force of friction, and the fr_{co} value of .724 for steel and the molded plastic nut material, they find the total force of friction for the three plain strings is

$$.724 (6.5113189 \text{ kg}) = 4.7141949 \text{ kg}$$

The total force of friction for the three wound strings is calculated the same way, except the coefficient of friction for the nickel-plated wound strings and the nut material is .589, which is lower than the fr_{co} for the plain strings.

$$.589 (8.0197196 \text{ kg}) = 4.7236148 \text{ kg}$$

The total force of friction in the nut, then, is 9.437809 kg.

After considering the values of the forces in the nut, the brothers realized they were actually looking at a ratio. The factors that determine the Normal force in the nut form one term; the factors that determine the force of friction in the nut form the other term. If they set the desirable loading force, which on their original headstock is 14.5310385 kg, against the undesirable friction force of 9.437809 kg, a ratio of 1.539 is formed. Perhaps, they decided, what they needed to do was redesign their headstock so that it met the conditions of a higher Normal to friction ratio.

Tom, who had done the legwork on the Normal force part of the equation, suggested that they increase the angle of tilt of the headstock in order to obtain a higher level of loading force in the nut, which would strengthen the tone. But Robert, who had been preoccupied with the friction side of the equation, noted that an increase in the loading force is always accompanied by a proportional increase in the force of friction. Robert argued that a reduction in friction, such as taking all R_2 values to zero and effectively making their headstock a single component model, would increase the ratio and make their guitars more usable and desirable.

They were getting ready to recalculate both points of view when their sister, Kitty, stepped into the equations. She had been listening to the discussion and suggested that

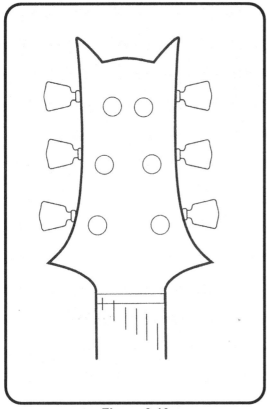

Figure 3.10
Cat Head Headstock (Narrow)

they might be able to define their ratio a little more precisely and save some time on their calculations.

Why not, first of all, set up the ratio according to the terms of Coulomb's general description of friction and Equation 3.9a:

$$F_{fr} \leq fr_{co} F_1 \sin\theta$$

The loading function will be on one side, and the friction function will be on the other, thus,

$$F_1 \sin\theta \,/\, fr_{co} (F_1 \sin\theta)$$

Reducing the ratio becomes

$$1 \,/\, fr_{co}$$

The headstock force ratio, then, is approximately equal to the multiplicative inverse of the coefficient of friction of the nut material and strings in use on the headstock and can be written as follows:

$$F_{rh} \approx (fr_{co})^{-1} \qquad (3.12)$$

If the coefficient of friction is the same for all the strings and the nut material, the headstock force ratio will be exactly equal to the inverse of their common coefficient. If there are two different coefficients, such as with steel and nickel strings, the F_{rh} will tend to shift away from the averaged value of the coefficients.

When Tom and Robert averaged the two coefficients of friction, .724 and .589, from their original calculations and took the inversion, the result was 1.539, which matched their original computations. Tom then agreed to convert the headstock to a single component design, but he still wanted to increase the angle of tilt to achieve more loading force. Robert agreed to an increase in tilt as long as they used a nut with a very low coefficient of friction. Robert felt that they needed to be cautious with higher levels of loading force in the nut due

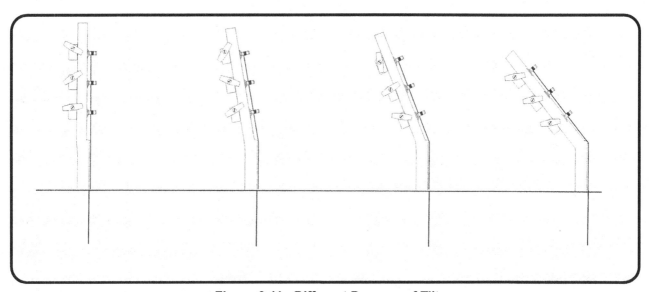

Figure 3.11 Different Degrees of Tilt

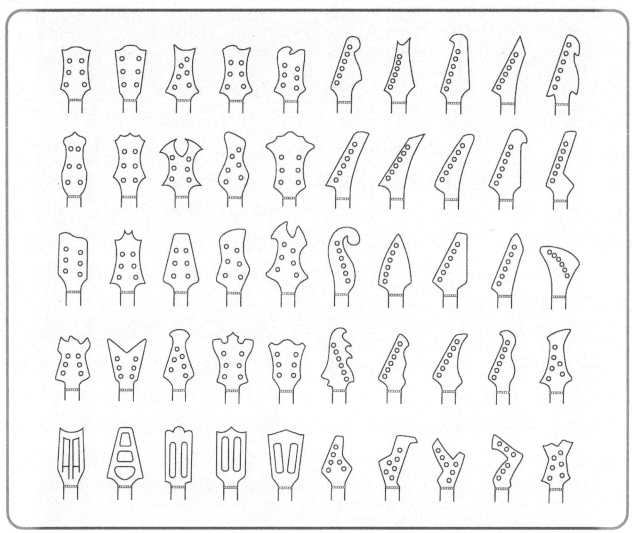

Figure 3.12 Headstock Designs

to the erratic nature of friction. In their coefficient testing there were rarely identical results for any material, and on occasion, there were uncharacteristically high levels. Using polished bone as the nut material and a fifteen-degree tilt, the headstock force ratio, F_{rh}, would become a respectable 3.65. Robert wanted no more than a fifteen-degree tilt; Tom wanted twenty degrees. Tom still wanted a twenty-degree tilt angle for the improved loading force.

    Kitty objected to any tilt angle above fifteen degrees. She hypothesized that the increased loading force would slightly deform the string in the nut slot area the same as a dual-component design. The compressed area of string would have a higher wave velocity than the rest of the string, resulting in a one- to two-cent increase in frequency on the first and possibly the second fret. Not only would that string be out of tune but the upper partials in all the rest of the register would be ruptured due to two dissimilar pitches being produced simultaneously in the same string.

    Tom reconsidered his objection, and everyone agreed to a temporary fifteen-degree tilt until they could devise an experiment to test Kitty's hypothesis.

    The brothers built a prototype neck with the redesigned headstock and showed it to Kitty, who wasn't impressed. It wasn't pretty. The original headstock had a cute nose in the center, and there was no room for a cute nose on the new headstock. Kitty felt that the trade dress had been compromised. There was room, however, to put extensions at either side of the base of the headstock so that it had the appearance of a mane, and this pleased everyone. Now the new headstock improved the tone of the guitar, made the guitar easier to tune, and helped the instrument stay in tune better even after more aggressive playing. The new styling of the headstock also retained the theme of their original design. Thus, the Cat Company partners successfully found a way to blend improved function with trade dress.

That leaves us with two challenges then, when dealing with headstocks. The first involves the creation of new headstocks. If you are trying to personalize a new headstock, whether it is for your own enjoyment or it is a work for hire, or it is for a new commercial application, you will be working with essentially the same issues that faced the imaginary Cat Head Guitar Company. We all want a headstock design that is both functionally efficient and stylistically distinctive. Plus, it must not look too similar to, or infringe upon, someone else's trade dress. For an exercise, you can study the many headstock shapes shown here and see if you can make some new, improved versions. Pick some shapes and tilt back angles and do the math and see what sort of headstock force ratios, F_{rh}, you can derive. If your new headstock design is intended for commercial application, do a thorough market investigation, familiarize yourself with the USPTO (United States Patent and Trademark Office), and consult with an intellectual rights attorney as necessary.

The second involves working with preexisting headstocks. Here you will encounter a fixed group of parameters, such as the tilt of the headstock and the positioning of the tuners in relation to the nut slots, that are generally best left unmodified. The task now lies in choosing the most effective strategies to simultaneously maximize the loading force in the nut while minimizing the friction force in the nut and at any points between the nut and the tuners. Common approaches involve using one or more string retainers to increase the loading force as well as changing the nut to a low friction material, such as polished bone. The string retainers can also be changed from metal to one of the lower friction synthetics, such as Teflon impregnated nylon.

Another common friction reducing strategy involves the use of lubricants. The earlier calculations in this chapter were all done in dry or non-lubricated mode, but with the addition of a lubricant, some of the coefficient values can drop to below one! Any substance that interferes with the quantum bonding mechanism between two interacting materials may be regarded as a lubricant and may be used between the nut and the strings as long as there are no undesirable consequences. Water, for example, would work as a lubricant, but it also would accelerate the oxidation rate on the strings as well as stress any exposed woods and possibly damage the finish. This makes it undesirable as a friction reducer on any instrument. (This example raises an important point: never waste an opportunity to exercise common sense.) There are several commercially available lubricants that can be applied to nut slots and retainers in very minute amounts, which will reduce friction. Probably the most popular home remedy I have seen players use in the nut slots is simple pencil lead. It is helpful, but it makes the instrument look dirty. I think if you are in a pinch for a bit of lubricant in a nut slot, try a crayon instead. The different colored waxes probably work just as well as pencil powder, they definitely look cleaner, and if you're going to mark up your guitar, it's more fun to do it with colors.

THE NECK AND THE FINGERBOARD

The fingerboard, supported by the neck superstructure, is the crossroad of the wave energy transfer between the nut and the bridge assembly and the area where the fundamental driving frequency is determined.

The neck structure, then, is tasked with vital musical and structural considerations.

MUSICAL CONSIDERATIONS

On the musical side, the historic record shows primary concern for the following: (1) *consonance*, and (2) the mathematical description for consonance. Consonance can be defined using the information in the first chapter of this book.

Consonance is the resonant condition where the constructive, or consonant, interference is the dominant feature of a tone. *Dissonance*, likewise, is the resonant condition where the destructive or dissonant interference is the dominant feature of a tone. There can be varying strengths of consonance as well as varying strengths of dissonance in a tone. These phenomena can be discerned aurally as well as demonstrated visually on a test device such as a spectrum analyzer.

On a string instrument with no stops, or frets, on the fingerboard, the string can be stopped at any point to produce consonance with a singer, another instrument, or another string on the same instrument. Placing predetermined stops, or frets, along the fingerboard enables the player to produce a more predictably pleasant tone more easily, which is more fun. So, which stops should be placed on the fingerboard and where exactly should they be placed? This is where the story of the modern fingerboard begins.

The woven fiber and gut strings of 2500+ years ago were crude compared to contemporary constructions. With the low level of homogeneity in those materials, the more powerful lower order waveforms would have consistently sounded the most consonant. The weaker higher order waveforms would have been corrupted with dissonants and sounded less desirable.

The test equipment, and string musical instrument most often referenced for interval experimentation in antiquity, was the *Kanon* (Greek), also known later as the *Qanun* (Arabic). The Kanon would hold one or more strings (four and eight were common) anchored at either end like the nut and bridge on a modern guitar and featured a movable bridge positioned beneath the strings. Positioning that bridge at different points along the length of the string(s) would allow for the exploration of consonant and dissonant length pairings.

Euclid's "Division of the Kanon," c. 300 BCE, references the instrument. Plato's "Timaeus" from the same era discusses the Kanon's tuning techniques, and Ptolemy's "Harmonics," c. 150 CE, describes the Kanon's string calculations.

It was demonstrated with largely nonhomogeneous strings and Kanons that the most consonant tones after the octave were the ones with simple integer ratios: the fifth, with a 3 to 2 ratio, and the perfect fourth, with a 4 to 3 ratio.

The Pythagoreans, c. 510 BCE, would only consider music made from the three octaves, 2 to 1, 3 to 1, and 4 to 1; the fifth, 3 to 2; and the fourth, 4 to 3. All other tones would be considered dissonant.

But what if you had been asked to play music for the Maenads at the Dionysian festivals? According to mythology, the Maenads were women who drank lots of wine during this celebration, danced into the mountains at night, and caught, tore apart, and ate wild animals raw. Would you have played only five combinations of tones for this crowd? I think I would have broken with the Pythagorean tradition and tried to fit in more notes to the octave.

Other players were using more tones than just the most consonant group; specifically, twelve of them per octave. Evidence of the twelve-interval octave was found in China in a set of chime bells recovered from the tomb of the Marquis Yi of Zeng, c. 500 BCE. This is roughly the same time in Greece that Pythagoras of Samos posited a mathematical argument that led to the tempering, or a small shifting of the pitch of notes, of the twelve-step octave. This suggests the twelve-step octave had been in use long enough to cause controversy about its consonance.

Pythagoras reasoned that the most pleasant-sounding intervals, the octave and the fifth, should be equal mathematically over a wide range. Specifically, twelve fifths should be equal to seven octaves. Looking at waveforms, which were unknown at that time, his instincts were correct. But factoring the string length math of the time used to describe intervals, he calculated

$$(3/2)^{12} = 531441 \text{ and } (2/1)^7 = 524288.$$

The fifths exceeded the octaves by a significant amount. In contemporary measurement the difference is 23.46 cents, which is almost a quarter of a semitone. This inequality became known as the *Pythagorean Comma*. (I will explain cents calculations later in this chapter.) This math reinforced the Pythagorean argument for consonance through simple integer ratios.

This marks the point in history, in my view, where the groundwork was established to fit twelve intervals into the octave in such a way that they would all sound pleasant enough to be usable. This system, incidentally, of using mathematical analysis and experimentation to explain observations would be later become known as the *scientific method*.

The scholar Aristoxenus of Tarentum, c. 330 BCE, advanced a theory that divided the note into twelve equal sonic parts instead of ratios. Using a twelfth of a tone, a semitone is equal to six steps, the fourth is 12 + 12 + 6 = 30 steps, the fifth is forty-two steps, and the octave is seventy-two steps. He was able to calculate the stops, or fret positions, on a scale length by use of the geometrical methods of his time, which involved constructing arcs and triangles and solving for a curvilinear locus.

Aristoxenus broke with the Pythagoreans' belief that ratios were the final judge of musicality. The following passage is from his work *The Harmonics*:

> "The geometrician makes no use of his faculty of sense perception. He does not in any degree train his sight to discriminate the straight line, the circle . . . But for the student of musical science accuracy of sense perception is a fundamental requirement."

Some music historians interpret Aristoxenus's work as an early example of tempering, but I believe his math demonstrates an attempt to explain musical consonance mathematically within the realm of human hearing.

In the meantime, the string instrument builders were tasked with positioning stops, or frets, along the length of the fingerboard in a manner that would make the most consonant tones. The stops themselves were made from gut tied around the neck, strips of bone and ivory glued to the neck or fingerboard, and eventually strips of metal enmeshed in the fingerboard. The instruments with an octave's worth of notes for each string or string group were the most popular, so the builds with twelve mostly accessible frets became the most common.

The builders had a shorthand method for calculating the positions for fret placement known as the *Rule of 18*. There were two ways of determining the fret locations.

1. The scale length, or distance from the nut edge to the front of the bridge/saddle was divided into eighteen equal parts. The first 1/18th distance was the location for the first fret. A measurement was taken from that position to the bridge and divided by eighteen; this second 1/18th was the location for the second fret. This process was repeated for the number of frets being used. The tones were satisfactory until the twelfth fret, which fell short of the octave.
2. The scale length is measured and divided by eighteen. The first 1/18th is the position of the first fret. The scale length minus the distance to the first fret is divided by eighteen; this becomes the location of the second fret. Next, the scale length minus the distances to the first and second frets is divided by eighteen; this is the distance to the third fret. This system is continued to the twelfth fret, which is very close to a perfect octave.

The rule of eighteen works a little more accurately using 17.82, or 17.817.

A cluster of events between 1584 and 1636 would establish the foundation for equal temperament tuning.

Zhu Zaiyu, China, published his work, "The Complete Compendium of Music and Pitch", in 1584, which included the mathematics for twelve-tone equal temperament, or *12-TET*. He showed that by dividing a length of string successively by the twelfth root of two, or approximately 1.059463, the length would be divided by two after twelve, or an octave's worth, of divisions.

Using the same math, after eighty-four divisions, or seven octaves, the length would be divided by a factor of 128, thus resolving the Pythagorean comma.

In Scotland, Baron Napier of Merchistoun, while trying to prove the reigning pope was the Antichrist, invented *logarithms*. He is known to have been working on them in 1594 and published his invention in his Descriptio in 1614. Coincidentally in Prague, J. Burgi also created a table of logarithms between 1603 and 1611, but Napier is credited with being the first to create them.

A logarithm (y) of a given number (x) to the base (a) is the exponent to which (a) must be raised to produce (x).

$$\log_a x = y \text{ and } a^y = x$$

Then, since

$$\sqrt[12]{2} \approx 1.05946, \text{ then } \log_{1.05946} 2 = 12$$
$$(\sqrt[12]{2})^{12} = 2, \text{ and } (\sqrt[12]{2})^{84} = 2^7 = 128$$

Our sense of hearing detects changes in pitch on a geometric, or multiplicative, basis. So, if we take a number that equals two when it is multiplied by itself twelve times, we will hear a uniform progression of pitches up to the octave when a string is divided in those proportions.

With this information a better system of fret positioning became available. The fret placement could be calculated by

$$\text{Fret (number)} = L \text{ (string length)} / \sqrt[12]{2}^{(y)}$$

where L is the string scale length measured from the nut to the bridge/saddle, the fret number is measured from the bridge/saddle to the fret position, and y is the power to which the irrational number 1.0594631 is raised, corresponding to the fret number.

The value of $\sqrt[12]{2}^{(y)}$ for the first 12 frets would be as follows:

$$(1.0594631)^1 = 1.0594631$$
$$(1.0594631)^2 = 1.1224621$$
$$(1.0594631)^3 = 1.1892071$$
$$(1.0594631)^4 = 1.2599211$$
$$(1.0594631)^5 = 1.3348399$$
$$(1.0594631)^6 = 1.4142136$$
$$(1.0594631)^7 = 1.4983071$$
$$(1.0594631)^8 = 1.5874011$$
$$(1.0594631)^9 = 1.6817929$$
$$(1.0594631)^{10} = 1.7817975$$
$$(1.0594631)^{11} = 1.8877487$$
$$(1.0594631)^{12} = 2.0000001$$

Then, in 1636, French mathematician Marin Mersenne completed the three basic laws governing string motion:

1. When the string's density and tension remain constant but the string's length is varied, the string's musical pitch (frequency) is proportional to its length. This is Pythagoras's law restated.
2. When the string's density and length remain constant but its tension is varied, the string's musical pitch is proportional to the square root of its tension.
3. For different composition strings of constant length and tension, the strings' musical pitches are proportional to the square root of the weight (density) of the strings.

Mersenne demonstrated that as tension is increased in the string, the forces tending to pull the string back to its original position are increased, and the motion of the string is proportionately increased. Conversely, if the mass of the string is increased and the same tension is applied, the motion of the string is proportionately decreased.

Recall the equations for determining frequency in a moving string from Chapter 1.

$$f = v/\lambda \quad (1.2)$$
$$\text{where } \lambda = 2l/h1 \quad (1.4a)$$
$$\text{and } v = (T/\mu)^{1/2} \quad (1.5)$$

These discoveries put in place the criteria used for fret placement in the majority of contemporary string instruments.

Finally, this discussion would not be complete without the inclusion of *cents*. Alexander Ellis described cents in his 1885 publication, *On the Musical Scales of Various Nations*, as a way to measure distance between frequencies. In an octave containing twelve hundred cents with twelve semitones, each semitone would have a hundred cents and each cent would be defined as the twelve hundredth root of two. This value, $2^{1/1200}$ or $\sqrt[1200]{2}$, equals 1.0005777895.

These *sonically* equal parts may have been what Aristoxenus was trying to express more than two thousand years earlier.

Since cents are logarithms, they can be added in the same way our sense of hearing combines tones.

Cents, then, are the logarithms of frequency ratios to the base 1.00057779.

$$c = \log 1.00057779^{fr}$$

where fr is a frequency ratio such as 3/2, a fifth.

A frequency ratio then can be calculated as

$$fr = (1.00057779)^c$$

Converting this function to log10 for easier calculations,
$$c = \log 1.00057779 fr, \text{ then}$$
$$c = (\log 10 fr) / (\log_{10} 1.00057779), \text{ and}$$
$$c = (\log 10 fr) / 0.00025086$$

which gives us an equation for calculating the cent value of any frequency ratio.

STRUCTURAL CONSIDERATIONS

The neck *superstructure* is tasked with providing a stable platform for the fingerboard, providing a low impedance pathway for the wave flow, and being comfortable to hold and play.

The neck, fingerboard, and the guitar body have historically been made from wood

Figure 3.13 Various Log Cuts

and virtually all contemporary constructions are still built from this amazing substance. Let's take a brief look at this material.

The body of a tree has two critical functions: It must support the weight of the canopy, or top of the tree, which can run into hundreds and thousands of pounds, and It must continuously circulate nutrients from the roots up to all of its parts. It grows and maintains its tremendous strength using a networking of structures:

1. *Wood vessels* are thin-walled cellulose tubes that carry sap from the roots up to the leaves.
2. *Tracheids* are short, thick, strengthening cellulose tubes running parallel to the wood vessels.
3. *Libriform fibers* provide stiffness for the trunk, and *medullary ray cells* run radially from the cambrium layer just under the bark to the *pith* in the center of the tree. They store fats and starches, the tree's building materials.

In the spring the cambrium fills up with sap rising from the roots. In the building season during the summer, it builds a thicker layer of cells inward and a thinner layer of bark outward. In the autumn at leaf fall time, the growth stops. The combination of the wide growth spring wood and the darker and harder summer growth creates the annual *growth ring*.

The trunk may be cut, for our purposes, three different ways:
1. Sawing perpendicularly to the grain direction will reveal the circular growth rings. This is called *cross cutting.*
2. Sawing radially into the center of the trunk will expose parallel grain lines. This is called *quarter sawn* and is valued for neck construction because of its stiffness.
3. Cutting parallel to the grain tangentially, or to the left, right, and through the center is called *flat sawn*. The center flat sawn cut is quarter sawn, and the grain lines on the rest of the cuts are wavy.

Cross cutting the trunk will reveal three types of tree structure:

1. Some trees have a core that is darker in appearance and harder than their sapwood. These are called *heartwood* trees. Some popular heartwoods include

ash, poplar, ebony, Indian rosewood, and mahogany.
2. Some trees have a uniform color throughout the heartwood and sapwood. These are called *hoopwood* trees. Spruce and field maple are examples.
3. Others have no heartwood and are uniformly hard. These are called *sapwoods*. Alder and birch are sapwoods.

Growth rings are visible in many woods, but in some they are barely noticeable or nonexistent. Ash, oak, elm, hickory, and pine have distinctive growth rings. Alder, maple, and poplar have subtle rings. Tropical trees that have uniform growth year-round, such as mahogany, show no growth rings.

The neck superstructure is typically made from quarter sawn or flat sawn pieces of wood. It can be one piece or a bonded structure of two or three or more pieces. Sometimes the headstock is continuous with the core element; sometimes it is spliced between the fingerboard and the core in a *kerf* joint. The goal is to keep the neck as stable as possible.

All woods contain some water after the initial *free water* has dried out. This bound, or *hygroscopic*, water is contained in the rows of micelles constituting the wood fiber. The wood releases this water when the surrounding atmosphere is drier and reabsorbs water from the air when the humidity is higher. This results in an expansion and contraction of the wood, which flexes the neck.

On April 5, 1921, Thaddeus McHugh of Michigan filed a patent for a neck for a musical instrument that contained an adjustable truss rod. The truss rod could be tightened to push

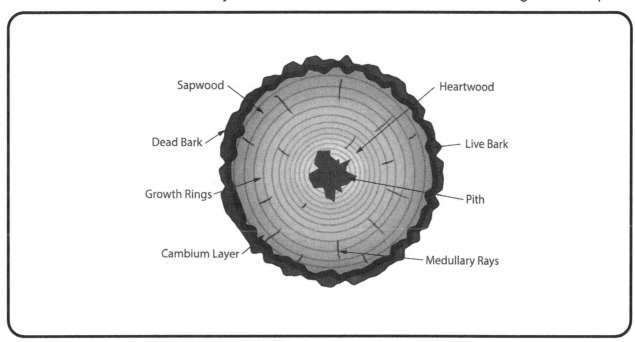

Figure 3.14   Log Cross Section

up toward the fingerboard to compensate for neck movement caused by changes in string tension and hygroscopic changes. The patent number 1,446,758 was assigned to the Gibson Mandolin-Guitar Company on February 27, 1923.

Over the course of the century the truss rod became a standard feature on almost all string instruments. A newer, two-way version came into use at the end of the century. The two-way truss rod pushes up toward the fingerboard when the adjusting nut is turned clockwise; it pushes away from the fingerboard when the adjusting nut is turned counterclockwise.

How will the waveform move through the neck structure?

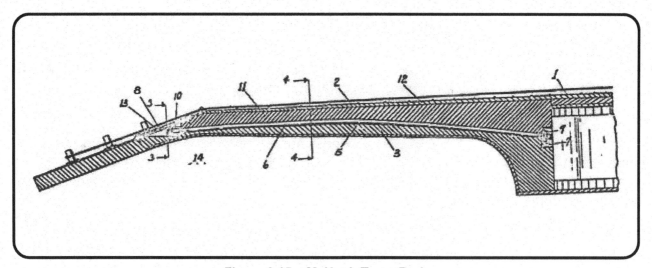

Figure 3.15 McHugh Truss Rod

From Chapter 1 we know the waveform will move with a predicted velocity through any homogenous material. For every change in density of a material, there will be a proportionate change in the wave velocity. How many different materials are there, then, in a neck?

The metal(s) in the truss rod will accommodate a specific velocity. The metals in the frets and tuners and screws will have their own identity. The velocity in the woods of the fingerboard and the neck superstructure will have multiple velocities depending on the densities of the wide growth and denser narrow growth grain lines.

These varying wave velocities will produce a resonant function in accordance with the resonant characteristics of these materials. The angled metal parts will produce dissonants; rounded parts will be more consonant. A square cut truss rod channel will produce dissonants; a rounded channel will be more consonant friendly. The wave flow will harvest the consonants from every component of the neck and take damage from the dissonant features of the neck. This resultant wave set, which is hopefully more consonant than dissonant, will merge with the resonant conditions presented by the body, bridge, and the rest of the instrument's parts in what is the instrument's *voice*. Our challenge, then, is to set the conditions that will allow the most favorable consonance.

Playing comfort is also a critical consideration.

The distance from the back of the neck, where the player's thumb anchors, to the tops of the strings above the frets can be considered the *working thickness* of the neck. It is a function of the physical thickness of the bottom of the neck to the top of the fingerboard plus the height of the fret wire and compounded by the setup of the instrument, which is a function of the arc of the fingerboard, string thickness, and tuning.

A thinner neck with taller frets, then, would have the same working thickness as a thicker neck with smaller frets, given that both would have the same fingerboard radius and the same gauge strings and tuning.

However, the neck with the larger fret wire will have an increased *coupling surface* between the fret and the fingerboard over the neck with the smaller fret wire, which will lower the impedance for the energy transfer. This will produce a more powerful tonal response than the smaller fret wire when the same amount of starting force is applied to the string.

Even though guitars have become a bit larger overall in the past three hundred years, the working thickness of necks has been relatively uniform. Even as guitar players in the last three centuries became larger, probably due to better nutrition, and guitar body styles grew dramatically in size in the nineteen hundreds, playability remained the top priority.

Obviously, the easier the guitar plays and the better it sounds, the more fun it is, so the working thickness should always be optimized. But not at the expense of the stability or wave flow features of the neck. No problem, right? Look at it as a challenge to your creative engineering.

THE BRIDGE ASSEMBLY

The bridge assembly can be regarded as a structure consisting of two key components: (1) the saddle, featuring the string intersection point, and (2) the string anchor, or termination point behind the saddle. The system in its entirety determines the wave path into the body.

The principal energy exchange point on the guitar is at the string/saddle intersection on the bridge. The nature of the energy exchange is a function of the following: (1) the loading force at the point of contact between the string and the saddle, and (2) the nature of the boundary conditions for the string at the point of contact on the saddle.

The loading force at the point of contact between the string and the saddle is described by Equation 3.1

$$f(F_r) = T_s \sin\theta \tag{3.1}$$

This is the same function that describes the loading force of the string in the nut slot and can be read similarly: the resultant line of force directed into the saddle is a function of the tension T_s in the string multiplied by the sine of the angle of interest θ, which is the angle of string descent behind the saddle away from the plane of the playing length of string.

As the string loading angle θ_l increases, the following happens: (1) the impedance to the exchange of longitudinal wave motion in the saddle decreases, and (2) the friction between the string and saddle material increases.

The force of friction is described by Equation 3.9a

$$F_{fr} \leq fr_{co} F_1 \sin\theta \tag{3.9a}$$

The strategy then becomes maximizing the loading force in the saddle and minimizing the friction force there. The primary working conditions for the string in the saddle are the same as those in the nut: a steeper angle of incline at the area of contact is preferable, a minimal friction component at the area of contact is ideal, and the point of contact between the working length of the string and the saddle/nut material must not move when the string is in motion.

The points at either end of the working string length determine the *boundary conditions* of the string. Just as the string leaves from a fixed position in the front of the nut, so should it leave from a similar fixed point on the saddle.

Recalling Equation (1.2a), which defines the frequency produced by a string as a function of the velocity per wavelength

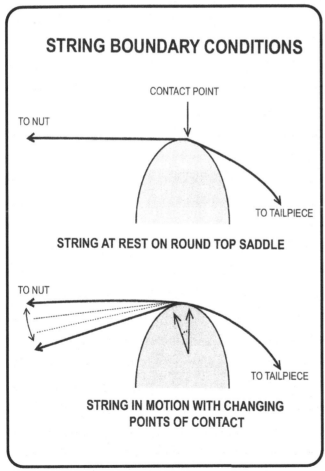

Figure 3.16
Unstable String Boundary Conditions

$$f = v/\lambda \tag{1.2a}$$

where the wavelength is determined by twice the vibrating string length per harmonic.

$$\lambda = 2l/h_n \tag{1.4}$$

This gives us the information for predicting the frequency for any length of string. If this length of string changes, the frequency produced will be changed as well. This has implications for the shape of the guitar saddle. (Figure 3.15)

The importance of the *fixed length* of string has been noted as early as c.1100 CE in Abu al-Salt's reference work on the construction of the kanon, Al-Qanun:

> . . . put a bridge made of a body with a broad seat and a *sharp edge* and let the . . . string ride on it in a notch.

This sharp edge would produce better defined lengths on either side of the bridge and more accurate string length ratios.

This didn't translate onto working instruments across the ages, however, as most string instruments had rounded top saddles. The rounded top saddle is still found on many contemporary electric guitars, basses, and acoustic instruments.

There are two dissonant issues associated with round top saddles.

The first involves multiple string lengths under the same tension. As the string restores itself to its original nonmoving state, it changes its point of contact on the curved part of the saddle, producing a changing frequency. The multitude of shifted frequencies in the string has the net effect of weakening the fundamental, disrupting the lower partials, and rupturing the weakest upper harmonics. Dissonance invades the structure and damps the overall resonance.

The second issue is the production of a nonmusical secondary frequency group as the string oscillates against the curved surface of the saddle. This droning effect, similar to the buzz produced by a worn fret, further disrupts the desirable harmonic structure, creating dissonance and its associated damping.

Using a saddle with a better defined, unmoving point of contact minimizes the introduction of dissonants and allows the string to produce stronger consonants. This stationary point of contact, or *SPC*, also reduces rounded top saddle noise and its associated damping to a minimum.

Use of an SPC allows the flow of the most consonant string information across the *bridge* and into the resonant systems of the body. Since the resonant systems of the body respond in kind to the structure of the incoming force, wouldn't the ear prefer a resonance derived from consonance over that of one created from dissonance? We will look at this in more detail in the following section on the body.

The second key component of the bridge assembly is the string anchor, which is located somewhere behind the string intersection point on the saddle. An examination of contemporary and historic bridge systems shows many approaches to string anchoring. The string anchor can most commonly be found as follows:

1. tied to some point behind and below the plane of the string intersection point;
2. secured to a separate fixture behind the saddle;
3. fitted in a receptacle on the back of the body so the string travels up through the body to the saddle;
4. locked in place directly behind the saddle;
5. seated in a moveable assembly behind the saddle, allowing for tension changes;
6. friction pinned in a hole behind the saddle; and
7. wrapped around and secured to a point beneath the saddle.

The string force loading and friction advantages and disadvantages of all these systems are readily apparent. When designing and building a new instrument, a higher force loading, lower friction bridge system is most desirable. If a variable tension string anchor system is to be used, then the friction issue must be addressed. All friction points must be minimized by means of a high polish, lubrication, or use of a lower friction synthetic material. Bear in mind that compromises in the wave path for the sake of tuning stability will reduce the tonal response of the instrument. Sometimes the fun of pitch shifting has to have its day, though. The challenge is to lessen the loading force as little as possible while maintain tuning stability.

The same principles apply to instruments that are already built, but there are different parameters. On new and used guitars and basses the bridge system has already been determined, so one must decide if it could be improved, and if so, how? If it has a plastic saddle, a polished bone saddle could be substituted. Could the loading angle be improved? If the saddles are rounded, could they be replaced with SPC style parts? Would it be more pragmatic to replace the entire bridge system? If the original parts are compromising the tonal and functional attributes of the instrument, then improvements can be made.

If the instrument is collectible, then the original parts are important to its long-term value. Every effort should be made to preserve them in optimum working condition, even if its performance could be improved by substituting better components.

After an assessment of the saddle and string anchor system of an instrument, a thorough review of the *wave path* should be made. You'll recall the nature of longitudinal motion from Chapter 1: the forcing function of the string information moves through all the parts of the bridge system that's in the line of force on its way into the body. The energy is taking the most direct route possible into the body; where must it go to get there, and how much energy is being dissipated along the way? Is the coupling area between the saddle and the body, or between the bridge chassis and the body, as large and flush as it can be? How about the mounting system? Are the screws or post anchors fit securely into the body?

It is desirable to familiarize yourself with as many brands and styles of bridge assemblies as you can find. Study how each one works with the string loading force and the associated friction. Bear in mind, though, that there are no brand names in wave motion; there are only interacting forces. Price is also not a gauge of performance; it's only an indicator of what it cost to bring that particular product to the marketplace.

THE BODY

The body is the structural centerpiece of the guitar; all of the key elements, which include the neck, the bridge assembly, and the pickup system (on amplified instruments), connect here.

It evolved historically as a resonant chamber and several thousand years later it is still, on many forms of the guitar, a resonant chamber. Even on solid body electric guitars and basses it still is a major contributor to the voice of the instrument.

The shape of the body is also important for playing comfort as it is being held. The body design is a factor in determining the center of mass of the instrument, which affects its balance.

The body then serves structural, resonant, and comfort functions.

Structurally, it is important for all the parts to be securely fastened to the body. Anything that moves out of synch with the musical function will damp the musical function. The neck, bridge assembly, all the components of the pickup system including the knobs and the strap mounts should be anchored firmly to the body. We want to make it as easy as possible for the wave flow to move unimpeded from one component into the next.

This great wash of wave information is what ultimately reappears in the string motion, which is then announced to the world through the air, with acoustics, and through the pickup system, with electrics. As explained earlier in the book, the resultant wave flow, or tone, is a conglomerate of all the resonant features in the instrument.

In a typical instrument, the resonant features are primarily a group of random structures. Each component is designed with the performance of a task in mind. The screws are designed to hold items together, the frets are designed to divide string lengths, and the tuning machines are designed to tension the strings, but none of these are designed to contribute a resonant function. Whatever manner in which they happen to resonate is purely unassigned and largely unmusical. The consonant qualities the instrument produces are diminished by the dissonant additives from all these random yet vital structures. So, what can be done about this?

Could the screws be built to resonate musically and still perform their bonding function? Could the frets be tuned? Could the tuning machines resonate harmonically and still tension the strings reliably? I'm sure you are thinking of a few ways this could work and a lot of ways that this couldn't work.

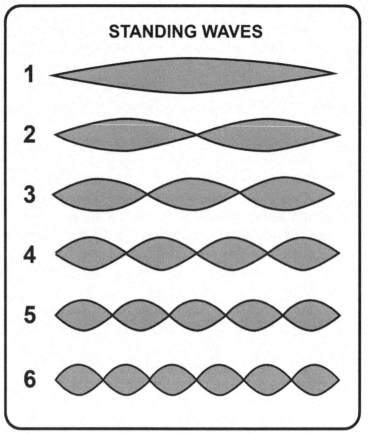

Figure 3.17   First Six Standing Waves

Let's look a little closer at the nature of musical resonance.

Back at the Cat Head Guitar Company, Tom and Robert were continuing the discussion on the meld of art and function in their instruments. They were satisfied with their neck design, and now they were exploring options for a body. They decided to start with the resonant musical function first and then engineer the structural and comfort features in accordance with the parameters necessary for the optimal musicality.

Tom and Robert began their examination at the string's sound energy's primary point of entrance into the body, which would be at the bridge anchor/body intersection. The forcing function at this point would be an energy package consisting of a fundamental frequency and its consonant overtone group propagating in a sinusoidal fashion.

Tom's initial reaction was since this energy group is a package of discreet sine waves that are round in nature, then the body and its associated internal structures must also be round in order for consonant resonance to occur.

That would mean that the body edges should be as round as possible, and the pickup, switch and control cavities, and any bridge routes should have rounded surfaces wherever possible.

Tom and Robert both agreed to keep the neck pocket square cut to make neck and body exchanges smoother. If the neck pocket on the body and the heel of the neck are interchangeable with other brand necks and bodies of the same scale, there would be more longevity for the parts.

Robert added that even with rounded external and internal body features, there is still a prevailing condition of resonant chaos in every instrument. The wave velocity in any two pieces of wood is unique. The resonant nature of the bridge, pickups, electronic components, knobs, screws, and other construction materials is completely random.

Tom referenced the historic record. The dominant body shape of guitar family and violin family instruments for several hundred years has featured upper and lower bouts of two different sizes. Usually there is a smaller upper bout that joins a larger lower bout at the waist, and the ratio of the sizes of the two bouts in some cases comes close to the ratio between a musical octave and a fifth.

The instrument family with this simple ratio predetermined resonant structuring has become the dominant style of string instruments. So, could the body's resonant conditions be more favorably structured, Tom wondered?

Robert roughed out a chart of the first six idealized standing waves on a string. The first drawing was an open string with a length ratio of 1/1, or an octave. The second drawing showed two equal standing waves with a length ratio of 1/2, which are octaves. The third drawing showed the string length divided into three sections with length ratios of 1/3, which is an octave and a fifth. The fourth drawing showed four equal sections with length ratios of 1/4, which are double octaves. The fifth drawing showed the string length divided into five sections with length ratios of 1/5, which are two octaves and a major third, and the sixth drawing showed six divisions with length ratios of 1/6, which are two octaves and a fifth.

Robert then suggested that they build rounded structures into the body with the proportions of the first six ratios.

Tom felt that there was some unnecessary duplication of the octaves and thought the 1/1, the 1/3, the 1/5, and the 1/6 might make the best grouping. That would enhance the resonance of the octave, fifth, and major third.

Kitty didn't like the potential look of the cavities, though. She didn't think the guitar should look like Swiss cheese or the moon. She thought the cavities could be cut concentrically into one area of the body which would save space for the other components.

The cavities could be cut into any solid part of the body as long as they were proportioned accurately, and the consonant resonance should be enhanced, Tom reasoned.

Robert suggested that the technique could also be applied to acoustic and archtop and violin family instruments as well. Instead of rounded, proportioned cuts in solid wood, proportioned rods, like sound posts in violin family instruments, could be positioned under the soundboard. There might be some loss of volume in some acoustics, but the consonance should improve.

This structuring, the Cat Head Guitar Company family agreed, should bring out the most desirable musical qualities of any instrument body. The body then could be shaped for balance, comfort, and aesth

CITATIONS AND REFERENCES

Statics The Physics Problem Solver, Dr. M. Fogiel, 1995 Edition, Chapter 2, Force Systems in Equilibrium

Vectors The Physics Problem Solver, Dr. M. Fogiel, 1995 Edition, Chapter 1, Vectors

Friction Engineering Mechanics, R. C. Hibbeler, 2007, The Feynman Lectures on Physics, Vol. 1 Richard P. Feynman, 1964, The Physics Problem Solver, Dr. M. Fogiel, 1995 Edition, Static and Kinetic Friction, pp. 49–60

Coefficient of Friction Engineering Toolbox.com, Friction coefficients and calculator

Coulomb Friction Charles-Augustin de Coulomb, 1756–1806, Recherches theoriques et experimentales sur la force de torsion et sur l'elasticite des fils de metal,1784

Division of the Kanon Euclid, c. 300 BCE

Timaeus Plato, c. 300 BCE

Harmonics Ptolemy, c. 150 BCE

Pythagoreans Pythagoras and the Early Pythagoreans, Leonid Zhmud, 2012, Pythagorean Women, Sarah B. Pomeroy, 2013

Marquis Yi of Zeng c. 500 BCE, Tomb of Marquis Yi of Zeng

The Harmonics Aristoxenus, c. 330 BCE

Complete Compendium of Music and Pitch Zhu Zaiyu, 1584

Descriptio Baron Napier of Merchistoun, 1614

Mersenne Marin Mersenne, 1588–1648, Mersenne's laws in Harmonie Universelle, 1636

On the Musical Scales of Various Nations Alexander Ellis, 1885

Science and Technology of Wood George T. Tsoumis, Manual of Guitar Technology, Franz Jahnel, 1981, pp. 55–96

Al-Qanun Abu al-Salt, c. 1100 CE

Chapter Four
Magnetism

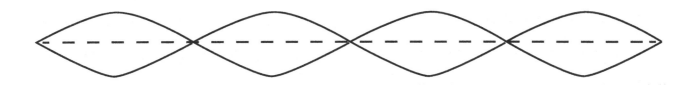

THE HISTORY OF DISCOVERY AND USE
PART I: 600 BCE TO 1900 CE

Have you ever played with a magnet and wondered, what is this stuff anyway? I wonder what the Greek philosopher Thales of Miletus was thinking in the sixth century BCE when he observed a rock that attracted pieces of iron to it? Diogenes, Aristotle, and others who attributed this discovery to him wrote that he believed part of the soul of the universe was in the material. Since he found the rock near the town of Magnesia, he subsequently called it "ho magnetes lithos," or the Magnesian rock. Although his investigations didn't reveal much about the phenomenon, his nomenclature was good enough that over two thousand years later the word "magnet" was still stuck to our language.

The Greeks, Romans, and Chinese of two thousand years ago were all aware of lodestone, or magnetite ($FE3O4$), a naturally occurring magnetized iron oxide. They knew that if you stroked a piece of iron with lodestone, the iron would take on the properties of the lodestone and be able to attract and magnetize other pieces of iron. It was interesting, but in the West there would be no practical use discovered for it for several hundred years.

As early as the second century CE, in China, someone had noticed that if a magnetized iron or steel needle was placed on a floating straw, the needle would align itself geographically north and south. By the eleventh century CE, compasses were in widespread use there, and by 1200 CE they had helped traders find their way to Western navigators.

In 1269, Petrus Peregrinus of France published his observations on the behavior of magnetized needles. He noticed that the tip that always pointed north, or the magnetic north pole, would repel another magnetic north pole. Also, the magnetic north pole of one needle would attract the magnetic south pole of another needle. Thus, similar magnetic poles repel; opposite magnetic poles attract.

In 1600, William Gilbert of England published "Of Magnets, Magnetic Bodies, and the Great Magnet of the Earth," the first scientific study of magnetism. He observed that our planet behaves like a giant magnet and also left us a record of the three main magnetizing techniques of the period. The first method involved touching the iron or steel with a lodestone. The second technique involved pointing the steel or wire in the north-south direction while it was being forged. Gilbert also noted that if vibrations were present during the first two magnetizing processes, the amount of magnetism would be increased. A third process involved heating a piece of iron to red hot, then leaving it to cool in the Earth's north-south magnetic field.

In 1750, John Michell of England used a balance of his own design to study attractive and repulsive magnetic forces. He discovered that magnetic forces decrease as the squares of the distance from the interacting poles increase. In other words, if you increase the distance between poles by a factor of x, then the resulting force decreases by $1/x^2$ of what it was originally. This inverse square law was coincidentally the same relationship that Newton had discovered for the force of gravitational attraction in 1687.

Although Charles Augustin de Coulomb of France later verified Michell's experiments with calculations derived from his torsion balance in 1777, it was Michell who first discovered a mathematical relationship between magnetic forces.

By the beginning of the nineteenth century some advancements in the description of magnetism had been made, but nobody was able to explain the nature of magnetism itself. Upcoming developments in electricity, however, would start to penetrate some of the mystery as well as begin to move magnet making toward a scientific footing.

In 1819, physicist Christian Oersted of Denmark put a compass close to a current-carrying wire and noticed that the needle pointed in a direction 90 degrees to the flow of current. Reversing the current made the needle point in the opposite direction, still at a right angle to the current flow.

In 1820, physicist Dominique Francois Arago of France demonstrated that while a current was flowing in a copper wire, the wire would attract iron filings. When the current stopped, the attraction stopped. This showed that iron didn't have a monopoly on magnetism. After his experiments, the new hybrid word "electro-magnetism" began making its way around scientific circles.

Also in 1820, physicist Andre Marie Ampere of France demonstrated that if two parallel wires had current going through both of them in the same direction, the wires would attract each other. If the current was going in opposite directions, the wires would repel each other.

Furthermore, if you wound the wire into a coil and sent current through it, all the coils would attract one another and produce the equivalent of a bar magnet with north and south magnetic poles.

In 1823, physicist William Sturgeon of England wrapped a coil of wire around an iron bar. When current passed through the wire, the iron amplified the magnetic field, creating the first electromagnet.

This was also a handy new way to magnetize materials, and Sturgeon started experimenting with both traditional and nontraditional materials. In particular, he magnetized alloys such as copper, silver, and gold with zinc, proving that the magnetic properties were not due to iron. Sturgeon's alloy experiments laid the groundwork for today's permanent magnet industry.

In 1831, Michael Faraday of England essentially reversed the concept of the electromagnet. He discovered that when you inserted a magnet into a coil of insulated wire, a current would be induced in the wire. The current would flow in one direction as the magnet moved in, and it would flow in the opposite direction as the magnet was pulled out. This is the principle by which guitar pickups work, and since all developments in pickup design must ultimately trace their origins to Faraday's experiments, Faraday must be credited as the grandfather of the guitar pickup.

The most historically significant contribution, however, came forty-two years later from James Clerk Maxwell, a British physicist and educator. In his "Treatise on Electricity and Magnetism," published in 1873, he presented his four equations describing the behavior of electricity and magnetism. Maxwell showed that electricity and magnetism are actually just manifestations of the same phenomenon, and that one cannot exist without the other. Any electromagnetic occurrence has both an electric and a magnetic element at right angles to one another.

Although Maxwell's equations unified electromagnetic theory and brought the world of classical physics to its apex, they didn't do a lot directly for magnet manufacturing at the time. Trial and error experimentation with different alloys had produced tungsten steel magnets by the mid-1850s, and chrome steel magnets were developed in 1870. These alloys were widely used throughout the end of the century.

Dramatic steps forward in magnet manufacturing would not take place until after German physicist Max Karl Ernst Ludwig Planck had advanced his quantum theory in 1900. Planck came up with the idea of energy packets he called quanta while working on a problem involving the energy levels of different wavelengths of radiation.

Planck's concept, which Albert Einstein used to explain the photoelectric effect in 1905 and led to the first proof that atoms really existed, revolutionized the world of physics. Everything developed up until 1900 is now called classical physics; everything that followed Planck's quantum theory from 1900 to the present is considered modern physics.

Much of modern physics in the twentieth century has focused on atomic and subatomic studies and discoveries. The understanding of quantum behavior that unfolded over the twentieth century is responsible for our current working knowledge of magnetism and the subsequent development of new and improved permanent magnets.

PART II:
THE QUANTUM ERA: 1900 CE TO THE PRESENT

The chronology of revelations of quantum behavior has not followed a step-by-step sequence into the workings of magnetism. So, to make an easier read, I've summarized our contemporary understanding of magnetism, which we owe to the work of many great minds in the twentieth century.

Our knowledge of atomic structure has mushroomed over the past hundred years. What was once considered the basic building block of matter has been shown to consist of many particles and sub particles, all bearing distinctly different characteristics.

Fortunately, we do not have to go far into the atom to discover the building blocks of magnetism, but a rudimentary understanding of atomic structure and behavior is very helpful. Let's take a brief review of what the Greek philosopher Democritus, circa 300 BCE, called atomos, which he believed was the smallest, unbreakable fragment of matter.

First of all, Democritus's definition of the atom has been updated a bit. We know now that an atom can be broken down into smaller fragments of matter—which include protons, neutrons, and electrons—and these particles can be broken down into even smaller fragments, which include quarks, photons, and virtual massless particles. Even though Democritus's atomos is no longer indivisible, he still had a very good concept.

In fact, if we just refine his definition to read that an atom is the smallest unit of matter that cannot be reduced chemically to any other form of matter, then we still have a pretty good contemporary definition of an atom. This definition provides us with a working concept, but it begs a question about the actual size of the atom: Just how small is this basic chunk of matter?

An atom of hydrogen, for example, is 10^{-8} cm—or 1 angstrom—in radius. This is one billionth of a centimeter, which is pretty tiny. If we had a traditional microscope that could magnify down to that level, we still could not see the atom because the smallest wavelength of light is only about 5×10^{-7} m. In fact, with the right equipment, we could place about fifty atoms in a row along the length of a single wavelength of light.

It gets even better. The nucleus, or center of the atom, has a radius of 10^{-13} cm. To put this into perspective, if this atom were the size of a small music store, the nucleus would be about the size of the period at the end of this sentence. With dimensions like these, it is apparent that we are dealing with a reality unlike anything we experience in our day-to-day life. This area is the quantum world, and it is very weird, but it is a good weird and a good exercise for the imagination.

Neglecting the multitude of elementary particles, the nucleus consists, simplistically, of protons and neutrons. The bulk of the mass of the atom is contained in the nucleus. The mass of the proton and the neutron are approximately equal, and can be measured in amu's, or atomic mass units, as well as Mev's, or million electron volts. One Mev equals 1.782×10^{-27}g. The mass of the proton is 1.6726×10^{-24}g. In atomic mass units, the neutron is 1.0086654 amu and the proton is 1.00734 amu.

The electron, with a mass of .511 Mev, circles the nucleus several billion times per second. Atoms can have one or more electrons orbiting the nucleus at different levels, called shells. Only certain numbers of electrons can occupy each shell, which are filled in a specific sequence.

Each electron has a negative electrical charge, which is attracted to the positive charge of the proton in the nucleus. If there are two protons in the nucleus, there will be an attraction for two orbiting electrons; if there are ninety-two protons in the nucleus, there will likewise be an attraction for ninety-two electrons.

If we consider the wave aspect of the electron, we'll see that each of the shells will have to consist of a whole number of wavelengths. The electron closest to the nucleus will have an orbit consisting of one wavelength. Each successive orbit away from the nucleus will contain progressively more whole numbers of wavelengths. If we couple the speed of the electron around the nucleus with the up and down motion of wave behavior, we will come up with something resembling a dimpled cloud.

Austrian physicist Erwin Schrodinger applied the mathematics of wave mechanics to the electron in 1926 and showed that there is a specific way each successive electron cloud fits on top of the previous cloud. There can only be certain distances between orbits, with each orbit containing specific ellipses. Each electron also will have a specific tilt and spin. Schrodinger's mathematical system, with some added refinements, is called quantum mechanics and is still in use.

The wave aspect of the electron, by the way, also explains why it doesn't simply dive and crash into the nucleus: it can't move any distance shorter than one wavelength.

Now that we have a nice, cloudy picture of the atom, and the electron in particular, you may have already guessed something about one of the universe's tiniest magnets. Remember that Oersted and Arago observed that a moving charge is accompanied by a magnetic field, and that Maxwell formalized the equations governing this behavior. We also know that the electron has a negative charge and a movement, since it has a spin and an orbit. The electron, being a moving charge, is therefore accompanied by a magnetic field called, at quantum level, a *magnetic moment.*

The magnetic moment itself is a force that is transacted by particles that have no mass. The electromagnetic effects of attraction and repulsion are caused by the exchange of lots of these zero mass particles referred to as virtual photons. These massless virtual particles, then, are the essence of the basic magnetic moment.

Most atoms do not have a magnetic moment because their electrons' moments all cancel one another. This includes, specifically, all the atoms with an even number of electrons. The atoms with an odd number of electrons are the ones of particular interest to us. The extra electron on these atoms gives the atom a spin and thus a magnetic moment. Furthermore, the extra electron needs to be in an inner shell. A loose electron in an outermost shell will quickly join with another atom having a vacancy in its outermost shell, forming a molecule. Loosely held electrons in the outermost shell also can become current in electrical applications, which we will look at more closely in the next chapter.

In the periodic table of elements, the atoms meeting this requirement are found in the transition elements, which include chromium (Cr), manganese (Mn), iron (Fe), cobalt (Co), nickel (Ni), palladium (Pd), and platinum (Pt). In addition, all the rare earth elements have unfilled inner shells and permanent magnetic moments.

From a magnetic perspective, matter may be classified into five different groups: (1) diamagnetic, (2) paramagnetic, (3) ferromagnetic (4) antiferromagnetic, and (5) ferrimagnetic. Of these five groups, the ferromagnetics are the ones that experience the most profound changes when exposed to a moderate magnetizing field. These include the aforementioned transition elements, rare earth elements, plus a variety of compounds.

In a typical ferromagnetic material, the atoms (magnetic moments) tend to group themselves into little clusters called *domains*. Each domain can consist of 10^{12} or more atoms and will have a uniform magnetic alignment. The domains tend to arrange themselves so that there is no overt magnetism to the material.

Each domain does not abruptly end where the next domain begins, however. There is a small boundary region called a domain wall of about a hundred atoms in diameter between the domains. The domain wall, which is also known as a *Bloch* wall, consists of a number of atomic planes that progressively rotate from the direction of one domain's alignment to the direction of the adjoining domain's alignment.

A *unit crystal* can be composed of 10^6 domains, and one cubic centimeter of a typical ferromagnetic matter would be made up of 10^2 crystals. That's a whole lot of magnetic moments that can be aligned by an external magnetizing force, which would then create a tiny permanent magnet, which could then possibly become a part of your guitar or bass pickup.

As you can imagine, magnet making has undergone tremendous advances since the advent of the quantum age, and the innovation process continues. There are special characteristics that are shared to some degree by all magnets, which include the following:

- The magnetizing force,
- Flux and flux density
- Permeability
- Reluctance
- Demagnetization and magnet stability.

BASIC MAGNET CHARACTERISTICS

Imagine that we have a cubic centimeter of ferromagnetic material that we want to magnetize. Let's see what happens when we apply forces.

There are many ways to apply a proper magnetic field. It can be done as simply as holding another magnet beside our ferro "magma," which is the oldest magnetizing technique. It is important, however, to use proper calculation and technique to achieve the desired magnetic effects from each different material. There are dc electromagnet magnetizers, dc open solenoids, iron bound solenoids, and capacitor discharge impulse magnetizers that can put a precalculated field into our ferromagma. Let's just imagine that we have a proper and controlled magnetic field that we can apply to our material.

Our ferromagma sample is composed of numerous domains, all positioned so that the net magnetic moment is zero. As we apply a magnetic field, or magnetomotive force, to the sample, the domains that are aligned in the direction of the mmf begin to grow. When we remove the mmf, something curious happens. Some of the domains spring out of alignment, and the magnetic force that remains is smaller than it was when the mmf was applied. This residual magnetism is what makes permanent magnets possible.

Now if we decide to demagnetize our little chunk of matter, something similar will happen. If we apply enough negative mmf to bring the sample back to zero magnetism, then remove the mmf, there will still be a bit of residual magnetism. If we increase the negative

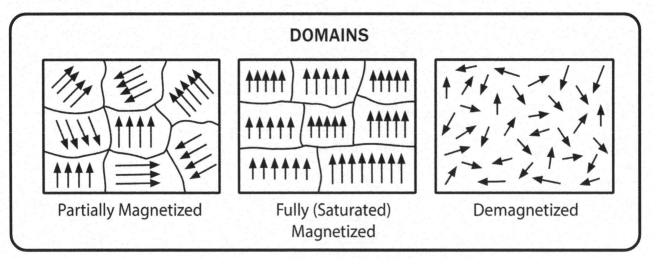

Figure 4.1 Domain States

mmf even more, then remove it, then we will achieve a zero level on the sample. The amount of force required to change the sample from its saturated state to a zero state is called the *coercive force*. The coercive force measurement will give you an indication of how well a material will retain its magnetism.

Coercivity is measured in Oersteds in the CGS system and ampere-turns per meter in the SI system.

You may have noticed that during both the magnetizing and demagnetizing states, the residual magnetism always lagged behind the magnetomotive force. This behavior is a characteristic of *hysteresis*.

If you plot a graph of a material's hysteresis curve from saturation to zero to negative saturation to zero and back to saturation again, you'll have a curve that is symmetrical on the left and right sides of the vertical axis. If you repeat this curve for several smaller values of mmf on the same material and connect the tips of each curve, you'll have the normal magnetization curve for the material.

The normal magnetization curve can be regarded as the fingerprint of a magnetic material. This curve will show how much magnetism a material will retain when different levels of mmf are applied to it.

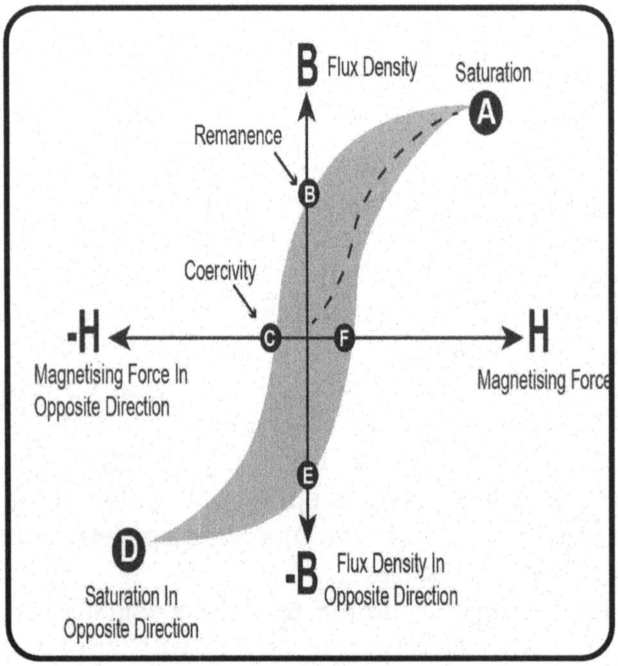

On a graph or chart depicting a magnetization curve, there will be two areas of measurement. One, H, will represent the magnetizing force and the other, B, will represent the material's magnetism, or, more precisely, the flux density. It's common to find the values of H and B expressed in both SI and CGS units, so it's prudent to be familiar with both systems, or at least have a conversion table or capability handy.

Let's look at H, the magnetizing force or pressure, first. In the older CGS system an arbitrary unit of magnetism called a unit pole was established. If two similar unit poles are placed 1 cm apart in a vacuum and repel one another with a force of 1 dyne, then the magnetizing force, H, is equal to 1 oersted.

In the SI system, H consists of the magnetomotive force per unit of length. The

Figure 4.2 Hysteresis Curve

mmf has its own symbol, F, and is defined as the external force or pressure required to establish magnetism in a material.

$$H = F / l \tag{4.1}$$

The magnetizing force is the mmf, measured in ampere-turns per length, measured in meters.

To convert at/m to oersteds, multiply by 1.257 X 10^{-2}. To convert oersteds to at/m, multiply by 7.958 X 10. Thus, 1 Oe equals 79.58 at/m; 1 at/m equals 12.57 X 10^{-3} Oe.

The magnetism a material acquires can be represented as magnetic flux, Φ. Faraday came up with a good idea, which is still in use, for representing magnetism with imaginary lines of flux. The flux lines are continuous, unbroken loops that concentrate in the material's interior, exit through the north pole, and travel the easiest route to reenter through the south pole. In a homogenous material, such as a commercial magnet, the flux lines are equally spaced within the material and symmetrically spaced outside the material.

The CGS unit of measurement for flux is the *maxwell*. The SI unit of measurement is the *weber*. One maxwell equals 10^{-8} webers. One weber equals 10^8 maxwells. The amount of flux, or flux lines, per unit of area is called the flux density, β. This is one of the key characteristics of any magnetized material.

$$\beta = \Phi / A \tag{4.2}$$

The CGS unit for flux density is the *Gauss*, G, which is a maxwell per square centimeter. The SI unit is the *Tesla*, T, which is a weber per square centimeter.

One gauss equals 10^{-4} teslas. One tesla equals 10^4 gauss.

The amount of magnetism or flux density, β, a material will experience when exposed to a level of magnetizing force, H, is related to its *permeability*, μ. Some materials, such as wood, plastic, glass, copper wiring, and your hands, that are found on and around your guitars are magnetically invisible. As far as the magnetizing force, H, is concerned, it may as well be passing through a vacuum. The permeability of a vacuum, or free space, is called the magnetic constant, μ_0, whose value in CGS is simply unity (lG = 1 Oe), or 1, and in SI is 4π X 10^{-7} wb/am.

Some materials, such as iron, nickel, steel, cobalt, and alloys of these metals, will retain high values of flux density, β, when subjected to a magnetizing field, H. These materials have high permeabilities and form the permanent magnets that are used in guitar and bass pickups.

Permeability can be defined as a material's susceptibility to magnetism.

Relative permeability is a term that is frequently used to describe magnetic materials. Relative permeability, μ_r, is the ratio of a material's permeability to the magnetic constant, μ_0.

$$\mu_r = \mu / \mu_0 \tag{4.3}$$

For nonmagnetic, low permeability materials, $\mu_r = 1$. For high permeability, magnetic materials, $\mu_r \geq 100$.

Flux density, permeability, and magnetizing force can be related in general form by this equation:

$$\beta = \mu H \tag{4.4}$$

The flux density of a material in a magnetizing field consists of two components:(1) the magnetizing field, and (2) the lines of flux induced in the material relative to the material's permeance. This is called the intensity of magnetization, I. A nickel or steel guitar string in the field of a pickup would have a quantity, I.

Equation 3.4 can also be written as

$$\beta = \beta_i \pm \mu_0 H \qquad (4.5)$$

where β_i equals $4\pi I$, the intrinsic magnetization, or magnetization due to the material.

Reluctance, the resistance of a material to the establishment of flux lines, is another important consideration in magnetization. It can be illustrated by the following equation:

$$R = l / \mu A \qquad (4.6)$$

R is the reluctance, l is the length of the magnetic path, μ is the permeability, and A is the material's cross-sectional area.

Obviously, calculating a magnetic circuit could get complicated in a hurry, but there are a few generalizations that can be drawn from the relationship depicted in Equation 4.6. First, reluctance is inversely proportional to the material's cross-sectional area: the bigger the area, the smaller the reluctance and the easier it is for flux lines to be established. Secondly, it is directly proportional to the material's length: the greater the length, the greater the reluctance and the harder it is for flux lines to get established. Finally, the reluctance is also inversely proportional to the permeability: the larger the permeability is, the smaller the reluctance will be, and the easier it is for flux lines to be established.

Thus, we can relate reluctance to flux by

$$\Phi = F / R \qquad (4.7)$$

We can also see that the magnetomotive force can be expressed as the product of the flux and the reluctance.

$$F = \Phi R \qquad (4.8)$$

Reluctance, R, is usually measured in rels or At / wb.

DEMAGNETIZATION

Once our little chunk of ferromagnetic material is magnetized, how long will it stay magnetized?

A stabilized permanent magnet requires no energy input to maintain itself. Once everything's atomically aligned, it will spin along, quantum wise, indefinitely, or realistically, until a demagnetizing force acts on it. Energy in some form must be supplied to the magnet before any change will take place. Let's look at some of the ways a magnet can become demagnetized.

The most fundamental form of demagnetizing energy that all magnets experience comes from within the magnet. Recall that the lines of flux exit through the north pole of the magnet and reenter through the south pole. The flux from the north is also attracted to the south through the inside of the magnet. This internal intrinsic magnetization, B_i, establishes a degree of demagnetizing field, H_d, in accordance with the geometry of the magnet.

If all the domains were perfectly aligned, this effect would be negligible. However, when a ferromagnetic material is released from its maximum magnetizing field, some of the domains always snap out of alignment. The magnet's own demagnetizing field, H_d, then pushes these domains into a reverse alignment, which then increases the net demagnetizing force. The magnet's own demagnetizing force will subsequently be additive with any other demagnetizing influences the magnet might encounter.

Demagnetizing energy can also be supplied to a magnet through thermal means. At a certain elevated temperature, every type of magnet reaches a point where the thermal agitation overpowers the exchange forces, called the *Weiss molecular field*, that hold adjacent atoms in parallel alignment. This scrambling point is called the *Curie point* and is way beyond room temperature for most magnets (900 degrees Celsius for cast and sintered Alnico 5). When a ferromagnetic material is taken above the Curie point, it becomes paramagnetic.

There is some change in magnetic properties with less extreme thermal conditions, but the degree of change varies from one magnetic material to the next, and it is not directly related to the magnet's flux or field. Specifically, the change of flux with temperature variation depends on the particle size, internal field, and domain structure of the material.

The old-style inclusion hardened steel magnets, for example, depended upon structural inconsistencies to maintain their magnetism. Domain wall motion was impeded by the presence of nonmagnetic materials, such as precipitated carbides, mixed in with the ferromagnetic material. It took coercive levels of 50 to 250 Oe to push a boundary through one of the nonmagnetic inclusions.

The newer style fine particle magnets, which include alnico, ferrite (ceramic), and rare earth materials, use a different approach to maintain their magnetism. The particles in these magnets are prepared so that their dimensions are less than the width of a domain boundary, thereby eliminating the boundary. Changing the direction of magnetization requires rotating all the atomic moments in each particle all at once, which requires quite a bit more energy than what it takes to move a domain wall. Fine particle magnets have coercive values, H_c, ranging from 500 Oe to more than 10k Oe.

It would appear that thermal disruptions would be easier in the lower coercive value materials, and it is somewhat true, but it is not linearly predictable. The material's composition as well as its physical shape contribute to the way in which temperature demagnetizes it; thus, direct measurements of the change of coercive force with temperature have to be made for each material and shape.

Short term temperature elevations aren't the only way a magnet can be changed by thermal activity. *Magnetic viscosity*, or the way a magnet yields to the stress of a constant temperature over an extended period of time, is another source of thermal demagnetization. Applying a small stress over a very long period of time can have the same demagnetizing effect as applying a large stress over a very short period of time. Magnetic viscosity is also referred to as *thermal after-effect*.

Magnetic field effects are another source of demagnetization. Ac and dc fields as well as sources such as other magnets can supply a demagnetizing pressure. Using a magnet's β/H information, the effects of a demagnetizing field can be calculated.

Magnet manufacturers use both field and thermal effects for demagnetization.

Mechanical energy including impact shocks, vibrations, and certain ferromagnetic contacts also demagnetizes. Impact shocks work against the viscosity much like thermal after-effects, except the length of time is replaced by the number of mechanical stresses.

You've probably had an Allen wrench, or a screwdriver, become inadvertently magnetized from being too close to a magnet, such as a pickup or speaker magnet. Soft ferromagnetic materials are easily magnetized and demagnetized. Knocking the wrench or screwdriver against a hard surface will usually demagnetize the material. If it has had a strong mmf applied to it, it won't demagnetize with just one rap. With successive blows, the magnetism will progressively weaken until it is unnoticeable.

Vibrational energy is a milder form of an impact shock; it just takes longer to effect a comparable degree of demagnetization.

Close proximity and direct contact with ferromagnetic materials, including other magnets, can also have a demagnetizing effect. If a ferromagnetic material is brought close to the length of a magnet, magnetic poles form along the surface of the magnet, which then alter the flux pattern.

Losses occurring from direct contact with ferromagnetic materials will vary according to the method and number of contacts. The smallest loss occurs when a ferromagnetic material contacts the pole end of a magnet and is removed either by a direct pull or by sliding off to the side. The largest loss occurs when a ferromagnetic material contacts the magnet parallel to the pole ends, or direction of magnetization, and is removed by a sliding motion toward either pole end. Demagnetization increases with the number of contacts.

Losses occurring from magnet-to-magnet contacts will also vary in the same way as ferromagnetic material contacts. Magnet-to-magnet contacts do produce more significant demagnetization losses, however. When two magnets are separated by a direct pull after repeated contacts in the repelling position, losses can go as high as 25 percent. When they are pulled apart in the direction of magnetization after repeated contacts in the repelling position, losses can approach 60 percent.

DEMAGNETIZING EFFECTS ON PICKUPS

Individual demagnetizing effects, then, include self-demagnetization; short- and long-term thermal pressures; external magnetic fields including ac, dc, and those from other magnets; mechanical energies from impacts and vibrations; and ferromagnetic proximity and contact effects, as well as magnetic contact effects. Studies have been done on all of these effects, so a magnet's performance over a specific period of time in any of these conditions can be predicted. This is very useful for some applications, but it does not present a complete picture for a magnet in a guitar pickup.

There are no comprehensive studies on the combined effects of demagnetizing influences, so there is no reference guide detailing how a specific magnet will behave under combinations of pressures. This raises several questions. What combinations of demagnetizing influences will have the greatest effect on different types of magnets? What combinations will have the greatest short-term or the greatest long-term effects? Will certain combinations enhance or even cancel one another?

Imagine the life of a magnet inside a pickup over a period of time. It's born, so to speak, with its own self-demagnetizing condition, and then things get complicated quickly. Thermal pressures abound in rides in trucks and cars and car trunks, hot stages and stage lighting, outdoor jobs under the sun, and unpredictable storage conditions, which can include attics. There's a never-ending wash of magnetic fields from amplifier transformers, speaker magnets, and most electronic devices. Impact energies are commonplace, from bouncy car rides to bumps inside guitar cases to the pounding many guitars get while being played. Since the guitar vibrates for its main occupation, there are also incessant mechanical vibrational energies acting on the magnet. In pickups with exposed magnet pole pieces, there are ferromagnetic proximity and contact effects from the guitar strings and random ferrous objects touching the magnets. It's normal for several of these conditions to be present at the same time.

It's not unreasonable to expect a pickup magnet to lose magnetism after it has been inside a working guitar for a while. This will affect the voicing of the pickup, of course. An upcoming section on electronics will explain how this happens.

MAGNET STABILITY

A magnet's susceptibility to demagnetizing influences can be minimized by a technique known as *pre-stabilizing*. All initially saturated magnets, at some higher temperature specific to their composition, will experience a 5 percent to 30 percent loss of magnetism within a short period of time. This primary loss is followed by a long period of stability.

By applying a limited ac or dc or thermal energy demagnetizing field to the saturated magnet, the magnet will be forced past its initial loss phase to its stabilized mode. Tests have shown that fully magnetized, unstabilized magnets will be subject to different degrees of demagnetization losses from thermal exposures, magnet-to-magnet contacts, and impact and vibration effects, while the same stabilized magnet will experience virtually no demagnetization from the same pressures.

It would follow, then, that the magnets in a typical pickup would have some losses after a period of time and would need to be saturated back to their original flux levels to achieve the pickup's original performance. At this point, it is simpler to replace the pickup with a new one, unless you like the voicing and performance of the worn pickup. The magnets can be tested with a gaussmeter and compared to the original specification of the magnet if that information is available from the manufacturer.

My own guess is most of the pickups made with ferrites will have very little change over a player's lifetime. The alnicos will be more likely to change the pickup's voicing and performance after a lot of exposures. Some testing will have to be done to see how accurate my instinct is, though.

MAGNETIC CIRCUITS

A circuit, paraphrasing the Random House Unabridged Dictionary, is an act of going around, a circular journey, or a path that has the beginning and the ending at the same place. I like the concept of a path because of the implication that something is supposed to travel on it and the implicit invitation for exploration.

On a magnetic circuit, the lines of flux, forming closed loops of the shortest length possible between the north and south poles of a magnet, are what occupy the circuit's path. The lines of flux will tend to follow the easiest path between poles. If a piece of ferromagnetic material intersects a flux line, the flux will route through the material for a distance before it hops back out on its way to the attracting pole. That's because the ferromagnetic material has a greater conductivity, or permeance, and thus less resistance, or reluctance, to the lines of flux than does air or free space.

There are a few basic relationships that govern magnetic circuits. The most basic of all is the relationship between the flux, the magnetomotive pressure trying to establish the flux, and the opposition to the establishment of flux. It can be expressed as

$$\Phi = F / R$$

from Equation 4.7, where flux, Φ, equals magnetomotive force, F, divided by reluctance, R. Since reluctance is difficult to calculate, it is usually easier to arrive at the magnetizing force per unit length of magnetic circuit.

$$F = H\,l \tag{4.9}$$

If we regard the relationship between flux, magnetomotive force, and reluctance as an interaction between effect, (Φ), cause, (F), and opposition, (R), then we can visualize any one of the three components in terms of the other two.

Thus, we would have flux as the quotient of magnetomotive force versus reluctance, as in equation (4.7), as well as

$$F = \Phi R \tag{4.10}$$

and

$$R = \Phi / F \tag{4.11}$$

Another relationship worth remembering is the magnetic circuital law,

$$\Sigma \sigma F = 0 \tag{4.12}$$

which says that the sum of the mmf rises and the sum of the mmf drops around the course of a magnetic circuit is equal, or, to put it another way, the algebraic sum of the rises and drops is zero.

Let's look at an imaginary, simple magnetic circuit consisting of a pole piece magnet, a length of ferromagnetic guitar string, and the air gaps separating the two. The magnetizing force of the pole piece magnet is equal to the magnetizing force across the air gap between the exiting (north) pole and string length, plus the magnetizing force across the air gap between the string and the returning (south) pole of the magnet. This is equivalent to saying that the magnetizing force across the magnet (rises) minus the magnetizing forces across the other three segments of the circuit (drops) is equal to zero.

This is purely an imaginary circuit, because in real life the mmf fans out in all directions and particularly toward materials of higher permeability. On an instrument, the mmf would route through adjacent strings, screws, springs, bridge parts, truss rod components, and similar materials on its way to the return pole of the magnet. The computation for this circuit is more complex, especially when the strings begin moving, but the outcome will be the same as for our imaginary circuit.

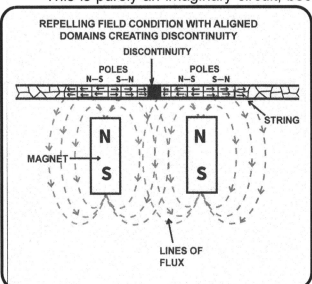

Figure 4.3 Repelling Field

On this complex magnetic circuit, we will also find that the sum of the fluxes entering a junction will equal the sum of the fluxes leaving a junction. This can be written as

$$\Phi_1 = \Phi_2 + \Phi_3 \tag{4.13}$$

where the flux divides between two materials of differing permeabilities. When the fluxes exit these materials on their way back to the magnet, we will have

$$\Phi_2 + \Phi_3 = \Phi_1 \tag{4.13.b}$$

as the flux converges at the return pole.

MAGNETIC FIELDS AND STRING MOVEMENT

Now that we have reviewed the fundamentals of magnetism, let's return to our examination of string movement. In particular, let's look at some examples of how

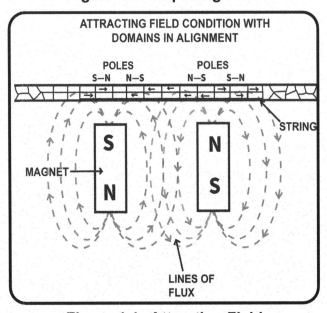

Figure 4.4 Attracting Field

string motion is affected by the presence and nature of magnetic fields. (See Figure 4.3 and 4.4)

There are three conditions that need to be considered that are commonly found on instruments:

1. **The No Field Condition**. The string encounters no magnetic field. Such a condition is found on an acoustic guitar that has no magnet-based pickup.
2. **The Repelling Field Condition.** The string length passes through two or more similar fields, as would be found on a guitar with two or more north pole facing-up pickups
3. **The Attracting Field Condition**. The string length passes through two or more opposite fields, as would be found on a guitar with a pickup with a north pole facing up, then a pickup with a south pole facing up, then another pickup with a north pole facing up toward the strings.

In the No Field Condition, the moving string couples both its own and the guitar's resonant information as described in Chapter 1. The domains are aligned randomly.

In the Repelling Field Condition, the same information attempts to form in the string, but something interesting happens. On a guitar with two pickups having the same polarities facing the strings, the lines of flux leave the up-facing magnet pole, travel in either direction

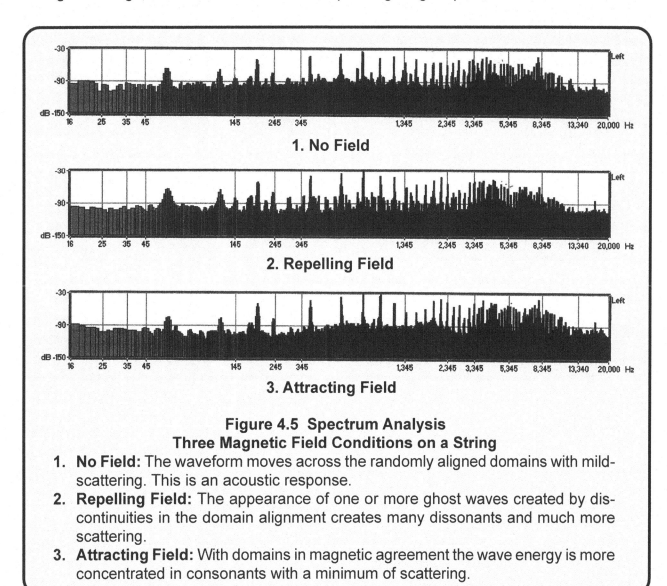

Figure 4.5 Spectrum Analysis
Three Magnetic Field Conditions on a String
1. **No Field:** The waveform moves across the randomly aligned domains with mild-scattering. This is an acoustic response.
2. **Repelling Field:** The appearance of one or more ghost waves created by discontinuities in the domain alignment creates many dissonants and much more scattering.
3. **Attracting Field:** With domains in magnetic agreement the wave energy is more concentrated in consonants with a minimum of scattering.

through the strings, and exit the strings to reenter the down-facing magnet pole. The flux from either pickup travels through the ferromagnetic string material, aligning the domains until the similar fields encounter one another at some point between the pickups. In this repelling zone a domain wall will form where the flux lines are exiting the string, effectively creating a crystalline discontinuity inside the string. This irregularity will be seen by the longitudinal wave motion as a speed bump of sorts.

The more powerful part of the wave motion will plow mostly undisturbed through this irregularity, but the weaker, higher frequency components will be more disrupted, with some energy reflection from the node. The reflected energies form what I call a *ghost wave,* which will establish between the boundaries formed by the discontinuity and the saddle edge. The interaction between the ghost wave and the normal wave function of the string will produce primarily dissonate information, which will result in an overall weakening of the musical structure.

Viewing this phenomenon on a spectrum analyzer will reveal a diminished fundamental and harmonic overtone series, with an increase in the number and strength of scattering, or adjacent nonharmonic features. On a guitar with three of the same repelling field upwards pickups, the situation is compounded by the addition of a second ghost wave, which disrupts the tone a bit more.

In the Attracting Field Condition, the string still carries the same original resonant information, but something even more interesting happens! On a guitar with two pickups with opposite attracting fields facing the strings, some of the lines of flux will exit one pickup's pole piece, travel along the string and enter the other pickup's pole piece, thus magnetizing the string length in a uniform direction. With the string's domains aligned in a more orderly sequence, the material's impedance to the wave motion is lowered, making it easier for the fundamental and overtone series to establish.

Viewing this condition on a spectrum analyzer will reveal a more pronounced fundamental and harmonic overtone series, with less scattering. On a guitar with a third attracting field pickup, the string's magnetic alignment becomes more enhanced, decreasing the string's mechanical resistance to the wave motion, and results in a strengthened harmonic tonal response.

Besides multiple pickup situations, there are other scenarios where the strings can encounter repelling fields.

On a typical pickup with six common alignment pole pieces, there are six repelling fields facing upward. As a string moves inside one field

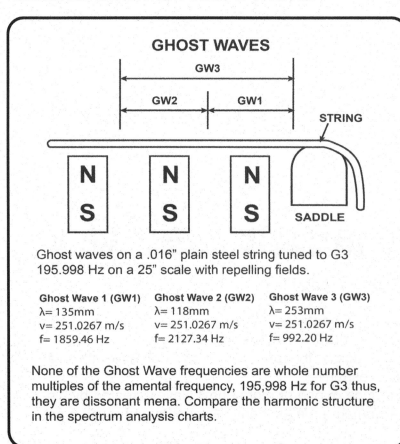

Figure 4.6 Ghost Waves

on a one pickup or an attracting field condition guitar, there will be an attracting field response. When the string is stretched from its home field into the repelling field zone of an adjacent pole piece, there will be a repelling field response with harmonic disturbance.

Leo Fender put this phenomenon to work in the design of his Jazz Bass pickup. By centering the string between two closely spaced repelling pole pieces, the percussive high frequencies associated with the initial attack of the note are disrupted. The Fender company in the late 1950s, according to Leo Fender, was having problems related to the punch of the Precision Bass pickups, so this design was conceived to soften the attack and instituted into their newer, deluxe bass model.

Another condition that is commonly found on guitars and basses is a tuning distortion resulting from improper string-to-magnet proximity. This is most prevalent on lower frequency tuned strings of higher permeance when they become very close to a neck or middle position pickup field. As the vibrating string passes close to the pickup, it accelerates as it approaches the field and decelerates it leaves the stronger part of the field, in accordance with the inverse square law of magnetic attraction. The deceleration is a little more pronounced, however, and results in a braking effect on the rate of the transverse wave through the field. When the string is played open, farther away from the field, it sounds in tune. However, as the string is played up the register and closer to the field, it sounds flat. Moving the saddle forward worsens the condition, though. Lowering the pickup to the level where its field will no longer interfere with the string motion will remedy this.

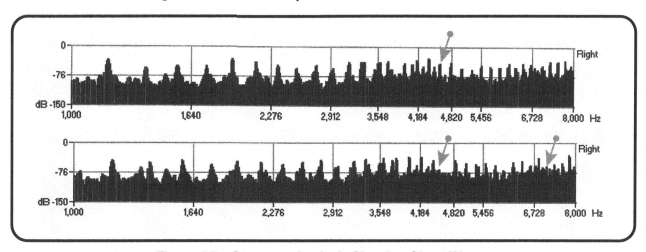

Figure 4.7 Spectrum Analysis Showing Ghost Waves

CITATIONS, REFERENCES AND FURTHER READING

Thales of Miletus, c. 624 BCE to 546 BCE, see Aristotle's De Anima.

Democritus, c. 460 BCE–c. 370 BCE, Greece, The Greek Atomists and Epicurus, C. Bailey, 1928, Handbook of Greek Philosophy from Thales to the Stoics, Analysis and Fragments, Nikolaos Bakalis, 2005

Lodestone The Book of the Devil Valley Master, Lushi Chunqiu, 400 BCE, China

The Letter of Petrus Peregrinus on the Magnet, AD 1269, a letter written by Petrus Peregrinus de Maricourt, translated by Brother Arnold, 1904

De Magnete, Of Magnets, Magnetic Bodies, and the Great Magnet of the Earth, William Gilbert, 1600, England

A Treatise of Artificial Magnets, John Mitchell, 1750, England

Der Geist in der Natur (The Soul in Nature), 1854, Christian Oersted, Denmark, 1777–1851

Annales de Chimie et de Physique, Dominique Francois Arago, 1824, France, also Oeuvres Completes de Francois Arago, 1856

Expose des Nouvelles Discouvertes sur l'Electricite et le Magnetisme, Andre Marie Ampere, 1822, France

British Royal Society of Arts, Manufactures and Commerce, 1822, William Sturgeon, England

Experimental Researches in Electricity, Vols. 1 and 2. Michael Faraday, 1839

Treatise on Electricity and Magnetism, James Clerk Maxwell, 1873, England

On an Improvement of Wien's Equation for the Spectrum, translation from the original 1900 publication by Max Karl Ernst Ludwig Planck, Germany, by D. ter Haar, 1967

An Undulatory Theory of the Mechanics of Atoms and Molecules, Erwin Schrödinger, published in The Physical Review, Dec. 1926, Vol. 28, No. 6

Physics Problem Solver, Fogiel, 1995, Magnetics, pp 742–779

Handbook of Magnetism and Magnetic Materials, edited by Coey and Parkin, 2021

A Guide to Understanding, Specifying and Using Permanent Magnetic Materials, MMPA Magnetic Materials Producers Association, 8 S. Michigan Ave, Suite 1000, Chicago, Illinois 60603

Standard Specifications for Permanent Magnet Materials, MMPA Standard No. 0100-00, available online

Chapter Five
Electricity

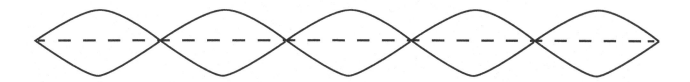

Let's review the group of events in our signal chain up to this point. First, the string is set into motion, producing a wave package consisting of the string's resonant information, which consists of its signature fundamental and harmonic overtone series. This energy group then washes through the string boundaries into the instrument where it gathers resonant information from all the components and reflects back up into the string. This information is further conditioned by the magnetic field(s) of the instrument's pickups. The moving string now carries this resonant information as it couples with the pickup's magnetic field and moves flux in tandem with its own motion.

Recalling Faraday's observation that moving magnetic lines of flux across a stationary wire produces an electrical current in the wire, we now are positioned to produce an electrical image of the string's information. All we need is some mechanical arrangement of magnets and wire in proximity to the moving string, right?

We will look at some of the ways magnets and wires have been put together to accomplish this task in the following chapter, but first let's take an overview of the basics of electricity as they pertain to pickups and guitar circuitry.

THE HISTORY OF DISCOVERY: THE QUEST FOR THE ELECTRON

As early as 600 BCE, in the time of Thales of Miletus, pieces of amber were known to acquire an unusual power. When the amber was rubbed, it could attract certain objects. The Greeks didn't name the power, but they did call the amber *elektron.*

Around 300 BCE, Greek philosopher Theophrastus observed that substances other than amber could also have this power.

William Gilbert of England was the first to publish a scientific study of this phenomenon in 1600 CE. He was also the first to derive the word *electric* from the old Greek word for amber, which he also distinguished from magnetic phenomena.

Otto von Guericke of Germany was the first to build a machine that could produce an electric charge. In 1672, his sulfur ball on a hand crank didn't have any practical application, but it must have sparked some curiosity among observers.

We don't know if Charles Francois de Costernay Du Fay ever handled von Guernicke's sulfur balls, but we do know he was the first to point out that there are two types of electric charges: positive and negative.

Pieter van Musschenbroek, in 1776, was the first to invent a device that could store a great amount of electric charge. This first condenser was called a *Leyden jar*, named after the University of Leyden, where he worked.

Benjamin Franklin, of colonial North America, charged a Leyden jar in 1752 by flying a kite in a thunderstorm. His experiment demonstrated that the electricity in lightning was the same as that in the condenser. I imagine that most, but not all, of Franklin's contemporaries were, contrary to standard scientific procedure, content to not try to duplicate his experiment.

The second half of the eighteenth century and the first half of the nineteenth century were filled with discoveries about the basic characteristics of electricity.

In 1766 Joseph Priestly established by experiment the inverse square law of the force between electric charges. Charles Augustin de Coulomb proved that the force between charges is also proportional to the product of the individual charges. Michael Faraday's work included the development of the concept of electric lines of force, as well as his experiments with electromagnetically induced charges. In 1840, James Prescott Joule and Hermann Ludwig Ferdinand van Helmholtz proved that electricity is a form of energy and that electric circuits obey the laws of the concentration of energy.

The major step down the path toward the discovery of the electron, however, was taken by Alessandro Guiseppe Volta in 1800 with his announcement of his discovery of the battery. By dipping two dissimilar metals in a saltwater solution, he was able to produce a current. By hooking multiples of these cells together, he was able to produce a high level, continuous current.

Everyone back then wanted to get a good look at raw, fundamental electricity in order to have a better understanding of it. Nobody knew what it was; Benjamin Franklin, in fact, speculated that it was a fluid that was part of all matter. The game plan, though, was to have the stuff reveal itself by forcing a large enough quantity of it through a vacuum.

Volta's batteries got everyone working to produce bigger and better ones, and eventually Faraday came up with a method for producing vast amounts of current, so the power supply problem was solved.

Johann Heinrich Wilhelm Geissler, a German glass blower, invented an air pump in 1855 for making vacuums. Geissler then blew a glass tube with a piece of wire in either end and sucked out as much air as he could with his pump. Faraday called the two wires the anode and the cathode from the Greek words for the upper way and the lower way, and these devices became known as Geissler tubes.

When current was passed through these tubes, a glow originated around the cathode. Everybody started calling this glow cathode rays, and the tubes were called cathode tubes. Better tubes were developed, namely by William Crooks in 1878. Eventually two parallel metal plates were used in the tubes.

Joseph John Thompson's experiments in 1897 showed that the cathode rays consisted of negative electric charges. With further experimentation, he was able to calculate the mass of a single cathode ray charge, which turned out to be considerably smaller than an atom. This was the discovery of the first subatomic particle, which Thompson called the *electron*.

The discovery of the electron was another piece of the puzzle that led to the development of quantum theory. It's also the star performer in every guitar circuit, so let's look at how it behaves.

BASIC CONCEPTS

In 1905 Albert Einstein published the first of his papers on mass/energy equivalency. In 1921, his equation appeared as

$$E_0 = mc^2 \tag{5.1}$$

This describes the relationship between mass in its resting state and energy. The value of a mass with no forces acting on it multiplied by the speed of light squared is the value of its energy equivalency.

If the mass of an electron is 9.1091 X 10^{-31} kg, then multiplying that by the speed of light squared, $(299,790,000 \text{ m/s})^2$, equals 1.602 X 10^{-19} joules, or one electron volt, eV. Putting this in a more familiar perspective, it takes about a trillion trillion of these little guys to equal one volt.

The electrons on the outer shell of an atom are the easiest to remove by an external force. At a larger distance from the attracting charges of the protons in the nucleus, they are the most weakly held and usually the first ones to be struck by an incoming force.

The force, in whatever form it may take, that moves these little quantum satellites around is referred to as an *electromotive force*. It is also known as *voltage* and is viewed as a difference of electrical potential. This difference between the most negatively charged point where there is a maximum number of electrons and the most positively charged point where there is a minimum number of electrons is measured in *volts*, V. Voltage when being referred to as an energy source is also designated as E.

A volt is the amount of *electromotive force*, EMF, or pressure it takes to move a one ampere quantity of electrons through one ohm of resistance. We'll look at these other quantities shortly. Most passive pickups have an EMF ranging in millivolts to just over a volt.

Before any electrons can go anywhere, they have to have a road that is electron friendly. A material that allows electrons to pass through freely is called a *conductor*. The word *freely* is used loosely here, because there is always some degree of *resistance* to

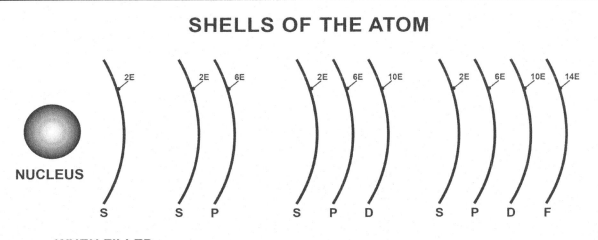

Figure 5.1 Shells of the Atom

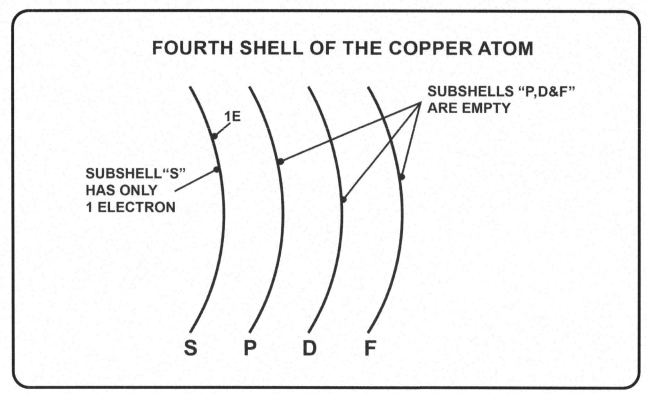

Figure 5.2 Fourth Shell of the Copper Atom

electron flow. Plus, you can get electrons to go through just about anything if enough force is applied. A material that won't pass electrons freely is called an *insulator*. Both conductors and insulators are necessary ingredients in electronic pathways or *circuits*.

If the conductive path has a large enough break in it, the electrons will be unable to move across it. When the circuit is *open*, nothing happens. If the opening is closed and the circuit forms a continuous path from beginning to end, the electrons will be able to travel. When an EMF pushes an electron loose from an atom, the electron scoots along in space until it bumps into an outer shell electron belonging to another atom. This knocks that electron loose, which in turn bumps into another guy, and the sequence repeats along the length of the conductor.

Each electron doesn't travel a great distance, but it does travel very quickly. Imagine a tube holding a row of marbles. If one new marble is pushed into the end of the tube, the marble on the opposite end of the tube would pop out "instantly" with a force proportional to the force of the incoming marble. This is similar to how electrons behave in a circuit.

The number of electrons travelling in a circuit is called *current* or electron flow. Like a number of cars travelling on a freeway, electron current is measured by the number of electrons going past a point in the circuit during a period of time. A *coulomb*, 6.25×10^{18}, of electrons going past a point in one second is called an *ampere*, A, and commonly called *amps*. Current is represented by the letter I and in guitars it is usually found in milliamps, mA. The designation for current, I, is taken from the French word for current, *intensité*.

When both voltage and current levels of a circuit are known, the *power*, P, or the total energy used by the circuit may be calculated. It follows the basic relationship that describes an effect as a ratio between the cause and its opposition, and may be written as

$$P = EI \qquad (5.2)$$

It takes one watt of power for one volt of pressure to push one ampere of electrons through a circuit. Since guitar circuits typically have millivolts of force and milliamps of current, milliwatts of power will also be found.

Since power equals voltage times current, we can derive that voltage equals power divided by current.

$$E = P/I \qquad (5.3)$$

Likewise, current equals power divided by voltage.

$$I = P/E \qquad (5.4)$$

RESISTANCE

As current moves along a conductor, there is a barroom brawl of sorts of electron activity. Electrons are knocking into and repelling other electrons from all angles, the atoms are having their outermost shells totally molested, and the insulator is having nothing to do with any of it. This activity produces a quantum rash, of sorts, much like the mechanical friction a body falling from a skateboard onto an alley encounters. Part of this energy of motion is converted into heat and is called *resistance*, R.

The effect-equals-cause-divided-by-opposition relationship can be applied here, too.

$$E = IR \qquad (5.5)$$

This is *Ohm's Law*, which in this form says that voltage equals current times resistance. It takes one volt of pressure to push one ampere of electrons through one ohm, Ω, of resistance.

We can also solve the equation for current.

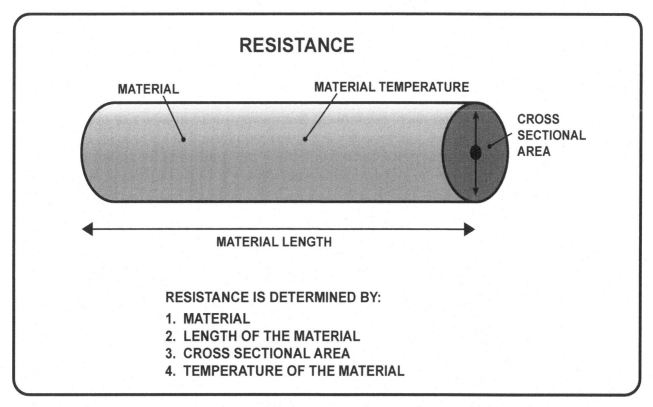

Figure 5.3 Resistance Factors

$$I = E/R \tag{5.6}$$

Resistance becomes

$$R = E/I \tag{5.7}$$

Combining the power and resistance equations, $P = EI$ and $E = IR$, we can solve for power when the resistance and current are known.

$$P = (IR)I = I^2 R \tag{5.8}$$

The power, resistance, and voltage relationship can be expressed similarly.

$$P = E(E/R) = E^2/R \tag{5.9}$$

RESISTANCE COMBINATIONS

Most circuits will have more than one resistance. Resistances are found in series, parallel, and series-parallel combinations. Resistances connected in series simply add their values. A series connection is formed when the end of one resistance connects to the beginning of the next resistance, giving the current only one path to follow.

The total resistance for any series-connected group of resistances can be represented by

$$R_t = R_1 + R_2 + R_3 \ldots + R_n \tag{5.10}$$

R_t is the total resistance, and R_n is the total number of resistances.

As current goes through each resistance in a series resistance circuit, the voltage pushing the current is used up proportionately to each resistance. Each resistance is called a voltage drop, and the value of the voltage drops can be calculated using Equation 5.5.

In general, for a series resistance circuit:

- The current value does not change throughout the circuit.
- Voltage drops at each resistance are proportional to the size of the resistance.
- The sum of the voltage drops equals the total voltage.
- The sum of the power dissipated by the resistances equals the total power.

In a circuit with only parallel resistances, the current will have two or more parallel paths to follow. In a circuit with equal resistances, the same amount of current will travel each path. With unequal resistances, more current will travel the path with less resistance. The voltage will treat each path as an independent circuit and will drop completely across each resistance.

The total resistance across a parallel circuit may be written as

$$1/R_t = 1/R_1 + 1/R_2 + 1/R_3 \ldots + 1/R_n \tag{5.11}$$

For two resistances in parallel, a quicker formula may be used:

$$R_t = (R_1 \times R_2) / (R_1 + R_2) \tag{5.12}$$

Voltage, current, and power calculations may be done with Equations 5.5, 5.6, 5.8, and 5.9.

In general, for a parallel resistance circuit:

- The voltage is the same throughout the separate paths.

- The current divides along the parallel paths inversely proportional to the size of the resistances.
- The total current is equal to the sum of the currents in parallel paths.
- The sum of the power dissipated by the parallel resistances is equal to the total power.
- The total resistance is always smaller than the smallest resistance of any individual path.

Series-parallel resistance circuits are very common, and although they look complex at first glance, they are very easy to analyze and solve. Once you have identified the series and parallel groups, subgroups can be formed. In other words, two series resistances can be grouped together to form one equivalent resistance circuit, then this subgroup can be added as one unit into the next series or parallel function.

Voltage, current, and power calculations can be solved for each path of a series-parallel resistance circuit just as they are done for individual series and parallel circuits. It just takes a few more steps to calculate values for the entire circuit.

DC AND AC

The electrical examples shown up to this point have all involved the flow of current in one continuous direction. This type of current flow is called *direct current*, dc, and is found in many simple low-voltage circuits. A flashlight, which has current flowing from the high potential side of a battery through a switch and a lamp (resistance) and back to the low potential terminal of the battery is an example of a dc circuit.

In a guitar circuit, however, there is a different kind of current. Just as the wave on a string moves through repetitive cycles, so does the current in a guitar circuit. This type of fluctuating current is called *alternating current*, ac. Like the fundamental waveform on a string, the ac waveform also graphs as the sine of an angle. This sinusoidal waveform is thus described in cycles, wavelengths, and hertz as defined in Chapter 1.

Since the current value is constantly changing in an ac circuit, it can't be described as simply as dc values can. The *Root Mean Square*, RMS, calculation gives an ac value that is equivalent to a dc value. The RMS value is derived by taking the square *root* of the *mean square* (the mean square is the arithmetic mean, or average, of the squares of all the values of the alternating wave form). For a sine wave, that is simply .707 times the value of the peak amplitude.

A guitar pickup, then, with a peak ac voltage of one volt would have an RMS voltage of 1 X .707, or .707 volts. That would be its equivalent dc voltage.

Here are some shortcut functions for sinusoidal ac values:

- RMS value = peak value X .707
- Peak value = RMS value X 1.41, or average value X 1.57
- Peak-to-peak value = peak value X 2
- Average value = peak value X .636, or RMS value X .9

DC AND AC COMBINATIONS

Circuits can have both multiple dc sources and multiple ac sources as well as combinations of dc and ac sources. Dc circuitry calculations are pretty straightforward. Two dc supplies connected in series simply add their voltages. If the two voltages have opposite polarities, the smaller is subtracted from the larger to determine the total voltage. With ac supplies, however, the phase relationship between the two signals must be considered. If the signals are both in phase with one another, the voltages will add. If one signal is 180 degrees out of phase with the other signal, the smaller value will subtract from the larger value. For any other out-of-phase values, the resulting voltage and phase angle can be calculated with vector diagrams.

Ac and dc voltages can also be combined. If a one-volt peak ac voltage is combined with a .5-volt dc supply, the total voltage will fluctuate. At 1-volt peak ac, the voltage will add with the .5-volt dc for a 1.5 voltage total. As the ac supply crosses the zero line, the ac has no influence, and the total voltage is just the .5 dc supply. At the bottom of the alternating current cycle, its value is -1 volts, which adds with the .5 dc to produce -.5 volts total.

The voltage values for this ac and dc combination will range from a high of 1.5 volts to a low of -.5 volts. Taking the rms value of the peak of the ac supply, .707 X 1 volt equals 707 volts. Adding this value to the .5 dc gives a total of 1.202 volts.

CAPACITANCE, INDUCTANCE AND IMPEDANCE

Like dc's resistance, ac has its own version of resistance called *impedance*. And like adding ac voltages, impedance is a little more complex than dc's resistance. Impedance, in general, is the total ac resistance of a component or a circuit. Specifically, it is the total of the capacitive reactances, the inductive reactances, and the dc resistances of the component or circuit. To explain this further, we need to look at the phenomena of capacitance and induc-

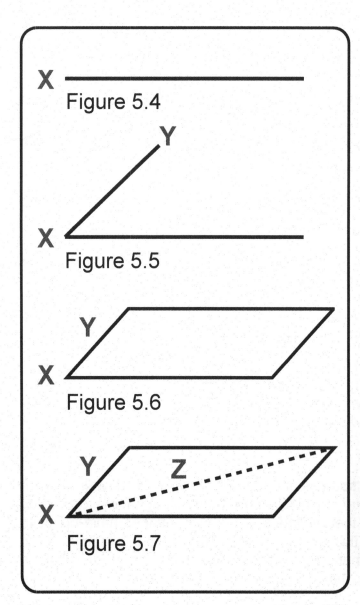

Figure 5.4
A 3-volt supply is represented by a 3 inch vector line, x.

Figure 5.5
The 1-volt supply is represented by a one-inch vector line, y, which is connected to the beginning of vector line x at an angle of forty-five degrees.

Figure 5.6
Now, complete a parallelogram out of vectors x and y.

Figure 5.7
Draw a resultant vector line, z, from the origin point, x,y, to the opposite corner of the parallelogram.
The length of the resultant vector line z corresponds to the new combined total ac voltage. The new angle xz is the phase difference between the original voltage and the new voltage. This same vector diagram technique can be used to illustrate pitch distortion created by compromised, rounded top saddles, as discussed earlier in the book.

tance, which, along with resistance form the building blocks of all circuits.

CAPACITANCE

Capacitance is the ability of a device to store a charge. This device, called a *capacitor*, consists of two parallel conducting surfaces usually in relatively close proximity separated by an insulator.

Capacitive devices can be found in many forms, both intentional and unintentional. The coils in a pickup separated by an insulating coating form a capacitor. A ground wire covered in insulating material pressed against a piece of shielding forms a capacitor. The braided shield and the center conductive wiring separated by a nonconductive insulator inside an instrument cable form a capacitor. Unwanted capacitances in a circuit are called *stray* or *parasitic* capacitances. These unintentional capacitors all have the same characteristics as the ones intentionally incorporated in a circuit.

To understand the capacitor as it is found in guitar circuits, we must look at the relationship between its components, namely, the parallel conducting surfaces, or *plates*; the electric field between the plates; and the insulating material, or *dielectric*, between the plates.

Imagine one plate of a capacitor connected to the negative terminal of a power source, V, such as a battery and the other plate connected to the positive terminal of the same battery. Electrons from the plate connected to the positive terminal will be attracted to the positive side of the battery. An equal number of electrons will leave the negative side of the battery and cram onto the plate connected to the negative terminal.

A little quantum tug-of-war begins. As more electrons try to leave the positively connected plate for the positive side of the battery, the now positively charged plate attracts them. The same thing happens on the negatively connected plate: as more electrons from the negative side of the battery try to crowd onto the plate, the now negatively charged plate repels them.

The battery will keep muscling the electrons until, after a period of time, a balance will be struck between the voltage source, V, and the capacitor's Q, or electric charge stored on its plates.

A few relationships can be surmised here. One is simply that the charge on a capacitor is proportional to the voltage applied to it.

$$Q \propto V \qquad (5.13)$$

Another is that the charge on the capacitor is the product of the voltage applied to it and the capacity of the capacitor's plates to store the charge.

$$Q = VC \qquad (5.14)$$

Likewise, capacitance may be defined as the amount of charge per unit of v

$$C = Q/V \qquad (5.15)$$

The basic unit of measurement for

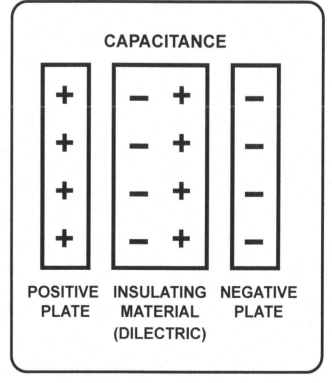

**Figure 5.8
Conditions for Capacitance**

capacitance is the *farad*, named after Michael Faraday. A farad is a large value, however. The microfarad, µF, which is equivalent to 10^{-6} F, and the picofarad, pF, which is equivalent to 10^{-12} F, are the units most commonly found in guitar circuits.

Sandwiched between the two plates inside the capacitor is the dielectric, which is used to enhance the charge on the plates. As both plates develop opposite charges, an electric field will radiate out from oplate to the other. Like a magnetic field, an electric field is represented by lines of flux, φ. Every electric charge is surrounded by an electric field. The density of this fiel can be represented by

$$D = \varphi/A \qquad (5.16)$$

The flux density is proportional to the electric charge. If the charge is increased or decreased, the flux per unit area will be increased or decreased by the same amount. Thus

$$\varphi \propto Q \qquad (5.17)$$

Coulomb's Law shows that the electric field strength, $\mathcal{E}$, at any point from a given charge is directly proportional to the size of the charge and inversely proportional to the distance squared from the charge. This can be written as

$$\mathcal{E} = kQ/r^2 \qquad (5.18)$$

In this relationship, k, a constant, equals 9×10^9; Q is in coulombs; and r is in meters.

While the dielectric, being an insulator, will not conduct any of the charges from either plate, it will be affected by the electric field of the charges on the plates. The atoms in the dielectric will reorient themselves so that their negative charges are facing the positively charged plate, and their positive charges are facing the negatively charged plate. When the dielectric becomes polarized by the plates' fields, the reoriented atoms are called *dipoles*.

The dipoles themselves now have their own electric field. The atomic layers inside the material cancel each other since the negative side of one dipole is adjacent to the positive side of the adjoining dipole. The guys on either outside edge, however, tend to neutralize a comparable value of field from the adjacent plates. Thus, the electric field between the plates is reduced by the dielectric.

However, when this happens, the voltage pressure will act to restore the original amount of field between the plates in accordance with the plate size and the distance between the plates. This will increase the charge and thus the capacitance on the plates. The dielectric, therefore, acts as a multiplier for the capacitance.

Different kinds of insulators will allow flux lines to set up with different degrees of ease. The measure of this ability is called *permittivity*, and is expressed by

$$\varepsilon_r = D/\mathcal{E} \qquad (5.19)$$

Permittivity is a ratio of the flux density to the electric field intensity. The bigger the value of ε, the more charge is put on the plates.

The factor that is actually used to calculate the value of a capacitor is the *relative permittivity* or the *dielectric constant*. This is the ratio of the dielectric value to that of air or a vacuum. It is expressed as

$$\varepsilon_r = \varepsilon/\varepsilon_0 \qquad (5.20)$$

If we take the permittivity equation, Equation 5.19, $\varepsilon = D/\mathcal{E}$, and insert the definitions of D and $\mathcal{E}$, we get

$$\varepsilon = (\varphi/A)/(V/d) \tag{5.21}$$

Since the flux is proportional to charge, Eq. 5.17, we can also express this as

$$\varepsilon = (Q/A)/(V/d) = Qd/VA \tag{5.22}$$

Remember the basic definition for capacitance is Eq. 5.15, $C = Q/V$, so we can rewrite the above as

$$\varepsilon = Cd/A \tag{5.23}$$

Solving for C gives

$$C = \varepsilon (A/d) \tag{5.24}$$

This is a more accurate description of the makeup of the values encountered in a typical working capacitor in a guitar circuit. This also presents some basic features about a capacitor, that is, capacitance will be increased if the following criteria are met:

- The area of the plates is increased,
- The distance between the plates is decreased, and
- The permittivity of the dielectric is increased.

CAPACITIVE CURRENT

Since the two plates inside a capacitor are separated by an insulator, virtually no current other than a few stray electrons will pass from one terminal to the other. However, the capacitor's nature of loading and unloading electrons on and off its plates pushes and pulls current through its circuit. This electron flow is referred to as *capacitive current*, i_c, and is essentially external to the capacitor, as opposed to a resistor where the current ripples in one end of the device and out through the opposite end.

Capacitive current is governed by two factors:

- The size of the capacitance, and
- The rate of change of voltage pushing the capacitor.

This can be expressed by

$$I_c = C (\partial v/\partial t) \tag{5.25}$$

Obviously, an increase in the size of the capacitor or an increase in the rate of change of voltage, or frequency, will result in an increase in the capacitive current. With the value capacitors used in a guitar circuit, mid and high frequencies will generate a usable capacitive current. Lower frequencies will not load onto the small-size plates used in guitars, so no usable current is produced by the capacitor.

Since an increase in capacitive current will be accompanied by a decrease in the opposition to the current, and the capacitive current is a product of the capacitance and the rate of change of voltage, the resistance to the capacitive current, or *capacitive reactance*, is directly proportional to the reciprocal of the capacitance and the frequency. Thus,

$$X_c = 1/\omega C \tag{5.26}$$

X_c is the capacitive reactance, which is measured in ohms; ω is the angular velocity, or frequency, which is measured in hertz; and C is capacitance, which is measured in farads.

What happens if direct current is put across a capacitor? If we take Equation 5.26 and plug a zero in the denominator (since dc is non-alternating and therefore has a frequency of zero), we come up with basically an infinite resistance, which is the same thing as an open circuit. After the capacitor has charged, there is no capacitive current when dc is applied.

CAPACITORS IN SERIES AND PARALLEL

Capacitive values can be changed by grouping capacitors together.

Grouping capacitors in series reduces the total capacitance. Capacitors in series will have the same charge on each one and will work against each other. The total is calculated by

$$1/C_t = 1/C_1 + 1/C_2 + 1/C_3 + \ldots 1/C_n \qquad (5.27)$$

Two capacitors in series may be calculated by

$$C_t = (C_1 C_2)/(C_1 + C_2) \qquad (5.28)$$

Capacitors in parallel will increase the total capacitance. Connected in parallel, the plates of each capacitor all act as one big plate, which essentially turns the capacitors into one big capacitor. Capacitances in parallel add their values.

$$C_t = C_1 + C_2 + C_3 + \ldots C_n \qquad (5.29)$$

Capacitors, then, differ from resistors in two key aspects:

- They do not dissipate energy like a resistor; they store it and return it to the circuit.
- They store and release their charges only when the applied voltage or current is changing.

In historical publications, you may encounter the term *condenser*. These devices were originally and appropriately named this because they do exactly that: they condense electrons. However, after working with these gadgets for over a century, the main focus has shifted from what they do to how much they can do what they do. The capacitor's storage capacity, and hence its *capacitance*, are the terms that have grown into popular usage.

INDUCTORS

You'll recall from the chapter on magnetism that a magnetic field accompanies a moving current. Likewise, a moving magnetic field will induce a current in a coupled conductor.

If a direct current passes through a straight piece of wire, a stationary magnetic field will surround the wire. If an alternating current passes through the same wire, a magnetic field will expand and collapse around the wire in step with the cycles of the ac.

If we take a wire and wrap it into a coil and begin to pass ac through it, a magnetic field will build around the part of the coil the current is passing through. As this field expands, it cuts across the adjacent coils and induces a current in them. This induced current, however, is in the opposite direction of the original current. The induced current also has, naturally, its own magnetic field that is in opposition to the original magnetic field.

Additionally, as the ac continues to progress through its cycle, the original magnetic field will peak, then collapse. As it collapses, the energy stored in the field will surge into the wire and increase the current, which again opposes the natural cycle of the original ac.

The inductor, then, opposes any change in current. For this reason, it is also known as a choke, since it tends to interfere with any change in current. Also, the faster the current changes, the more opposition the inductor creates, making it an effective high frequency filter.

Inductance, L, is measured in Henries, H, and is commonly found in Henries in guitar pickups and mH and µH in circuit devices. One Henry is the inductance required to produce one volt when the ac changes at a rate of one ampere per second. One Henry also equals one ohm per second.

Inductors, like capacitors, can be grouped together.

Grouped together in series, their values add like resistors.

$$L_t = L_1 + L_2 + L_3 + \ldots L_n \tag{5.30}$$

In parallel, inductor values add by reciprocals.

$$1/L_t + 1/L_1 + 1/L_2 + 1/L_3 + \ldots 1/L_n \tag{5.31}$$

A quicker formula for two inductors in parallel is

$$L_t = (L_1 L_2)/(L_1 + L_2) \tag{5.32}$$

If two inductors are placed in the same proximity, the magnetic field from each one can induce a voltage in the other one in addition to their own self-induced voltage. This interaction is called mutual inductance. It is represented by the letter M, which is also known as the coefficient of coupling.

If two adjacent coils are wound in the same direction, their mutual induction, M, will add to their self-induction. Connected in series, their inductive value becomes

$$L_t = L_1 + L_2 + 2M \tag{5.33}$$

Connected in parallel, their reciprocals add

$$1/L_t = 1/(L_1 + M) + 1/(L_2 + M) \tag{5.34}$$

If two adjacent coils are wound in opposite directions so that their magnetic fields oppose one another, their mutual inductance will be negative.

Connected in series, two opposing inductors' value becomes

$$L_t = L_1 + L_2 - 2M \tag{5.35}$$

Connected in parallel, the same two inductors will have a value of

$$1/L_t = 1/(L_1 - M) + 1/(L_2 - M) \tag{5.36}$$

The inductor's opposition to the flow of current is called *inductive reactance*, X_l, and is expressed in ohms. Inductive reactance may be expressed by

$$X_l = 2\pi f L \tag{5.37}$$

There is a straight linear relationship between inductive reactance and frequency. In other words, the higher the frequency becomes, the more inductive opposition there is.

RESONANCE

Just like mechanical resonance discussed earlier in the book, there is also an electrical resonance. Just as in mechanical resonance, electrical resonance occurs when the energy released by one element in a system is equal to the energy absorbed by another element in the same system.

This is a good place to shine a light on the nature of force. Compare the similarities between mechanical and electrical phenomena from the perspective of force.

- Force flow: in mechanical systems it is described simply as $\partial x/\partial t$, or the rate of travel.

In electrical systems it's described as current.
- Force level: in mechanical systems it's called force; in electrical systems it's called voltage.
- Force storage: in potential energy perspective, the mechanical version is called spring, or k. The electrical version is called capacitance, C. In kinetic energy perspective, the mechanical version is called mass, while the electrical version is called *inductance.*
- Force dissipation: the mechanical version is called *damping*; the electrical version is called *resistance.*

In addition to the two systems covered in this book, there are other similar equivalencies found in thermal and fluid systems. It's the same force wearing different costumes for different gigs.

Now imagine the mechanical equivalency of electrical resonance.

For electrical resonance to occur, the three elements of resistance, inductance, and capacitance must be present. The resonance will happen at a specific frequency that is determined by the R, L, and C values. Resonant conditions will be different in series and parallel R, L, and C configurations.

In a series resonance, since the inductance and capacitance are swapping energy on an equal basis, there are no capacitive or inductive reactances. In other words

$$X_l = X_c \tag{5.38}$$

The inductive reactance is equal to the capacitive reactance at resonance. In this situation, the impedance, Z, is at a minimum, and the current, I, is at a maximum, limited only by the resistance, R, in the circuit.

Since $X_l = 2\pi f L$ (Eq. 5.37) and $X_c = 1/2\pi f C$ (Eq. 5.26), and the reactances are equal at resonance, then

$$2\pi f L = 1/2\pi f C \tag{5.39}$$

Solving for f, which becomes the resonant frequency, f_r, gives

$$f_r = 1/2\pi\sqrt{LC} \tag{5.40}$$

Like mechanical systems, electrical systems also have a *quality factor*, Q, which is an expression of how much energy is placed in capacitive and inductive storage compared to how much energy is dissipated by the resistive element.

This can be expressed as

$$Q = X_l/R \tag{5.41}$$

If we plug Eq. 5.40, which is the equation for the resonant frequency, into Eq. 5.41, it will reduce to

$$Q = (\sqrt{L/C})/R \tag{5.42}$$

As stated earlier, the current at the resonant frequency is at a maximum, and the impedance there is at a minimum. At frequencies increasing and decreasing from the resonant point, impedances progressively increase, which diminishes the current proportionately. The group of frequencies closest to the f_r will have the most current, but there is a cutoff point beyond which the current is insignificant. These cutoff points are calculated by multiplying the maximum current value, I_{max}, by 707. These cutoff frequencies are also referred to as *half-power* frequencies because the power there is one half what it is at the resonant point.

The cutoff frequency below the f_r is designated by f_1; the cutoff frequency above f_r is designated by f_2. The range of useful frequencies between f_1 and f_2 is called the *bandwidth*, BW.

In general, a small value of Q means a wider bandwidth, while a large value of Q means a narrow bandwidth.

Looking at Eq. 5.42, $Q = (\sqrt{L/C})/R$, we can determine that for a larger value of R with a fixed LC ratio, we will have a smaller Q and a wider bandwidth. Also, if the LC ratio decreases with a fixed value of R, the Q value will become smaller, and the bandwidth will increase.

A parallel resonant circuit has a more complex path than a series resonant circuit. Unlike the series configuration, the parallel resonant circuit has the current dividing across the elements, but not in three typically separate paths.

Ideally, the LCR elements would each have an independent path for the current to follow. However, an inductor, being a coil of wire, has a resistance of its own, so the path the current actually sees is more of a parallel path across a capacitance and a series-joined inductance and resistance.

There are also two variations on this related to the Q of the coil.

For high Q conditions (quality factor of ten or higher) in a parallel resonant circuit, the resonant frequency is defined the same way as in a series resonant circuit. From Eq. 5.40, $f_r = 1/(2\pi\sqrt{LC})$.

However, for low Q conditions, specifically for coils with a quality factor of four and under, an additional factor must be entered into the equation for resonance.

$$f_r = (1/(2\pi\sqrt{LC}))(\sqrt{1-((R^2C)/L)}) \qquad (5.43)$$

The bandwidth calculations for both series and parallel resonant conditions are basically the same.

$$BW = f_2 - f_1 = f_r/Q \qquad (5.44)$$

CHAPTER SUMMARY

This chapter illuminates the rudiments of force behavior from the electronic perspective. Before there can be any useful electron movement in a guitar system, there must be a complete path, or closed circuit, for the electrons to navigate. There also needs to be a push of some sort, or an electromotive force, to get them moving. This pressure is called voltage, and the quantity of moving electrons is called current. The material that the current travels through most easily is called the conductor. Opposition to current is called resistance. Materials with very high resistance are called insulators.

Current that flows continuously in the same direction is called direct current, or dc. Current that changes direction of flow in regular time intervals is called alternating current, or ac. Ac behaves as a sine wave with characteristics including cycles per second, or frequency. A dc equivalent of ac is the rms value.

Capacitance and inductance are often found in circuits. When there is a change of current, as found in an ac circuit, capacitors and inductors store energy that can be returned to the circuit. They differ from resistors, which dissipate energy. Capacitors and inductors have a frequency-related opposition, called reactance, to current flow. Capacitors have higher reactance to lower frequencies and pass higher frequencies; inductors have higher reactance to higher frequencies and pass lower frequencies. Summed with resistance, the total capacitive and inductive reactance in an ac circuit is called impedance.

In a circuit with resistive, capacitive, and inductive elements, there will be a frequency where the energy stored by one reactive element will be equal to the energy released by the other reactive element. This is called the resonant point. The power transfer through the circuit is at a maximum at the resonant frequency, and it subsides as the frequencies fall away on either side of the resonance. The bandwidth is the range of frequencies on either side of the resonance that measure at least half of the power level at resonance. The quality factor, or Q, of a resonant circuit is a ratio that indicates the bandwidth of the circuit. The lower the Q, the wider the bandwidth; the higher the Q, the narrower the bandwidth. There are series and parallel resonant circuits, each having slightly different characteristics in low and high Q situations.

So, what would happen if we took a coil of wire with resistive, capacitive, and inductive elements, loaded magnetic flux inside it, and linked the flux field with a ferrous, tensioned moving string? The next chapter will look at the device that has become known as a *pickup,* which is the gateway to the electronic world external to the guitar, and some of the last century's key intellectual history on its design.

CITATIONS, REFERENCES AND FURTHER READING

DeMagnete, William Gilbert,1600

Otto von Guericke, Germany, Ottonis de Guericke Experimenta Nova Magdeburgica de Vacuo Spacio, 1672

Charles Francois de Costernay Du Fay, Histoire de l'Academie Royale des Sciences, memoirs 1–6, 1733–34

Pieter van Musschenbroek, the Leyden jar condenser, letter dated Jan 20, 1746, to Rene Reaumur, translated by Abbe Nollet

Benjamin Franklin, Experiments and Observations on Electricity made at Philadelphia in America, 1751, a booklet of five letters on Franklin's experiments, published by Peter Collinson

Joseph Priestly, The History and Present State of Electricity with Original Experiments, 1767

Charles Augustin de Coulomb, seven papers each titled Memoire sur l'Electricitie published in the Histoire de l'Academie Royale des Sciences, 1785–1791

Alessandro Giuseppe Volta, On the Electricity Excited by the Mere Contact of Conducting Substances of Different Kinds, Philosophical Transactions of the Royal Society, 1800

Michael Faraday, Experimental Researches in Electricity, Vols. 1, 2, 1839; Vol. 3, 1855; Experimental Researches in Chemistry and Physics, 1859

James Prescott Joule, On the Heat Evolved by Metallic Conductors of Electricity, Philosophical Magazine, 1841, On the Caloric Effects of Magneto-Electricity, Philosophical Magazine, 1843

Hermann Ludwig Ferdinand van Helmholtz, On Electrical Oscillations, 1869

Johann Heinrich Wilhelm Geissler, 1815–1879, the Geissler tube, 1857

Joseph John Thompson, 1856–1940, Philosophical Magazine and Journal of Science, Vol. 44, Oct. 1897, "Cathode Rays," pp. 293–316

Albert Einstein, Relativity, The Special and the General Theory, 1916, Crown Trade Paperback, 1995 edition

Introductory Circuit Analysis, Robert Boylested, 6th Edition, Atoms and Their Structure, pp. 29–32; Resistance, pp. 55–68; Capacitance, pp. 343–381; Inductance, pp. 427–449

Chapter Six
Pickup Design

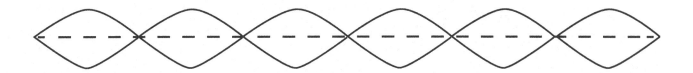

The guitar pickup is a very common item, but not much more than a century ago there were no pickups. The earliest published use I have found of the word pickup in an electromagnetic context comes from the Pall Mall Gazette, dated Oct. 20, 1891:

"The experiments for Mr. Edison's new electric tramcar were conducted at his laboratory at West Orange, NJ . . . Its chief feature is the 'pickups' which take the current from one line of rails."

It is evident from the first pickup patents of the 1930s that the pickup pioneers of the 1920s had adopted this word for guitar usage. The fundamental elements of what would later make guitar pickups possible were first discovered by Faraday at the beginning of the nineteenth century. His experiments with a magnetic field and a piece of wire demonstrated that a current can be produced when a field is pushed through a conductive wire.

In the latter part of the 1800s, patents began to issue for inventions with electromagnetic features. One of the earliest inventions to show Faraday's concept in a practical, working embodiment is shown in Patent # 370,477, awarded on Sept. 27, 1887, to H. V. Hayes. It is called the telephone. Although it is not a working guitar pickup as set forth in this invention, it is relevant prior art.

Not long after that people started getting ideas about putting electromagnetic devices in guitars. If you can amplify the human voice, why not guitars, too?

One of the best resources for studying the guitar pickup and its development is the US Patent Office. This is the grand repository of US intellectual property registered and granted from July 31, 1790, to the present. A patent is a deed to intellectual property. The deed to this property, or invention, is granted by the government and essentially gives the owner a seventeen-year monopoly on the rights to manufacture and sell the invention.

There are three types of patents: utility, design, and plant. Utility patents are the most common and include inventions such as guitar and bass pickups.

For a patent to be awarded for a new invention, such as a new guitar pickup, the idea must meet four very stringent requirements.

1. It must fit into one of five statutory classes. The invention must qualify to be called either a process, a machine, a manufactured item, a composition, or a new use of one of these classes. This is one of the easiest requirements to fulfill. A pickup fits into the manufactured item class.
2. The pickup, for example, must be useful. This is known as utility and is also a pretty easy requirement to fulfill. This requirement helps weed out ideas like invisible pickups for air guitars.
3. The invention must be *novel*. That is, it must be different in one or more ways than all other previous inventions and knowledge. All the previous inventions and knowledge is known as prior art, and in the case of pickups, would include all known makes of pickups plus any published or public knowledge having to do with pickups. Sometimes something someone thinks is new turns out not to be new after some research is done. The existence of prior art will get a patent
4. The invention must be *unobvious*. In other words, would the new pickup provide one or more new and *unexpected* results to someone skilled in the art, such as a luthier or pickup manufacturer? This is the toughest requirement and ends up knocking out more patent applications than any other reason.

In addition to meeting the above requirements the patent application must be submitted in a very specific form. Each application must include the following:

1. Drawings of the invention
2. A specification of the invention that includes the name of the invention, background of the invention, objects and advantages of the invention, descriptions of the drawings, a list of reference numbers for the drawings, a description of the structure of the invention and an explanation of how it works, and a conclusion.
3. The *claims*, or key descriptions, of the invention
4. An abstract, or summary, and
5. A list of relevant prior art.

If and when a patent is approved, it will contain all this information and will be available to the public upon request. Patent searches can be done online at the United States Patent and Trademark Office, or USPTO.

I've included a group of some of the most interesting electromagnetic pickup patents, but not all of them, to illustrate the many ways people have envisioned generating a signal from a guitar. They are organized into three groups:

1. The Early Designs: 1931–1942
2. The Golden Age: 1951–1971
3. The 70's, 80's and 90's

There's quite a bit of information in every patent application, so I've picked out key elements from each one that includes the inventor(s) names, the invention title, the patent number, and filing and issue dates. I've also including some of the illustrations and highlights of the text from the body of the document. Patent text is organized by page number, column number (usually two to a page) and sequential line number from the top to the bottom of each page. You can download the full versions of any of these that especially pique your interest from the USPTO.

THE EARLY DESIGNS: 1931-1942

The 1930s saw the first wave of guitar pickup patents. A recurring theme in the bulk of these patents, including the earliest ones, is a quest for improvements in fidelity, or tonal quality. For many inventors, part of this better tone production included a reduced susceptibility to interfering signals, or noise.

C. T. Jacobs, in Patent No. 1,906,607, filed April 30, 1931, and issued May 2, 1933, shows a musical instrument pickup and one of the first hum cancelling, or humbucking, pickups on record. This patent was registered to Charles T. Jacobs of New Providence, New Jersey, assignor to Miessner Inventions, Inc.

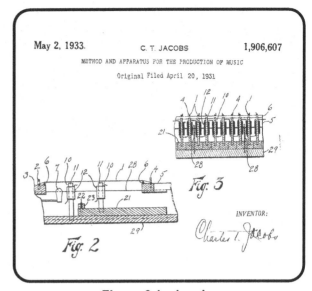

Figure 6.1 Jacobs

[Page 1, Lines 1–17]

This invention relates to musical instruments and systems, with particular reference to those in which the vibrations of mechanical vibrators are translated into electric oscillations. Mechanical vibrators as contemplated in the invention are those whose vibration contains not only a fundamental frequency component, but also coincident higher frequency components harmonically related to the fundamental. The fundamental and these higher frequency components may each be termed a partial of the composite vibration. Typical of such vibrators are, of course, strings under longitudinal tension; and strings are shown as the vibrators in the accompanying drawings.

[Lines 21–25]

It is an object of my invention to provide the method and means for translating the vibration of mechanical vibrators into electric oscillations of a harmonic structure selectable within wide limits.

[Lines 41–44]

A further object is the provision of such means characterized by relatively low susceptibility or sensitivity to stray electrostatic and electromagnetic fields.

[Page 4, Lines 76–99]

In Figures 1 and 3, I show each of the rows of coils 10 and 20 electrically connected within themselves in a certain manner. This is such that, viewing the coils say from the top, an electric impulse passing through either of the two series of coils will travel in a clockwise direction in one coil, counterclockwise in the next, clockwise in the next, etc. As shown in the figures, the coils are similarly wound, similarly terminalled, and similarly mounted, and the top of one is connected to the top of the next, the bottom of this to the bottom of the next, the top of this to the top of the next, etc. This greatly reduces the susceptibility or sensitivity of the coils to stray electromagnetic fields such as those emanating from the nearby power apparatus. Such fields, as they intersect two adjacent coils, which are very close together, are almost identical in strength and configuration and hence induce similar voltages in the two coils, which voltages are caused to buck each other by the arrangement shown.

Benjamin F. Miessner came up with quite a few different ways to establish a voltage in a coil via string movement in his Patent No. 1915858, also titled Method and Apparatus for the Production of Music, filed April 9, 1931, and issued on June 27, 1933. His patent shows several kinds of pickup arrangements and discusses their tonal implications. This was registered to Benjamin F. Miessner of Millburn Township, Essex County, New Jersey, assignor to Miessner Inventions, Inc.

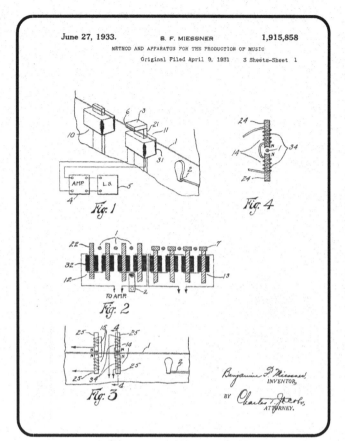

Figure 6.2 Miessner

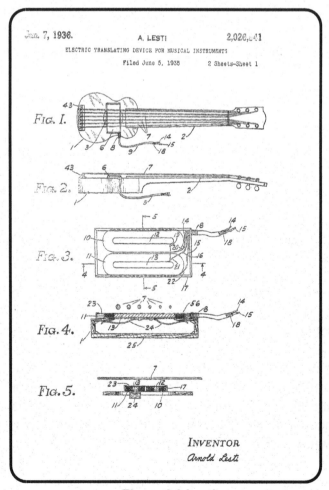

Figure 6.3 Lesti

Arnold Lesti's "Translating Device for Musical Instruments" is the first pickup to use two side-by-side ferrous loaded coils in a shape that would later become a mainstay of the pickup industry. Patent No. 2026842, filed June 5, 1935, and issued on Jan. 7, 1936, also concerns hum cancelling. This patent was registered to Arnold Lesti of Los Angeles, Calif.

[Page 1, Lines 1–10]

My invention relates to an electrical translating device for use with musical instruments that are not sufficiently loud when played in the normal manner. This device translates the musical vibrations into corresponding electrical values, and these are electrically amplified and then translated into corresponding sounds by a loudspeaker. The invention is particularly adapted to steel stringed musical instruments such as the guitar.

[Page 1, Lines 34–48]

Another important objective of my invention is to provide, along with the above-mentioned features, a translating device that is free from pickup action engendered by extraneous electrical and magnetic influences. These last-mentioned influences are found to produce extremely objectionable noises. In the construction of my invention, I have found that two or more solenoids may operate together so that each neutralizes the effects of the other insofar as extraneous unwanted magnetic influences are concerned, but that their positions with respect to the vibrating magnetic portions of the musical instrument causes an addition or summation of their respective translating currents.

[Page 1, Col. 2, Lines 34–55]

Referring to the drawings wherein similar characters represent similar parts throughout, 1 is the body of a guitar and 2 the fingering board. Character 3 represents the sound hole at which is held the translating device designated generally by 6. 7 represents generally the steel strings that are vibrated during the act of playing. Translating device 6 is held to the guitar by spring 24. The small spring 8 around the cable 9, where it enters the translating device 6, safeguards 9 from excessive wear at that point. In Fig. 3 the coils 10 and 11, having iron cores 12 and 13, are shown connected to insulated leads 14 and 15 and their center connection 16 is shown connected to the case 17, made of magnetic material. A shielding 18 around leads 14 and 15 constitutes a return lead, also connected to the case 17. The windings in coils 10 and 11 are in opposite directions, as can be seen from the direction of the ends 19, 20, 21, and 22. The case 17, made of magnetic material, aids in the pickup action by reducing the magnetic

[Page 2, Col. 1, lines 1–4]

Reluctance, giving greater field strength from the relatively weak inductive fields surrounding strings 7. Character 23 is a nonmagnetic top cover.

Guy Hart's "Electrical Musical Instrument" shows a pickup with a bar magnet for three strings and individual pole pieces for the other three strings. His pickup is also height adjustable. Patent No. 2087106 was filed Feb. 8, 1936, and issued July 13, 1937. Guy Hart, Kalamazoo, Mich., assignor to Gibson, Inc., Kalamazoo, Mich.

[Page 2, Col. 1, Lines 5–19]

In operation, when the strings are set to vibrating by the player, the variations in the air gap between the strings and the magnet fingers 22 set up corresponding variations in magnetic flux, which cause varying electromotive force to flow in the coil windings. The electrical impulses are transformed into sound waves by the loudspeakers 29, which may be manually modified as to tone or volume by the controls 26, 27. The adjusting screws 15 permit the magnets 18 and the extensions 22 thereof to be shifted in position, as indicated by the position shown in dotted lines in Fig. 6. The adjustability provided by the shifting action permits the instrument to be readily tuned.

George Beauchamp's Patent No. 2089171, "Electrical Stringed Musical Instrument," shows a section of the guitar strings immersed in a flux field. What's intriguing about this design is that as the string moves up and away from the pole piece, it

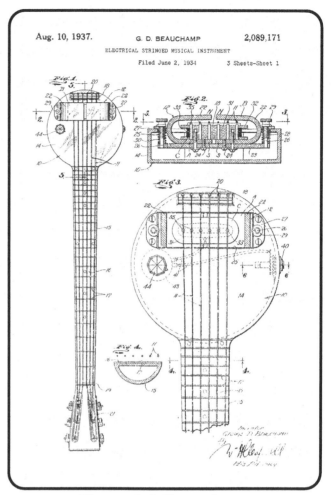

Figure 6.4 Beauchamp

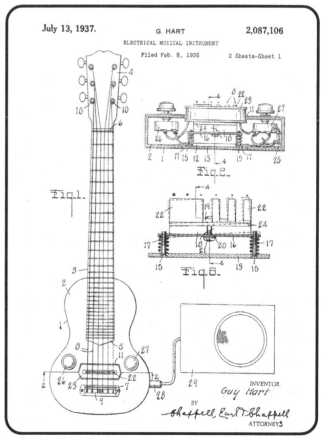

Figure 6.5 Hart

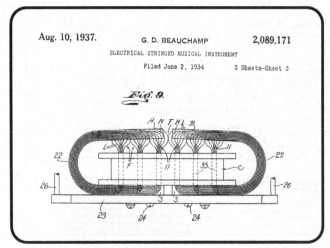

Figure 6.6 Beauchamp

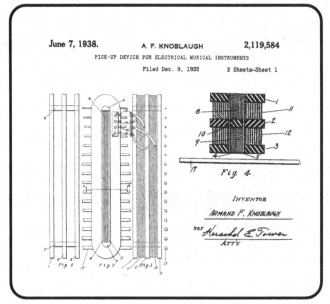

Figure 6.7 Knoblaugh

is still pushing a rather powerful amount of flux due to the magnet overhead. This produces a consistently textured tone no matter which direction the string is rebounding in.

This patent was filed June 2, 1934, and eventually issued on Aug. 10, 1937. It was assigned to Electro String Instrument Corporation, which later became Rickenbacher, which became Rickenbacker.

[Page 1, Col. 2, Lines 15–19]

Another objective of the invention is to provide an improved electro-magnetic pickup unit capable of embodiment in stringed musical instruments of various characters with little or no modification.

This is the first mention I've seen of the nonexclusive use of a pickup, which foreshadows the replacement pickup industry to come several decades later.

Armand Knoblaugh shows a hum cancelling pickup in his "Pickup Device for Electrical Musical Instruments." His application was filed Dec. 9, 1935, and Patent No. 2119584 was issued June 7, 1938. His invention shows one coil stacked on top of the other coil. Armand F. Knoblaugh of Cincinnati, Ohio, assignor to the Baldwin Company, Cincinnati, Ohio.

[Page 2, Col. 1, Lines 1–17]

The motions of the magnetized strings and the consequent motions of the flux from the magnetic poles on the strings, cyclically toward and away from the pickup device, induce corresponding electromagnetic forces in the coils 11 and 12 by electromagnetic induction, which can be amplified and reproduced as musical tones. It is to be noted particularly, in this respect, that essentially all of the induced electromagnetic forces are generated in the coil 12, which is nearer to the strings 17 (see Figs. 3 and 4) and that very little of the electromagnetic forces are generated in the farther coil 11, because of its greater distance from the strings and the magnetic isolation effected by the nonmagnetic piece 10.

[Page 2, Col. 1, Lines 30–35]

The induction of electromagnetic forces by stray magnetic fields into coil 12 is then counterbalanced, part by part, by the induction of equal and opposite electromagnetic forces into coil 11, with the result that any reproduced extraneous noises, such as hum, are essentially eliminated.

Herbert Sunshine's "Magneto-Electric Pick-Up Device for Stringed Musical Instruments," Patent No. 2175325, shows height adjustable pole pieces. Filed on Nov. 10, 1937, the patent was issued on Oct. 10, 1939 to Herbert S. Sunshine of New York, NY, assignor to Epiphone, Inc., New York, NY.

[Page 1, Col. 1, Lines 16–27]

Another objective of the invention is to provide in a stringed musical instrument, a pickup unit that is adjustable for each string of the instrument. A further objective of the invention is to provide in a stringed musical instrument having strings of different diameters, a pickup unit including a plurality of individually adjustable core-members adjacent respective strings that are adapted for adjusting the air gaps therebetween, to compensate for the ordinary spacing variation that is due to the difference in the diameters of the strings.

Walter Fuller devised a movable pickup for use on archtop guitars in Patent No. 2294861. His application was filed on Aug. 14, 1940 and was granted on Sept. 1, 1942. It's titled "Electrical Pickup for Stringed Musical Instruments," Walter L. Fuller of Kalamazoo, Mich., assignor to Gibson, Inc., Kalamazoo, Mich.

[Page 1, Col. 1, Lines 3–16]

The main objectives of my invention are as follows:

First, to provide an improved electrical pickup for string instruments having provision for readily and quickly mounting the same on and removing the same from the instrument toward its selective adaptation for electrical reproduction.

Second, to provide a pickup device of the type described, which is characterized by the simplicity and compactness of its parts.

Third, to provide a pickup that is selectively adjustable to various positions relative to the strings or bridge of the instrument to enable the tones reproduced to be varied as desired.

There is a gap in the guitar pickup history spanning the years from the early 1940s to 1950 due to the world being at war. Although World War II ended in 1945, it took several years for the industry to reconvert to civilian purposes.

"In the emergency of war our nation's powers are unbelievable. I have heard soldiers say a thousand times, 'If only we could have created all this energy for something good.'" Ernie Pyle, 1944.

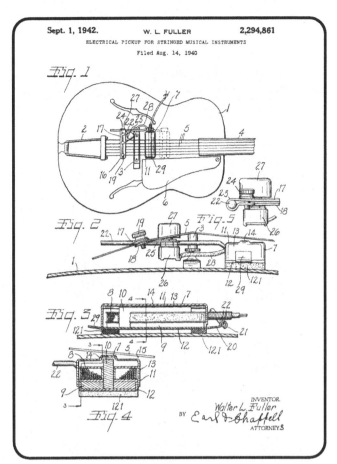

Figure 6.8 Fuller

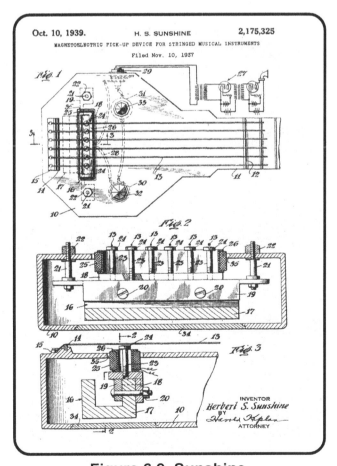

Figure 6.9 Sunshine

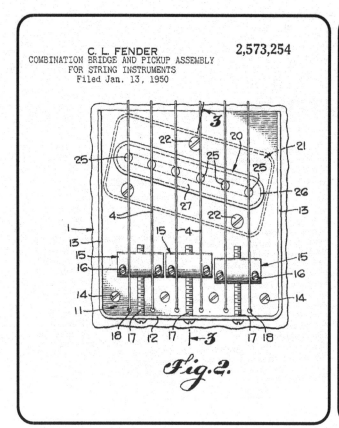

Figure 6.10 Fender

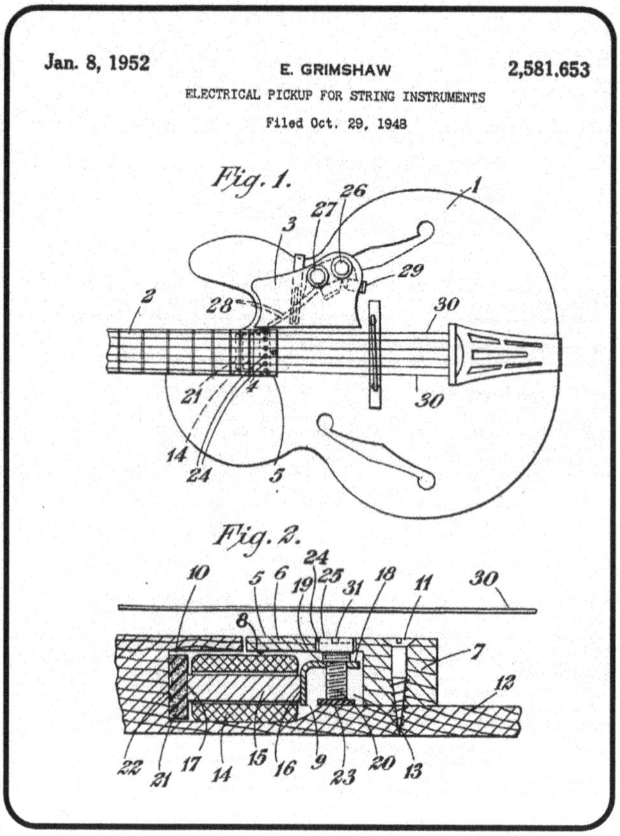

Figure 6.11 Grimshaw

One has to wonder what kinds of ideas never came back from the killing grounds. We can look to the historians to learn what was won for all that effort. What we don't know is what was lost.

"And that's all I have to say about that." Forrest Gump, 1994.

THE GOLDEN AGE: 1950-1970

This era saw the creation of many guitar and bass pickups that were destined to gain widespread acceptance. Many of these models outgrew the instruments they were originally designed for and spawned endless variations for use in many manufacturers' guitars and basses. They became templates of sorts for many creative new manufactures and gave rise to a replacement pickup industry.

On Jan. 13, 1950, Leo Fender filed an application for a "Combination Bridge and Pickup Assembly for String Instruments." Patent No. 2573254 was issued Oct. 30, 1951, to Clarence L. Fender, Fullerton Calif.

[Page 1, Col. 2, Lines 3–30]

The plate 11 is provided with a clearance slot 19 in registry with the recess 2. Mounted in the clearance slot 19 and extending particularly in the recess as well as protruding in the plate 11, is a pickup unit

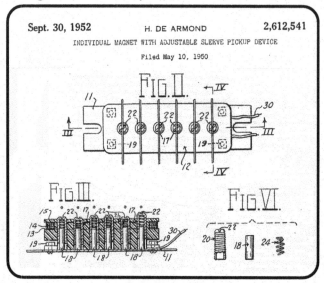

Figure 6.12 Armond

20. The pickup unit includes a base plate 21 of nonmagnetic material mounted within the recess 2 and adjustably suspended from the plate 11 by screws 22. Surrounding the screws 22, between the plate 11 and the base plate 21, are coil springs 24. The base plate 21 supports upstanding permanent magnet armatures 25 adapted to be located in alignment with the strings 4 of the guitar. The armatures are surrounded by a solenoid coil 26. Suitable leads electrically connect the solenoid coil to a conventional amplifier. The upper extremities of the armatures 25 are retained in a head plate 27, also of nonmagnetic material.

The pickup unit is preferably suspended by three screws, so positioned that the pickup unit may be tilted slightly either about an axis traversing the strings or about an axis parallel with the strings, so that each armature may be brought into the proper relationship with its corresponding string. Furthermore, it has been found desirable to set the pickup unit in acute angular relation with the strings rather than at right angles thereto.

Emile Grimshaw of London, England, filed "Electrical Pickup for String Instruments" in the US on Oct. 29, 1948. His application shows a covered pickup for archtop guitars with the controls mounted on the pickguard. His patent no. 2581653 was granted Jan. 8, 1952.

[Page 2, Col. 4, Lines 1–15]

A stringed musical instrument of the kind having a body part and a neck in combination with an electric pickup comprising a recess in the end of the neck adjacent to the body, a coil accommodated in the recess, a magnet surrounded by the coil, a plurality of pole pieces for the magnet each adjacent to a wire of said instrument, a guard plate adjacent to the neck of the instrument, control means attached to the guard situated between the guard and the body of the instrument, connections between said coil and said controls, a jack for outside connections attached to the guard situated between the guard and the body of

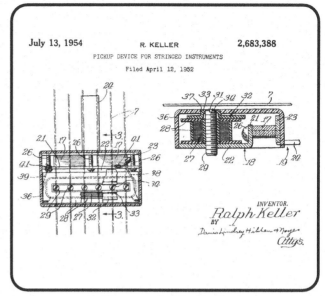

Figure 6.13 Keller

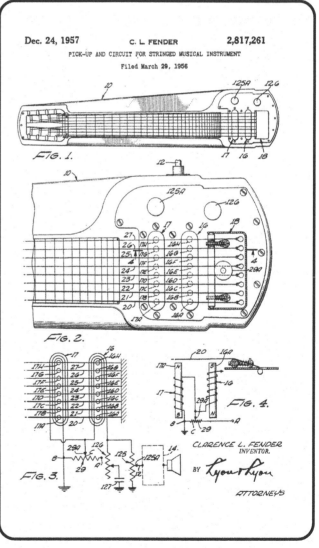

Figure 6.14 Fender

the instrument, and connections between the controls and jack.

Harry DeArmond filed "Individual Magnet with Adjustable Sleeve Pickup Device" on May 10, 1950. His invention shows height adjustable sleeves or pole pieces. The patent was issued Sept. 30, 1952, as No. 2612541 to Harry De Armond of Toledo, Ohio, assignor to Rowe Industries, Toledo, Ohio.

[Page 1, Col 1, Lines 7–19]

The objective is to provide a simple construction for the adjustability of the magnetism of each individual magnet in which, in the specific embodiment of the invention herein illustrated, a telescoping soft iron sleeve may be moved toward and away from the strings of the instrument in contact with a magnet, one for each string of the musical instrument, and spring means are interposed between one end of the magnet and the closed end of the sleeve to tension the friction and keep the magnet and sleeve held in proper adjusted position for producing the desired results.

Ralph Keller's "Pickup Device for Stringed Instruments" shows a pickup with an extended magnetic field. Filed April 12, 1952, Patent No. 2683388 issued July 13, 1954, to Ralph Keller of Elmhurst, Ill., assignor to Valco Manufacturing Co., Chicago, Ill., a partnership.

[Page 1, Col. 1, Lines 1–14]

The invention relates to pickup devices for stringed musical instruments, and its general objective is to provide a novel pickup device that is highly sensitive to the vibrations of the associated strings, which pick up not only the fundamental note of each string but also the harmonics or overtones to a high degree, and which faithfully respond to the string vibrations.

More specifically, an objective of the invention is to provide a device that establishes a magnetic field extending for a substantial distance along each string, with the magnetic lines of force lying substantially parallel to the strings for the major portion of the said distance.

[Page 2, Col. 4, Lines 16–27]

Another important performance factor in the present invention resides in the fact that there is a desirable flux concentration at the tips of the adjusting screws 29 because of the fact that the screws are in effect one pole of a horseshoe magnet, as hereinbefore described. It is also known that with respect to a horseshoe magnet, the most effective position for the pickup coils is surrounding the tips of the magnet poles. Consequently, the arrangement in my device is such that the coil 27 can be readily mounted immediately adjacent the tips of the screws 29.

Leo Fender shows two single coil pickups being used in conjunction to get a broader tonal response, cancel hum, and achieve a little more powerful output in Patent No. 2817261. "Pickup and Circuit for Stringed Musical Instrument" was filed March 29, 1956, and approved Dec. 24, 1957. It was registered to Clarence L. Fender, Fullerton, Calif.

[Page 1, Col. 1, Lines 21–29]
[Page 1, Col. 1, Lines 54–65]

In general, the present arrangement involves two coils that are positioned so that one reproduces the fundamental frequency of a vibrating string or strings more than the other, while the other coil reproduces the harmonic content of the same string or strings more than one such coil. These two coils are interconnected in a novel manner in the input circuit of a vacuum tube amplifier and with different magnetic polarities as is described in detail hereinafter.

Using these techniques, a single control, i.e., an adjustable potentiometer resistor, serves to shunt out the so-called rhythm coil in varying degrees while the output of the lead coil remains substantially constant, thereby varying the balance between the fundamental content and the harmonic content of the signal.

Greater signal amplitude is realized because of the two coils and their relatively close

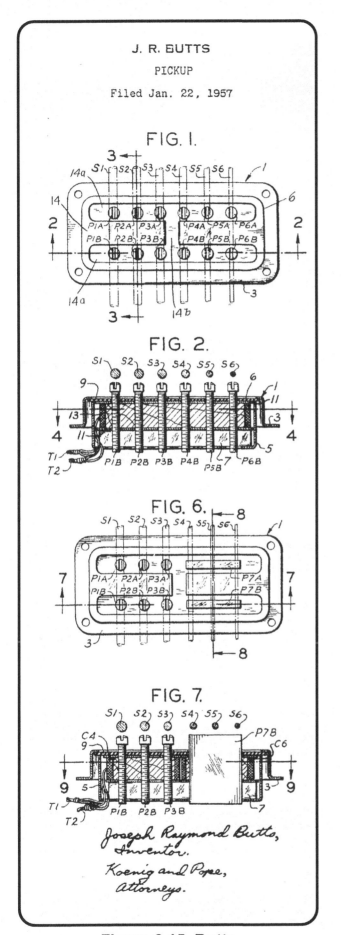

Figure 6.15 Butts

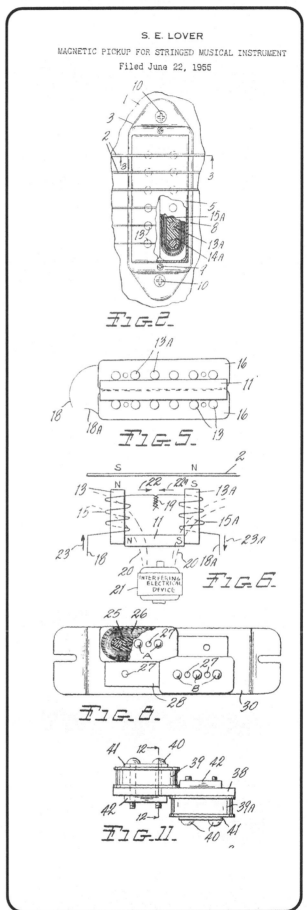

Figure 6.16 Lover

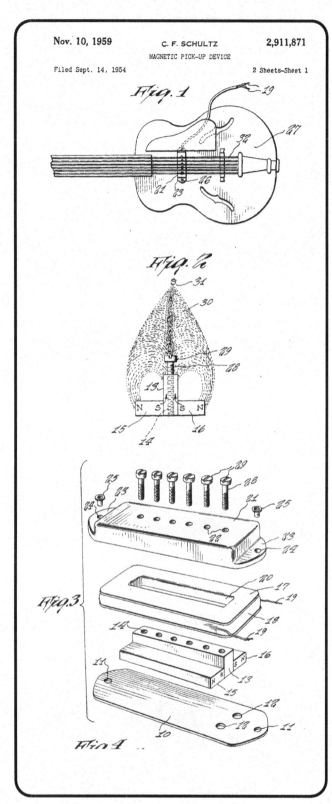

Figure 6.17 Schultz

spacing. This close spacing allows the steel string to both attract and conduct the magnetic flux between the two coils because of opposite magnetic polarity, resulting in a total signal amplitude greater than that produced by a single coil, or two coils not so closely spaced.

J. R. Butts also shows a pickup design centered around improvements in fidelity. He raises the pickup's resonant frequency, gives it height-adjustable pole pieces, makes it hum cancelling, and introduces a novel shield around it. His application, titled "Pickup," was filed Jan. 22, 1957, and was granted as No. 2892371 on June 30, 1959. This pickup design, which would be known as the Gretsch Filtertron, was registered to Joseph Raymond Butts of Cairo, Ill.

[Page 1, Col. 1, Lines 18–35]

Among the several objects of this invention may be noted the provision of pickups that have an increased magnetic coupling with vibrating musical members, thereby producing a higher amplitude output voltage; the provision of such pickups that have a smooth linear response over the audible range; the provision of pickups of the class described that have an electrical output that is unaffected by external hum and noise pulses; the provision of pickups of the class described that are capable of a wide variety of tonal effects; the provision of pickups in which the relative volume of each vibrating musical member can be independently adjusted over wide latitudes; the provision of such pickups that have a resonant frequency greater than 20 kc.; and the provision of pickups of the class described enclosed in a metal casing without undesirable frequency discrimination effects. Other objects and features will be in part apparent and in part pointed out hereinafter.

[Page 2, Col. 4, Lines 24–33]

This embodiment has the advantage of decreasing the tonal coloration (i.e., the inclusion of strong harmonics relative to the fundamental due to the interaction between the pole pieces and the vibrating strings) as to the higher frequency portion of the spectrum. This is due to the modified magnetic field resulting from the use of elongate pole pieces P7A and P7B, which diminish the sensitivity of the pickup to transverse or lateral vibration modes of the strings lying thereover, which modes generate these harmonics.

Seth Lover filed a design titled "Magnetic Pickup for Stringed Musical Instrument" on June 22, 1955. The Patent No. 2896491 was approved four years later on July 28, 1959. His design featured a hum cancelling pickup that was lightweight with an enhanced magnetic field around the string. Seth told me the application got knocked out twice by the patent office for prior art, but it got approved on the third, and final, rewrite. Even though there were other hum cancelling pickups in the marketplace, this one became known as the "humbucker" in popular vernacular. It was registered to Seth E. Lover of Kalamazoo, Mich., assignor to Gibson, Inc., Kalamazoo, Mich.

[Page 1, Col. 1, Lines 1–39]

This invention relates to improvements in magnetic pickup for stringed musical instruments. The principal objectives of this invention are as below:

First, to provide a magnetic pickup for a stringed musical instrument that is not affected by adjacent electrical devices and that does not pick up and transmit to the amplifier the hum of such devices.

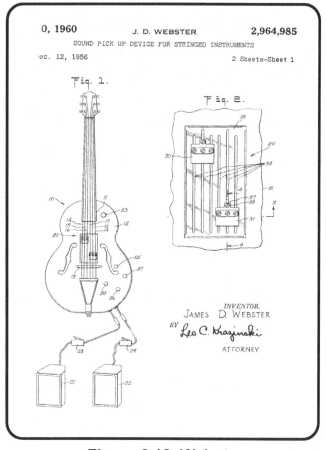

Figure 6.18 Webster

Second, to provide an electromagnetic pickup for stringed musical instruments with magnetically opposed pickup coils that neutralize the effect of currents induced by adjacent electrical devices.

Third, to provide a hum neutralizing magnetic pickup that is efficient in producing electrical vibrations in response to the playing of a stringed instrument.

Fourth, to provide a magnetic pickup that effectively employs relatively small masses of permanent magnet material and is easily mounted on a stringed musical instrument in proper relation to the strings of the instrument.

Fifth, to provide a magnetic pickup having a metallic magnetic return circuit between a pole of the permanent magnet and a coacting string of a musical instrument to increase the strength of the magnetic field around the string and improve the efficiency of the permanent magnet.

[Page 2, Col. 3, Lines 3–22]

By applying the familiar right-hand law of magnetism to the coil 15 it will be noted that an external magnetic field such as indicated at 20 emanating from an electrical device such as the motor 21 will tend by induced voltage to create a current in the coil 15 in the direction of the arrow 22. However, the same magnetic field at the same instant will tend by induced voltage to create an approximately equal and opposite current in the coil 15A as indicated by the arrow 22A so that the induced currents cancel each other and cannot create a hum in the pickup and its associated amplifier. If the source of the interfering magnetic field is not centered between the coils, or if the coils are not of identical construction, cancellation of hum will not be complete but will be substantial. It should be noted that the particular winding of the coils illustrated is not critical because cancellation of interfering voltages can be obtained

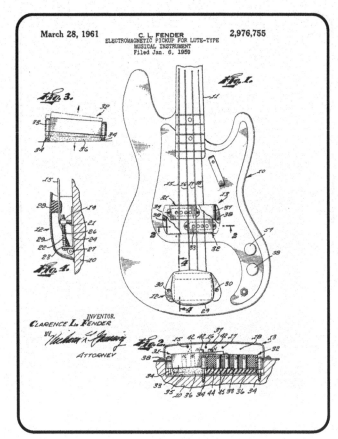

Figure 6.19 Fender

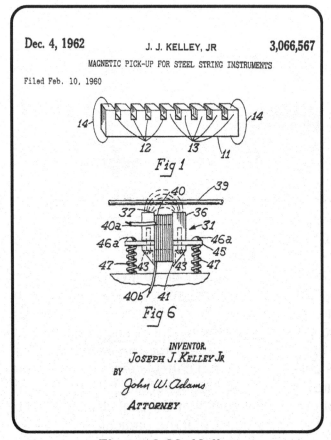

Figure 6.20 Kelley

when the direction of winding of one coil is reversed if the inner or upper end of one coil is connected to the outer or lower end of the other coil.

Charles Schultz shows a method of putting a lot of flux up in the air around the string's path of movement in Patent No. 2911871. "Magnetic Pickup Device" was filed Sept. 14, 1954, and approved Nov. 10, 1959, and registered to Charles F. Schultz of Lindenhurst, NY. This pickup would be known as the P-90.

[Page 1, Col. 1, Lines 17–26]

It is an objective of the present invention to provide an electro-magnetic pickup device for individually varying the amplitude of the reproduction of the various strings of a stringed musical instrument or the like wherein permanent magnets are arranged so as to provide a controlled and increased density of space extension of lines of force that are adapted to be cut by the string vibrations and to induce modulated currents in a coil element connected to a tone control and amplifier for the instrument.

[Page 1, Col. 2, Lines 56–58]

Adjustability of screws 28 permits the variation or control in the amplitude reproduced from any one string.

Jimmy Webster put together a sliding stereo pickup system in his "Sound Pickup Device for Stringed Musical Instruments." Filed Dec. 12, 1956, Patent No. 2964935 was issued Dec. 20, 1960, to James D. Webster of Northport, NY, assignor to the Fred. Gretsch Mfg. Co., Brooklyn, NY.

[Page 1, Col. 1, Lines 63–72]

In accordance with the present invention, the foregoing objects in general are accomplished by providing a device that comprises transducer means adjacent the bass strings adapted for electrical connection to one amplifier and transducer means adjacent the treble strings adapted for electrical connection to another amplifier.

For example, in a six-string instrument, such as guitar, the sound pickup is split into two sections, each having its own volume and tone control. One section covers the first, second, and third playing strings, and the other section covers the fourth, fifth, and sixth playing strings.

[Page 1, Col. 2, Lines 1–25]

Each pickup section is slidably mounted on the soundboard, so that the bass and treble sections can be placed at points where tonal reproductions can be best balanced to suit the most critical player. Thus, by placing the bass section near the lower end of the fingerboard and placing the treble section near the bridge, a pure tonal scope between bass and treble is attained with separate volume and tone control to give a substantially perfect balance between bass and treble. By the same token, the player can bring out the bass and subdue the treble. The volume shadings between bass and treble together with the tonal colorings so derived enable the instrument equipped with the device to produce exceedingly pleasing music.

To further clarify this principle of tonal control, when the bass section is at the fingerboard, and the treble section is at the bridge, a well-rounded bass side and a crisp sharp treble side will be heard. When the instrument is played in full chord form, it gives the effect of two guitars. When single string solos are played, the crossover between bass and treble creates a fresh sound and affords the player greater variation in solo work, once again giving the effect of two guitar parts.

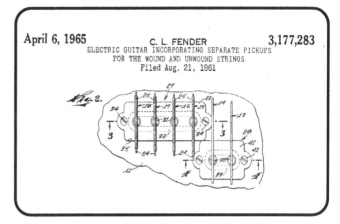

Figure 6.21 Fender

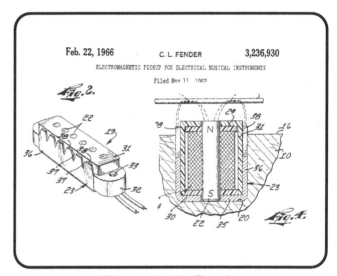

Figure 6.22 Fender

Leo Fender shows an innovative design for basses in his "Electromagnetic Pickup for Lute-Type Musical Instrument." In addition to being hum cancelling, this offset pair of pickups uses an opposing magnetic field to damp the string vibration. These pickups became known as Precision bass pickups, and the same design concept was used for his Jazz bass pickups. Clarence Leo Fender's application was filed Jan. 6, 1959, and was approved as Patent No. 2976755 on Mar. 28, 1961. The patent was issued to Clarence L. Fender of Fullerton, Calif.

[Page 1, Col. 1, Lines 50–60]

In view of the above and other factors and problems relative to electromagnetic pickups for bass guitars and the like, it is an objective of the present invention to provide an electromagnetic pickup construction and circuit that may be readily adjusted for the desired response to each string of the guitar, which operates to buck or cancel out signals produced by extraneous sources, which does not produce a beating effect due to rotation of the plane of string vibration, and which adequately senses the string vibrations despite the wide excursions and large sizes of the strings.

Joseph J. Kelley Jr. shows how a single coil pickup can have increased output and

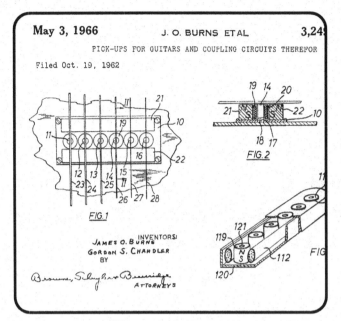

Figure 6.23 Burns

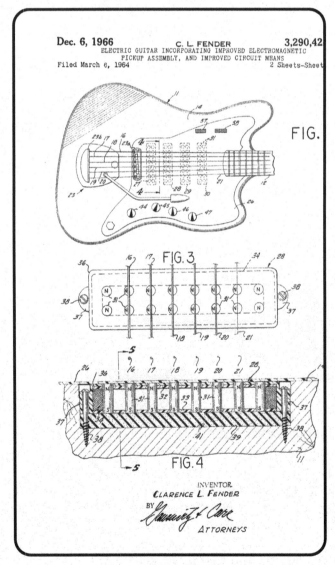

Figure 6.24 Fender

decreased susceptibility to noise by using a novel magnetic arrangement. His "Magnetic Pick-Up for Steel String Instruments" was filed Feb. 10, 1960, and approved as Patent No. 3066567 on Dec. 4, 1962.

[Page 1, Col. 2, Lines 16–26]

According to the preferred embodiment of the present invention, the pickup apparatus generally designated 10 is provided with a magnetic body or mass 11 having a plurality of spaced grooves 12-12 arranged along a major face thereof, the spaces between the grooves forming a plurality of pedestal members 13-13. The magnetic body is permanently polarized across the thickness dimension thereof, thereby rendering each pedestal in effect a pole-face for a specific string. The flux lines 14-14 are utilized to illustrate this polarization arrangement.

Leo Fender filed "Electric Guitar Incorporating Separate Pickups for the Wound and Unwound Strings" on Aug. 21, 1961. His invention shows two coils forming a hum-cancelling unit with one coil for the wound strings and the other coil for the unwound strings. Patent no. 3177283 was issued on Apr. 6, 1965, to Clarence L. Fender of Fullerton, Calif.

[Page 1, Col. 2, Lines 9–24]

If a single pickup were employed for all of the guitar strings 13–18, and the guitarist were to play a chord by picking each of the strings with uniform pressure, the notes produced by the unwound strings 13 and 14 would be much more dominant than those generated by the wound strings 15–18. Even if the picking pressure is not uniform, the wound and unwound strings produce sounds having audibly different characteristics. This is because the windings on the magnetizable cores of the wound strings have the effect of dampening harmonics, particularly the higher harmonics. Thus, the unwound strings produce notes that contain a much larger proportion of harmonics, in relation to the fundamental, than do notes produced by the wound strings. The notes produced by the wound and unwound strings therefore sound differently, which is a highly undesirable condition.

Leo Fender devised a pickup with a creative magnetic circuit to provide a fuller tone with reduced susceptibility to noise in Patent No. 3236930. "Electromagnetic Pickup for Electrical Musical Instruments" was filed May 11, 1962, and issued Feb. 22, 1966, to Clarence L. Fender of Fullerton, Calif., assignor, by mesne assignments, to Columbia Records Distribution Corporation, New York, NY.

[Page 1, Col. 1, Lines 34–39]

An additional objective is to provide an electric guitar incorporating a pickup that generates a relatively high current and voltage in comparison to prior-art pickups, and which is relatively insensitive to extraneous electromagnetic fields so that the amount of noise generated in the pickup and associated circuitry is minimized.

[Page 1, Col. 2, Lines 25–34]

Stated generally, pickup 19 comprises permanent magnet means 22, and magnetic circuit means 23 adapted to cause the lines of force generated by magnet means 22 to pass longitudinally through portions of strings 12 whereby such strings act as magnet keepers or armatures. Coil means 24 are operatively associated with the means 22 and 23 in such a manner that the variations in magnetic flux caused by vibrations of strings 12 generate in the coil means an electrical signal corresponding to the sound produced by the vibrating strings.

James Burns and Gordon Chandler show a low impedance pickup connected to an impedance matching transformer in Patent No. 3249677. They show the pickup composed of six individual coils that may be grouped in various combinations for tonal variations. Their application was filed in the US Oct. 19, 1962, and was granted May 3, 1966. "Pick-Ups for Guitars and Coupling Circuits Therefore" was issued to James Ormston Burns of Buckhurst Hill, England, and Gordon Spencer

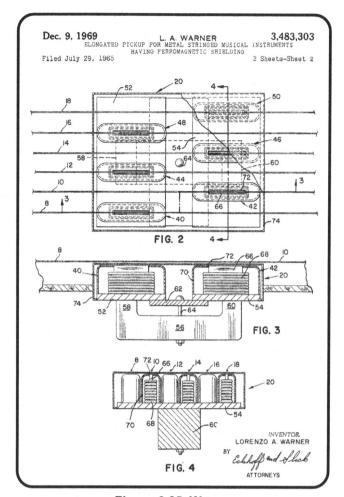

Figure 6.25 Warner

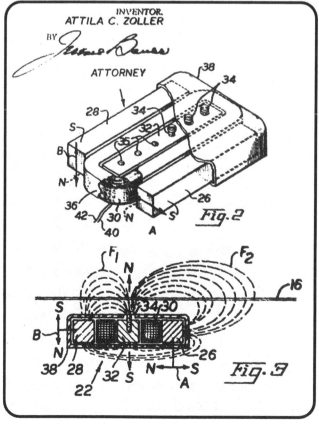

Figure 6.26 Zoller

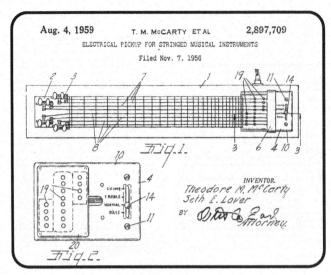

Figure 6.27 McCarty

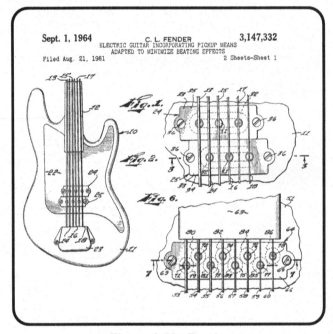

Figure 6.28 Fender

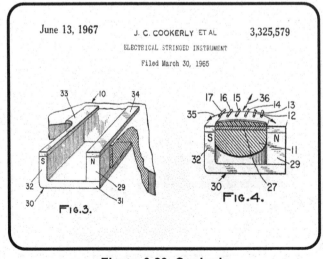

Figure 6.29 Cookerly

Chandler of Frimley, near Aldershot, England, assignors to Ormston Burns Limited, London, England.

[Page 1, Col. 1, Lines 13–30]

It is an established practice to provide a pickup on a guitar for deriving electrical signals from the vibrations of steel strings and to feed signals from such a pickup to an amplifier and loudspeaker system for production of audible sounds. Conventional pickups used hitherto have embodied a magnetic system and one or two coils of relatively high impedance wound around part of the magnetic system, each coil being disposed around part of a magnetic system associated with more than one string when the pickup is in situ on a guitar. A disadvantage of a pickup with a high impedance coil is a strong tendency to provide a peak output signal with the first wave when a string is struck or plucked. Moreover, there is a risk of stray capacitances and a high impedance coil producing a tuned circuit having a resonant frequency within the audible range with resultant peaking around certain frequencies in the audible range.

[Page 5, Col. 9, Lines 47–55]

We claim the following: A pickup for a guitar comprising a magnetic core structure, a permanent magnet in the said core structure, a plurality of pole pieces in the said core structure equal in number to the number of guitar strings from whose vibration electric signals are desired to be derived, and a plurality of low impedance coils having a dc resistance not greater than about one ohm disposed one around each pole piece.

In Patent No. 3290424, Leo Fender buries the pickups beneath the pickguard. By bunching a double row of magnets together, the magnetic field is projected higher than usual, thus allowing a reading of the string movement. This application was filed Mar. 6, 1964, and issued Dec. 6, 1966. "Electric Guitar Incorporating Improved Electromagnetic Pickup Assembly, and Improved Circuit Means" was registered to Clarence L. Fender of Fullerton, Calif., assignor, by mesne assignments, to Columbia Records Distribution Corp., New York, NY.

[Page 1, Col. 1, Lines 16–23]

An objective of the present invention is to provide a practical, commercial, and economical pickup assembly incorporated in a guitar or the like, which assembly is so sensitive that it may be disposed on the order of one-half inch or more from the strings and completely concealed beneath the pickguard or face plate of the instrument yet responds in a musically satisfactory manner to all generated frequencies, including high frequencies.

[Page 1, Col. 2, Lines 40–68]

As best shown in Figures 3–5, each pickup component comprises two rows of permanent magnet pole pieces 31, the rows of pole pieces being parallel to each other and transverse to the strings 16–21. Each row contains eight pole pieces 31, six of such pole pieces being generally beneath the respective strings 16–21. The remaining two pole pieces in each row are outboard of the strings, there being one outboard pole piece at each end of each row. The pole pieces in each row are spaced substantially equal distances apart. Thus, each row of pole pieces is similar to what would be found in a conventional pickup for an eight-stringed guitar.

The pole pieces are preferably elongated cylindrical permanent magnets. The axes of such magnets are perpendicular to the plane of the strings. All portions of all the magnets lie on only one side of the lane of the strings and are spaced a substantial distance from such plane. The spacing between the two rows of pole pieces is sufficiently small that the pole pieces (which have the same magnetic polarity, as will be described below) definitely interact with and repel each other, bunching up the lines of magnetic force in such a manner that many lines of force extend upwardly from face plate 26 a much greater distance than would be the case if only one row were present. Because of this bunching-up of the lines of magnetic force, the strings 16–21 may be spaced on the order of one-half inch from the upper ends of the pole pieces 31 and still achieve a highly satisfactory musical response.

Lorenzo Warner shows an elongated pickup placed in a parallel relationship to the string in Patent No. 3483303. "Elongated Pickup for Metal Stringed Musical Instruments Having Ferromagnetic Shielding" was filed July 29, 1965, and issued Dec. 9, 1969, to Lorenzo A. Warner of Saratoga, Calif. 95070.

[Page 1, Col. 2, Lines 10–40]

The pickup itself, 20, includes six individual pickup assemblies designated 40, 42, 44, 46, 48, and 50, which underlie the strings 10 to 18, respectively. It will be noted that each pickup lies generally parallel to a string and also that adjacent pickups are staggered with respect to its neighbor as is most clearly shown in Figure 2. The individual pickups are mounted on bars 52 and 54, which are made of a magnetic material such as soft iron and each of which extends the entire width of the pickup. Underlying the bars 52 and 54 is a permanent magnet 56 having poles 58 and 60. The bars 52 and 54 are supported by a strip of nonmagnetic material such as brass or plastic, 62, held to magnet 56 by means of a bolt 64.

The individual pickups are identical so that only one pickup, namely that designated by the general number 42, is described in detail. The pickup consists of a thin, elongated pole piece 66, surrounded by a suitable winding 68, connected by suitable wiring to the switch 26. The wiring is not shown in Figures 2 through 4 but is shown in Figure 5.

Surrounding each of the pole pieces is a magnetic shield 70 of a suitable material such as metal having an elongated slot 72 at the top thereof, which slot directly underlies string 10. It will be noted that the top of the pole piece is flush with the top of the shield. Thus, from a magnetic standpoint, the pole piece 66 is exposed only by means of the slot 72. The whole assembly of six pickups is covered with an electrostatic shield 74 of a nonmagnetic material such as brass. If desired, a plastic potting material may fill the space inside shield 74. It will be noted that each pickup is staggered with respect to its neighbor; this minimizes

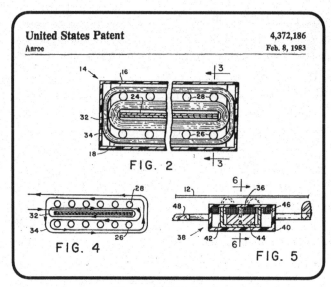

Figure 6.30 Aaroe

cross talk between the strings.

Attila Zoller came up with an innovative design in his "Bidirectional Electromagnetic Pickup Device for Stringed Musical Instruments." His pickup uses two differently focused magnetic fields to improve fidelity. Patent No. 3588311 was filed Jan. 6, 1969, and was granted June 28, 1971.

[Page 1, Col. 1, Lines 73–75 and Page 1, Col. 2, Lines 1–9]

Briefly, the present invention provides a pickup device simply comprising a coil adapted for connection to a current amplifier and magnetic means for generating a bidirectional flux pattern about the coil having one component extending essentially longitudinally of the vibratable elements and a second component extending essentially vertically of the vibratable elements. The flux pattern encompassed substantially all of the vibrations of the vibratable element, which then induce a single integrated current in the coil.

[Page 3, Col. 6, Lines 5–23]

I claim this: A pickup device for a musical instrument having a plurality of magnetizable metallic vibratable elements between a forward end and a rearward end, the said device comprising the following: a pair of transverse polar magnets spaced parallel to each other for positioning adjacent the elements; the said magnets being arranged transversely of the said elements with the polar axis of one horizontally parallel to the said elements and the polar axis of the other vertically normal to the said elements producing in combination a bidirectional flux pattern encompassing the elements; a coil between the said spaced magnets and within the flux pattern thereof; and means for connecting the said coil to a current amplifier system, whereby on vibration of the elements the said flux pattern is modulated, inducing within the said coil a current directly responsive to the said vibrations for transmission to the said amplifier.

Other patents of interest from this era include No. 2897709 by Ted McCarty and Seth Lover, "Electrical Pickup for Stringed Musical Instruments," filed Nov. 7, 1956, and issued Aug. 4, 1959. It was registered to Theodore M. McCarty and Seth E. Lover of Kalamazoo, Mich., assignors to Gibson, Inc., Kalamazoo, Mich. It shows multiple pickups on a guitar with different switching arrangements.

[Page 1, Col. 1, Lines 17–28]

The principal objects of this invention are as follows:

First, to provide an electrical pickup for a multiple stringed metallic string instrument that can easily be adjusted for various tonal effects. Second, to provide a pickup and circuit by means of which a single switch may be shifted between four positions to provide four different tonal effects. Third, to provide an electrical pickup in which the impulses induced by the strings of the instrument are variously combined and modulated to effect various combinations of the tones induced by all of the strings together and the treble and bass strings separately.

Leo Fender designed a hum cancelling pickup where alternating strings were routed into two different amplifiers to minimize "beating" effects. This patent, No. 3147332, was filed

Aug. 21, 1961, and issued on Sept. 1, 1964. It was titled "Electric Guitar Incorporating Pickup Means Adapted to Minimize Beating Effects" and registered to Clarence L. Fender of Fullerton, Calif.

[Page 1, Col. 1, Lines 11–15, Lines 22–27]

An objective of the invention is to provide an electric guitar system in which there is a minimum of intermodulation or beating effects, so that the resulting sound is relatively free of distortion and is more musically satisfactory than in prior-art systems.

Another objective is to provide a pickup containing separate elements adapted to sense the notes produced by alternate strings, such elements being offset only a short distance longitudinally of the strings and being so constructed and related that voltages induced from extraneous electromagnetic fields are cancelled out.

J. C. Cookerly and George Hall put two magnets down on either side of the fingerboard and then amplified the current induced in the strings in their Patent No. 3325579, filed March 30, 1965, and issued June 13, 1967. It was titled "Electrical String Instrument" and registered to Jack C. Cookerly, North Hollywood, Calif. 91605, and George R. Hall, Sherman Oaks, Calif. 91403.

[Page 1, Col. 1, Lines 11–30]

This disclosure relates to an improved electrical guitar wherein a uniquely designed magnet is employed to provide a magnetic field cutting across the strings over a portion of the length of the strings between the guitar nut and the bridge. The magnetic field configuration is such that the resulting current induced in the strings as a consequence of vibration will have frequencies and amplitudes proportional to the frequencies and amplitudes of the vibrations themselves and may be passed through suitable wave-shaping circuits and amplifier means to loudspeakers. The magnetic-field-generating arrangement extends a sufficient distance along the length of the strings to result in a long sustaining output signal. In addition, the electrical circuitry involved, together with other features, provides for proper dampening of undesired resonances in the neck structure of the guitar. In this respect, the guitar neck includes a laminated conducting plate that serves to dampen resonances in the neck and also serves to provide a current path for the current induced in the strings.

THE 70s, 80s AND 90s

The last three decades of the twentieth century saw more new pickup innovations, but the marketplace by then was dominated by variations on the "template" models invented during the Golden Age. There were lots of designs built to fit into the preexisting footprint of pickups created in the fifties and sixties that became a mainstay in many popular guitars and basses.

On Aug. 5, 1974, Willi Lorenz Stich, known commercially as Bill Lawrence, filed "Electrical Pickup for a Stringed Musical Instrument." Patent No. 3902394 was issued on Sept. 2, 1975, and assigned to Norlin Music, Inc., Lincolnwood, Ill.

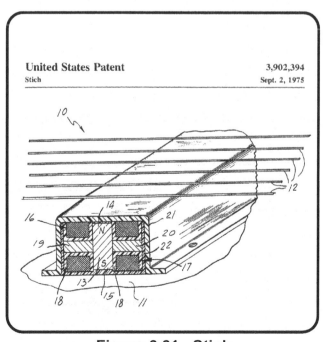

Figure 6.31   Stich

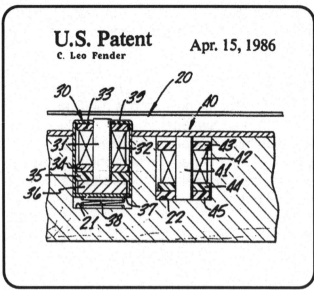

Figure 6.32 Fender

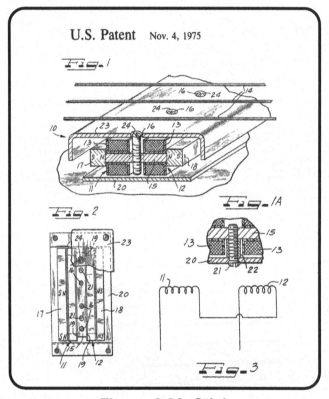

Figure 6.33 Stich

ABSTRACT

An electrical pickup for a stringed musical instrument includes a permanent magnet having one field polarity intersected by the string, a pair of coils, and each coil having a pole piece so arranged that the pole pieces are magnetically neutral and are thus not loaded magnetically but serve merely as inductors.

[Page 1, col. 1, lines 18-21, 25-28]

In this invention, the pole pieces of the pickup coils are disposed so as to be located in a neutral part of the magnetic field of the permanent magnet so that such pole pieces are not loaded magnetically. Another objective of the present invention is to provide a guitar pickup that can be produced with virtually no additional tooling other than that which the manufacturer in this field already has.

On Jan. 9, 1975, Willi Lorenz Stich, of Antioch, Tenn., filed another patent application for a similar pickup with a hum cancelling specification. Patent no. 3916751, "Electrical Pickup for a Stringed Musical Instrument," issued Nov. 4, 1975, and was assigned to Norlin Music, Inc., Lincolnwood, Ill.

[Page 1, Col. 1, Lines 10–35, 38–52]

It has been conventional to use a coil underlying the strings of a guitar with the axis of the coil being perpendicular to the top side of the guitar and perpendicular to the strings. This construction causes hum when there are stray magnetic fields nearby, such as emanate from an amplifier transformer, fluorescent lights, or the like.

A prior solution has been proposed to use a second coaxial pickup disposed beneath the main pickup and separated therefrom by a magnetic shield. Such a pickup has been effective in eliminating such hum, but it has a disadvantage in that it doubles the resistance if the wiring through which the signal must pass, and therefore the signal is weakened.

It has also been proposed to use a pickup with two coils side by side with their axes parallel. Constructions of this type have eliminated hum, but they have a disadvantage in that string vibrations are not sensed at a narrow point on the string but along a rather wide range of string length. Both such coils can pick up or sense the fundamental vibration, but for higher frequencies, the phase difference in the signals induced in the spaced coils can cause partial or even total cancellation of signals at these frequencies. These pickups thus have good fundamentals but are poor in reproducing desired overtones and sometimes have a resonance or boost effect in the midfrequency range.

In this invention two coils are employed to eliminate hum, but they are so arranged and disposed so that they are both active, preventing loss of signal from use of the second coil. The boost and cancellation problems resulting from spaced coils are eliminated by sensing string vibration at a rather narrow spot on the string.

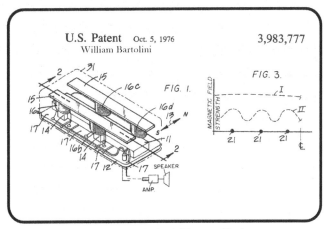

Figure 6.34 Bartolini

To effect the foregoing, a pair of coils are arranged to have their axes extend in the same direction as the string, and a ferromagnetic pole piece is disposed in the coils and spans the space between them, it having a portion between the coils projecting toward each string, and permanent magnet means are disposed at opposite sides of the coils and direct a magnetic field of a single magnetic polarity into the pole piece from opposite sides thereof.

Bill Bartolini devised a pickup with a highly asymmetrical magnetic field to produce tonal effects more like those of an acoustic instrument. Patent No. 3983777, filed Feb. 28, 1975, and Patent No. 3983778, filed Aug. 21, 1974, both issued on Oct. 5, 1976. "Single Face, High Asymmetry Variable Reluctance Pickup for Steel String Musical Instruments" was registered to William Bartolini, Livermore, Calif.

ABSTRACT

A single-face, variable-reluctance pickup for steel string musical instruments is described, which provides a highly asymmetrical magnetic field for preferentially sensing and generating electrical signals responsive to string vibrations perpendicular to the string plane. The described pickup features a single bar magnet, common shaping faces, oriented parallel the string plane and perpendicular the strings, and a plurality of sensing circuits having cores that magnetically and mechanically couple the shaping faces and the bar magnet. The described pickup provides a magnetic field in the string plane having a large flux gradient perpendicular the string plane and a minimum flux gradient parallel the string plane. The pickup is insensitive to "bending" and provides amplified musical instruments with tonal characteristics similar to the tonal characteristics of acoustic string instruments.

Leo Fender devised a way to increase the magnetic flux in the coils and provide shielding from magnetic interference at the same time in his "Electromagnetic Pickup for Stringed Musical Instruments." This design enabled a higher-output, lower-noise single coil pickup. Filed June 20, 1979, Patent No. 4220069 issued Sept. 2, 1980. This patent also shows examples of the flux distribution characteristics of the common prior-art pickups.

ABSTRACT

A pickup for an electrical musical instrument of the stringed type including first and second pickup assemblies, each pickup assembly including a plurality of metallic, unmagnetized pole pieces operatively associated with the strings of the instrument, the pole pieces being aligned in parallel, spaced-apart relationship, generally perpendicular to the plane of the strings, first ends of all the pole pieces being closely adjacent to the plane of the strings, and second ends of all the pole pieces being flat and planar. Each pickup assembly

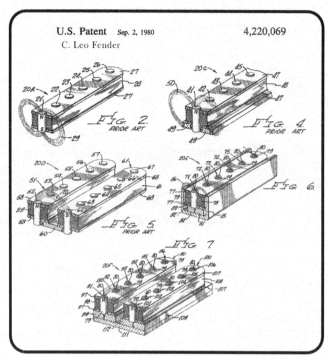

Figure 6.35 Fender

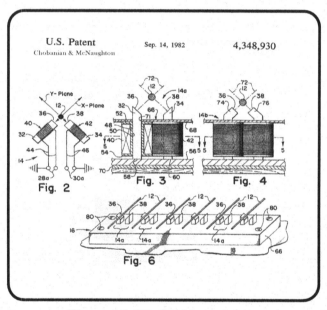

Figure 6.36 McNaughton

further includes a rectangular bar magnet having a first surface defining a north pole and an opposite second surface defining a south pole, the bar magnet of the first pickup assembly being positioned with the first surface thereof in surface contact with the second ends of all the pole pieces of the first pickup assembly, the bar magnet of the second pickup assembly being positioned with the second surface thereof in surface contact with the second ends of all the pole pieces of the second pickup assembly. Each of the pickup assemblies further includes coil means wound around the pole pieces thereof. A keeper is positioned in contact with the second surface of the bar magnet and the first surface of the second bar magnet. In another embodiment, the pickup includes only a single pickup assembly.

Dan Armstrong shows yet another way to load coils with flux in "Magnetic Pickup for Electric Guitars." His application was filed Jan. 26, 1979, and issued as Patent No. 4283982 on Aug. 18, 1981. It was registered to Daniel K. Armstrong of Santa Monica, Calif. 90402.

[Page 1, Col. 2, Lines 1–19]
The magnetic pickup for a stringed musical instrument disclosed in the present invention includes a polar magnet having its polar axis extending across the thinnest dimension of the magnet, and a coil having a magnetically permeable pole piece extending upwardly toward an instrument string. The magnet is positioned longitudinally parallel to the coil with the polar axis of the magnet perpendicular to the winding axis of the coil. The device may be constructed using one or more magnets arranged with one or more coils and has either a magnet or a pole piece positioned within the coil. Various embodiments include one magnet arranged between two coils, one coil between two magnets having like poles facing opposite each other, and two coils arranged between two magnets having unlike poles facing each other. Another embodiment utilizes two coils arranged with three magnets having like poles facing opposite each other, with a first coil positioned between the first and second magnet and a second coil positioned between the second and third magnet.

Dennis Chobanian and Alan McNaughton show a novel pole piece arrangement in Patent No. 4348930. "Transducer for Sensing Vibrational Movement in Two Mutually Perpendicular Planes" was filed Jan. 25, 1980, and issued Sept. 14, 1982. It was registered to

Dennis A. Chobanian of Eldorado Springs, Colo. and R. Alan McNaughton of Golden, Colo.

ABSTRACT

Two magnetically permeable pole pieces have pole faces of predetermined configuration formed thereon, and the pole pieces conduct magnetic flux that interacts with a magnetically permeable string of a stringed instrument. The positioning of the pole faces, the geometric configuration of the pole faces relative to the string, and the predetermined pattern of magnetic flux emanated from the pole faces are arranged so that vibrational movement of the strings in one plane creates significant magnetic flux changes in a first pole piece and minimal or no flux changes in the second pole piece. String vibrational movement in a second plane mutually perpendicular to the first plane creates significant magnetic flux changes in the second pole piece and minimum or no flux changes in the first pole piece. The magnetic flux changes are sensed, and electrical signals related to the flux changes are derived. The electrical signals are supplied directly to audio-amplifying equipment.

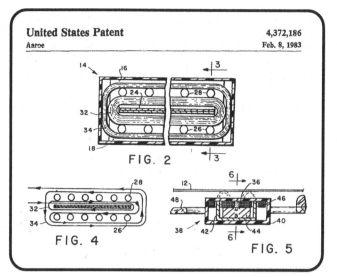

Figure 6.37 Aroe

Kenneth Aaroe shows a hum cancelling, two-coil pickup with one coil inside the other. His Patent No. 4372186 for "Humbucking Electromagnetic Pickup for Stringed Musical Instruments" was filed Feb. 17, 1981, and issued Feb. 8, 1983. It was registered to Kenneth T. Aaroe of Castro Valley, Calif.

ABSTRACT

A humbucking electromagnetic pickup for musical instruments, such as guitars having ferromagnetic strings. The pickup includes a permanent magnet for generating a flux path through the strings, a sensing coil in the flux path, and a humbucking coil substantially out of the flux path and concentrically wound closely around the periphery of the sensing coil and in opposition thereto

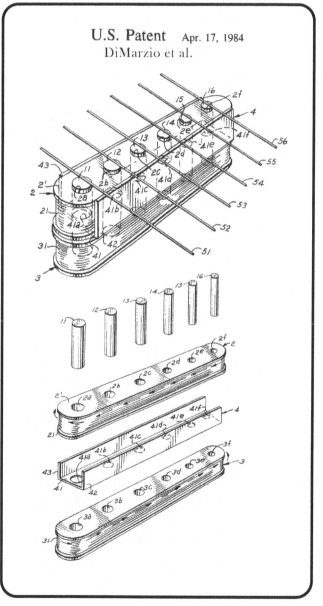

Figure 6.38 DiMarzio

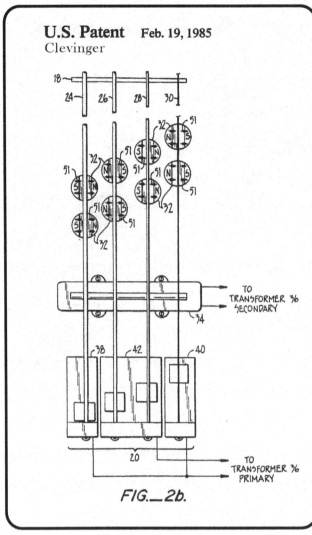

Figure 6.39 Clevinger

to cancel radiating extraneous interfering electromagnetic hum from the sensing coil.

Larry DiMarzio and Steve Blucher created a classic design with their "Electrical Pickup for a Stringed Instrument Having Ferromagnetic Strings." Patent No. 4442749, which was filed Aug. 6, 1982, and issued Apr. 17, 1984, shows two coils stacked in a single-coil-sized space with a ferrous plate situated around the top coil so as to load the coil with flux. This patent was registered to Lawrence P. DiMarzio of Staten Island and Stephen L. Blucher of New York.

ABSTRACT

An electrical pickup device for a stringed musical instrument having ferromagnetic strings comprises a pair of superposed coaxial bobbins, each axially wound with a coil having its axis perpendicular to the instrument strings. An integral plate of magnetic material is provided comprising a base disposed between the two bobbins perpendicular to the coil axis and two side walls extending upwardly and perpendicularly from the base to at least immediately below the top face of the upper bobbin. A plurality of rodlike permanent magnets extend through at least the upper coil parallel to the axis thereof and contact the base of the integral plate, and the magnets have like polarities at the tops thereof.

Martin Clevinger shows a way to blend the current generated in a vibrating string with the signal from the pickups in his "Dual Signal Magnetic Pickup with Even Response of Strings of Different Diameters." Filed July 11, 1983, Patent No. 4499809 issued Feb. 19, 1985, to Martin R. Clevinger of Oakland, Calif.

ABSTRACT

A transducer adapted to fretless musical instruments, instruments with non-conductive frets or non-conductive string wrapping, with two or more vibratable strings of magnetically permeable material. The strings pass through a magnetic field. Motion of the strings generates current in the strings. The magnetic field is provided by magnets shaped to concentrate the field across the signal-generating portions of the strings. In a preferred embodiment, the coils are wound around the specially shaped magnets to utilize the same magnetic field used to generate current in the strings. Means are provided to passively mix both signals generated in the coil and signals generated in the strings. The circuitry electrically connected to the strings incorporates a method of balancing the uneven output caused by differences in string diameter. There is no special "return" wiring of the neck required. A wide variety of tonal differences are obtainable without active circuitry or signal processing. The signal level and impedance is such that it can be connected through a convenient length of cable to a standard musical instrument amplifier.

Steve Blucher designed a hum cancelling pickup with two coils using different wire diameters on each coil in Patent No. 4501185. "Transducer for Stringed Musical Instrument," filed July 29, 1983, and issued Feb. 26, 1985, was assigned to DiMarzio Musical Instrument Pickups. The patent was issued to Steven L. Blucher of New York, NY.

[Page 1, Col. 2, Lines 1–16]

SUMMARY OF THE INVENTION

The present invention avoids the shortcomings of prior two-coil humbucking pickups by winding the coils such that both coils of the pair have substantially the same number of turns but are wound with

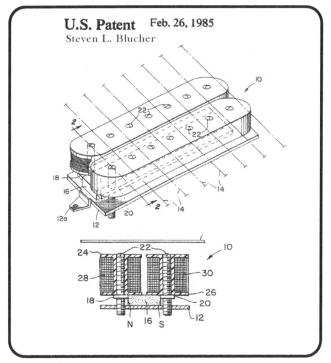

Figure 6.40 Blucher

wire of different diameter or gauge. It has been found that by means of this construction, low frequency cancellation is emphasized, providing more effective elimination of the sixty-cycle hum without affecting the higher harmonics of the sixty-cycle signal, which may contribute to the desired tonal qualities. Moreover, because of the differences in impedance characteristics resulting from different diameter wire on the respective coils, overall frequency response can be selectively adjusted to provide improved tonal qualities.

Leo Fender designed a way to get the tonal balance of a single coil pickup with a hum cancelling arrangement in Patents No. 4581974 and No. 4581975. Both applications were filed Apr. 9, 1984, and both issued Apr. 15, 1986. "Pick-up for an Electrical Musical Instrument of the Stringed Type" was issued to C. Leo Fender of Fullerton, Calif.

ABSTRACT

A pickup assembly for stringed musical instruments including a pair of pickup assemblies, only one of which is magnetized. The first and second pickup assemblies are physically disassociated so that the reactance of the unmagnetized pickup assembly does not interfere with the magnetized pickup assembly. The unmagnetized pickup assembly is lowered further into the body of the instrument than the magnetized pickup assembly for the same purpose. The outputs of the two pickup assemblies are summed at the negative input of an operational amplifier, which negative input is a virtual ground so that neither coil acts as a load for the other coil.

Donald Lace shows a novel way of concentrating flux into the coil in his "Magnetic Field Shaping in an Acoustic Pickup Assembly." This invention also uses the flux arrangement to skew interfering signals, thus providing some shielding against noise. Filed July 14, 1987, Patent No. 4809578 was issued Mar. 7, 1989, and was assigned to Donald A. Lace of Huntington Beach, Calif.

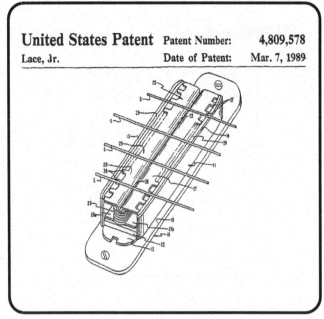

Figure 6.41 Lace

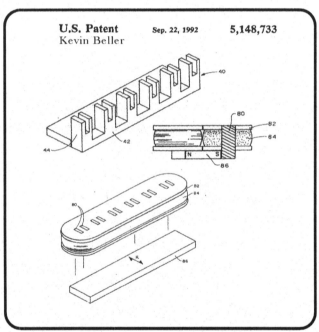

Figure 6.38 Beller

ABSTRACT

An electromagnetic pickup for use in sensing the mechanical motion of strings includes a ferromagnetic housing of elongate, longitudinally recessed form in which a ferromagnetic core is received. The core includes a plurality of coplanar, spaced, finger-like projections directed at the walls of the recess. Both the walls of the recess and the finger-like projections of the core are permanently magnetized to a common magnetic polarity and thus will concentrate by magnetic repulsion the flux into the gap between the projections. A coil wound around the core then senses the flux changes of these concentrated flux fields due to string motion.

Kevin Beller uses a different pole piece arrangement to improve the tone of the string in his "Pole Piece for an Electric String Instrument to Decrease Magnetic Flux Intensity Around Strings." This application was filed Mar. 8, 1990, and issued as Patent No. 5148733 on Sept. 22, 1992, to Kevin Beller of Santa Barbara, Calif. and was assigned to Seymour Duncan Corporation, Santa Barbara, Calif.

ABSTRACT

A pole piece for an electric string instrument comprises a block of ferrous material having a slot formed therein. The string of the string instrument passes over the pole piece in aligned relationship with the slot, thereby allowing vibration in a zone that is substantially free of any in tense magnetic flux lines.

Reading through all these creations, I keep seeing a recurring theme. There's been a never-ending quest, spanning generations, to improve the fidelity, or tonal quality, of musical instruments. It's very apparent in the pickup patent record.

In the pickup domain, the approach to this theme is dominated by two, sometimes concurrent, strategies. The first and primary focus is by way of improvements in the way the pickup reads the string movement. The second consideration is in the reduction or elimination of interfering signals, or noise. The ultimate goal is to achieve the most representative electronic picture of the string's motion without any harmonic disruption and the accompanying resonant damping created by interfering fields. It's quite a challenge.

Bear in mind that not all inventors work with the same set of tools. Some do not have the same vision of string motion, or flux patterns, or string behavior in magnetic fields. In fact, the Patent and Trademark Office does not require the inventors' opinions to be factual or the claimed invention to even work as claimed in the patent application. An application has only to meet the standards for receiving a patent in order to have a patent issued, which is no easy task. Regardless of whether or not the inventors' visions can be proven or disproven, the fact stands that once approved by the PTO, the patents are legally on record for trying to create better functioning pickups.

With this in mind, I decided that each of the patent excerpts chosen for inclusion in this chapter would have to have some teaching value demonstrated by one or more of these three requirements: (1) The patent would have to illustrate valid scientific principles, (2) The pickup resulting from the patent would need to be historically significant to guitar history, and (3) the invention would have to be at least interesting. In regard to Requirement No. 3, there were some creations that were very humble, scientifically, and did not attain any commercial success, but nevertheless were very intriguing in their inception, and thus are intellectually noteworthy.

If any of the patent highlights in this chapter piques your interest, I encourage you to download the entire version of it from the PTO and study it in full. In addition to what I have included, there are many other pickup patents to study if you want to broaden your base of knowledge in this area.

Thus far, we have seen how the musical note is developed on the string, how that information travels throughout the instrument structure, harvesting tonal information, and reflects back into the string. Now we can appreciate how that information is translated into an electrical signal. At this point, it could be delivered directly to a source of processing or amplification, or it could be adjusted somewhat before it is sent downstream.

The next chapter will focus on the components typically found in guitar circuits for making these adjustments.

ADDITIONAL READING

Patent It Yourself, David Pressman, Nolo Press, 1986

Chapter Seven
Guitar Circuit Components

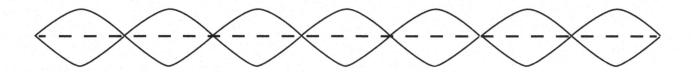

The interpretation of the guitar's tone that is generated from the pickup can be delivered directly to an external source, or it can be combined with one or more other pickup signals and voiced via combinations of switches, potentiometers, resistors, capacitors, and inductors before it leaves the instrument. Most electric string instruments will have some arrangement of circuit components to allow for a variety of tonal coloration. This chapter will look at the most common circuit components; the following chapter will outline their combinations.

SWITCHES

A switch is a device that is used to make and break connections. In terms of the signal path, it is used to direct the route of the signal. Switches are described in terms of their two main components: poles and throws. The pole of a switch is the moving component that contacts the terminals. The throw of a switch is the completion of a path between terminals by the pole. The simplest kind of switch found in guitars is the *single-pole/single-throw* variety. The one moving element, or pole, connects the terminals in one position only. The *SPST* switch is made in slider, mini-toggle, and push-button versions.

What's more commonly found in instruments is the *single-pole/double-throw* switch. The one moving conductor closes a path in two different positions. This type of switch in a three-

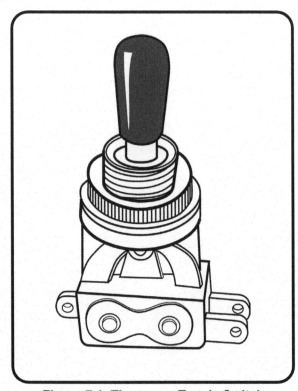

Figure 7.1 Three way Toggle Switch

way configuration can also have an off position in the center. It is more commonly referred to as an on-off-on switch, and is found in slider, toggle, and mini toggle versions.

One of the most widely used switches is the *double-pole/double-throw*, or *DPDT*. This model has two moving poles and six terminals, making it two SPST switches in one housing. The DPDT slider and mini-toggle also come in center-off as well as center-on varieties. Like the SPDTs, they are referred to as on-off-on and on-on-on switches. The DPDT can also be found in combination with a potentiometer and is called a push-pull or a push-push pot.

Slider switches can be found in configurations up to double pole/four-throw, but the most commonly found multi-position switches in guitars are lever, toggle, and rotary models. Double pole three-, four-, five-, and six-way levers and rotaries are very popular.

POTENTIOMETERS

Another electro-mechanical component found in nearly all electric guitars and basses is the *potentiometer*. Commonly called a *pot*, this device is a variable resistor. The potentiometer is used in circuits where low levels of ac are present. A beefed-up version of a pot is called a *rheostat* and is used in high power applications. Rheostats are often two-terminal devices, whereas pots nearly always have three terminals.

Pots can be divided into two groups: trimmers and panel types. Trimmers are the little guys, generally ¼ in. to 3 mm, that are used on circuit boards for test adjustments and calibration. These are usually turned by a small flathead or Phillips screwdriver. Panel types have a threaded bushing for installation on instruments through an opening in the body or pickguard. These pots are adjusted by means of a spindle, which can be insulated or non-insulated. A knob, insulated or non-insulated, is usually attached to the spindle to make it easier to operate.

The pot itself has an inner conductive path of resistive material connected to the two outer terminals. This material is generally either carbon or cermet, which is a ceramic substrate with a metal film attached to it. The conductive *wiper*, which is affixed to the center terminal, is able to slide along this resistive path. This assembly is loaded into a small container that can be sealed or, more commonly, left open to facilitate cleaning.

The way in which the resistance changes as the wiper moves across the track is called

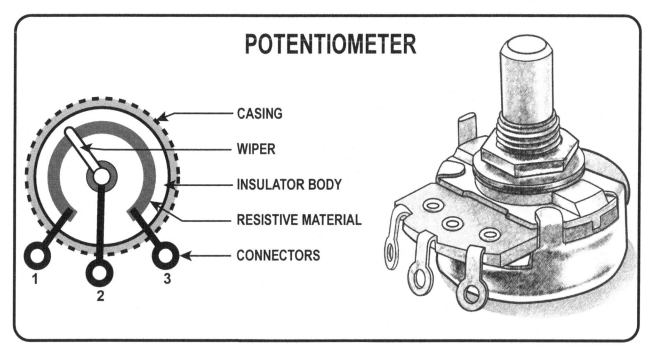

Figure 7.2 Potentiometer

the *taper*. Two types of tapers are commonly used: linear and logarithmic. A linear taper simply varies the resistance in direct proportion to the position of the wiper. A logarithmic taper varies the resistance logarithmically, much the same way our sense of hearing perceives volume changes.

The specification tolerance of a pot is a measure of how close the end-to-end resistance of the conductive resistance path will be to the target value of the pot. A batch of 500k pots with a 5 percent tolerance rating will have resistance track values ranging from 475k to 525k, and an overall average value of 500k.

The law accuracy specification of a pot indicates how close to linear or logarithmic taper the pot may be. With no specification at all, the pot is linear with no better than 10 percent tolerance to linearity. If a logarithmic pot has a worse tolerance rating than a linear pot, there may not be a big difference to the ear. I notice that most of the time a linear pot sounds more like an on/off function, whereas a logarithmic pot will have some sort of taper. I thus stick with logarithmic pots for most circuits. Some active circuits require linear pots, so always check the manufacturer's recommendation when replacing them.

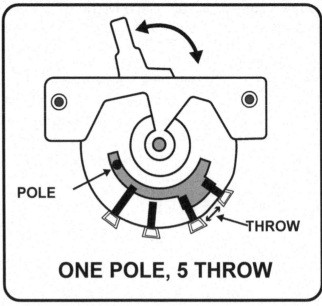

Figure 7.3 Five Way Switch

In addition to the everyday panel pot, there are also combination pots such as *push/pull* or *push/push* and *ganged pots*. The push/pull pots are a combination of a pot and a switch. Pulling up on the spindle changes the switch mode; the spindle works the pot by turning in either up or down positions. Ganged pots are two pots stacked together with their wipers moving in tandem, much like the pole movement of a double pole switch. Some ganged pots' wipers traverse the resistive track from one end to the other; other ganged pots have a détente in the center position and a resistive track on either side. The start-to-finish taper of the resistive track also comes in two varieties. These pots are used for blend controls and for boost and cut functions on active circuits. There are also concentric ganged pots; each pot has its own spindle, one located inside the other. Concentric ganged pots require two knobs.

RESISTORS

Although not widely used in guitar circuits, resistors are the most common of all the passive electronic devices. They consist of two leads, a resistive material, and an insulating covering. They are built with resistive values ranging from .1 ohms up to 22 megohms.

The first commercially available resistors were carbon composition types. Their performance was poor, and they are therefore not used in very many applications now. The most common, and inexpensive, resistors in use now are carbon film types. These are fine for general use.

The quietest low-cost resistors are the metal film types. They are price competitive with carbon film models, but they have better temperature coefficients and greater power-handling abilities. They are typically made out of a nickel-chromium alloy. There are also wire-wound resistors, which are used in circuits ranging from two watts on up. They are also inductive and not normally used in guitar circuits. The resistor specifications most commonly encountered are power-handling capability, tolerance, and temperature coefficient.

The power-handling rating is measured in watts, which of course is the prod-

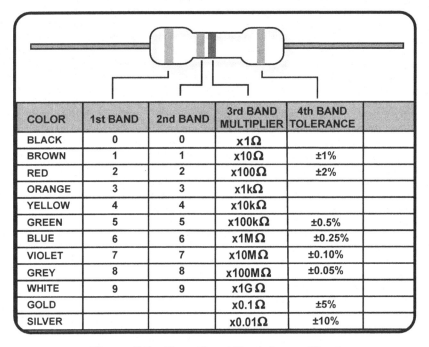

Figure 7.5 Four Band Resistance Chart

uct of voltage times current, P = EI. A good rule of thumb to remember is always double the calculated power rating of your guitar circuit when choosing a resistor. This greatly increases the odds of dependable resistor operation. A typical guitar circuit will usually be okay with ¼ to ½ watt resistors.

The tolerance rating is a measure of how close the resistor's value will be to the target value. Common carbon composition types are usually ±5%. Metal film types average ±1%, and precision metal film types average ±.1%.

The temperature coefficient is a measure of how far the resistance value will change as the temperature changes. It is measured in ppm/°C, or parts per million per degree centigrade. The *tempco* of a typical 1 percent metal film resistor will average ±50 ppm to ±100 ppm. A .1% precision metal film resistor can run ±25 ppm.

Other specifications will include the operating temperature range, insulation resistance, moisture resistance, and terminal strength, as well as the unit's physical dimensions. It's wise to pick the type that is the best overqualified for the job. In a guitar, a compact component with good leads, good specs, and a reasonable price is the preferred choice.

Resistors have an identification code marked on them. The code consists of four bands of different colors. The first two bands, starting from the end of the resistor, correspond to the first two significant numbers of the resistor's value. The third band is the multiplier, which, when factored with the first two numbers, will be the target resistance of the unit. The fourth band represents the tolerance value. Precision resistors oftentimes skip the banding and simply print the value right on the component. If you don't work with resistors enough to memorize the color code, you can always measure their resistance with a resistance tester.

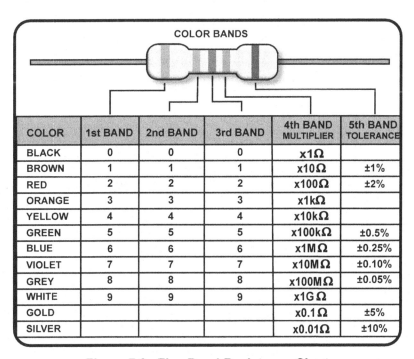

Figure 7.6 Five Band Resistance Chart

115

CAPACITORS

Capacitors, like resistors, are very common passive devices that are found in practically all electronic circuits. In guitar circuits, they are used primarily as part of filter circuits, or tone controls. Capacitors can be categorized according to their dielectric component. The three main groups are these: (1) metallized film and paper, (2) ceramic, and (3) electrolytic. There are several subtypes of each group, and each subtype can be found in several styles of construction.

The metallized film capacitors are basically a sandwich of dielectric layers and electrodes. These are found in polyester, polycarbonate, polypropylene, and polystyrene varieties. Metallized paper was one of the earliest widely used capacitor constructions, but they are not used much anymore due to their problems with humidity.

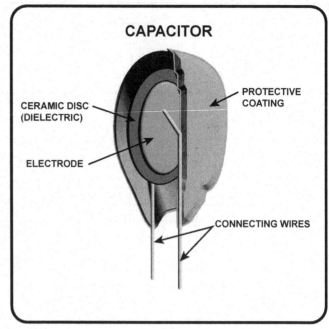

Figure 7.7   Capacitor Structure

There are two main types of ceramic capacitors: single-layer and multilayer. Single layer types simply have different thicknesses and types of dielectrics and are inexpensive to manufacture. Multilayer types are made much like the multilayer film types except that the layers are built up individually instead of being wound.

Multilayer ceramics are found in three grades: (1) COG, which is also known as NPO; (2) X7R; and (3) Z5U. The designations are internationally recognized classifications established by the EIA-US and the IEC-Europe.

NPO is the best quality of the three, but it doesn't have very high capacitance values, which makes it ideal for guitar circuits. X7R attains higher capacitance ratings, but its value fluctuates with temperature, frequency, and voltage. Its main usage is in coupling and decoupling applications. Z5U is the worst performer overall, but it does have some of the highest capacitance values. It is limited to primarily IC coupling.

Single-layer ceramic capacitors are basically just cheaper versions of the Z5U multilayers. The most notable of the single layers are the Type 1, low-K (permittivity) and the Type Z, high-K. Also known as Class 1 and Class 2 capacitors, these varieties exhibit a more stable performance overall. The Type 1s have the best characteristics, but have low capacitance values, typically ranging from 1 pF to 500 pF.

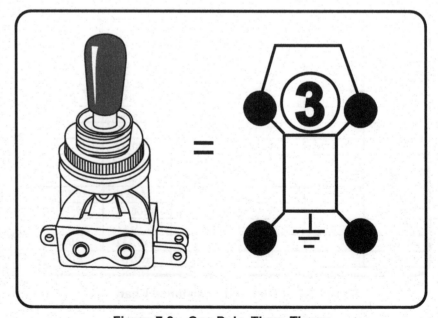

Figure 7.8   One Pole, Three Throw

The Type 2s range in values from 100 pf up to 47 nF, but their performance fluctuates with temperature, voltage, frequency, and age, much like the multilayer Z5Us.

The electrolytic capacitors have the highest capacitance values, ranging from .1 µF in miniature form to 1 µF to 4700 µF in normal sizes. These polarized firecrackers, which is what they sound like when they explode, are used in guitar amplifiers. Except for some of the smallest value miniatures, they are never used in guitar circuits.

Some of the specifications you will see used to describe capacitors include the tolerance; tempco, or temperature coefficient; tan δ, insulation resistance, or time constant; dielectric absorption; voltage coefficient and aging coefficient. The tolerance rating is the same specification as used for resistors. It describes how close to the printed value the actual value of the capacitor will be. The temperature coefficient gives the change in capacitance the unit will experience with change in temperature. It's written in parts per million, or ppm/°C—the same as for resistors. Sometimes this information will be listed simply as an operating temperature range, such as -40 °C to +100 °C.

Tan δ is a measure of dissipation. It's the ratio of the resistance and capacitive reactance of the capacitor. This is commonly found as the dissipation factor in sales literature and will be written as a maximum percentage at some frequency and temperature, such as 1 percent @ 1kHz, 25 °C.

Insulation resistance is a measurement of the dc leakage and is expressed in ohms. It will usually have a minimum resistance rating, and sometimes a rating per capacitance, and a maximum rating. This is also known as the time constant and is calculated by multiplying the dc resistance by the capacitance per second. In electrolytic capacitors, this measurement is commonly called leakage current.

The dielectric absorption is a measure of the rate at which the dielectric stores its charge. It is also known as the voltage memory of the capacitor and is usually listed as a percentage of change over a given amount of time.

The voltage coefficient indicates how much capacitance will be lost as the applied voltage approaches the capacitor's voltage rating. The aging coefficient tells what percentage of the capacitor's rated value will be lost after a given number of operating hours.

It's quickly apparent that the listed capacitance rating on a capacitor will not be the same under changing conditions and time. Its value will fluctuate. Part of the skill of choosing the best components for any circuit is knowing which specifications are relevant to the circuit's applications.

In a guitar, which is not usually played in temperatures drastically different from room temperature, the tempco at extremes is not important. The tolerance is a notable spec, however. I look for 5 percent to 10 percent tolerances. The tan δ and time constant are negligible, but the voltage rating and physical size are important. Fifty-volt versions are more than sufficient, and compact is what's needed inside a guitar control cavity. The aging coefficient is interesting but not extremely important. Ideally, when a capacitor gets beyond 10 percent tolerance, it should be replaced. That's simple enough on newer instruments, but a negative on a vintage, collectible guitar. Fortunately, the capacitor's job in a guitar's tone circuit isn't vital to the instrument's functions, so if the value drifts a bit, most listeners either don't notice, or they just get used to it.

Many capacitors have their capacitance value and voltage rating printed on their casings. Others have a color code either in dots or in banding, like resistors. If you encounter one that is defaced, you can always simply test the capacitance value.

INDUCTORS

Inductors are the third most common passive device, after capacitors and resistors, that are used in circuits. They are not found very often in guitars and basses, but when they are, they are generally part of a filter, or tone, circuit.

The three main applications where inductors are commonly used include energy storage in power supplies, filtering in suppression circuits, and frequency routing in resonant circuits.

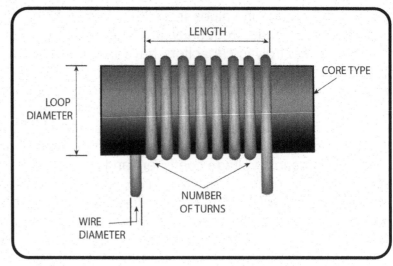

Figure 7.9   Inductor Structure

There are fixed and variable inductors. Fixed inductors include air core and high-permeability core versions that have a set inductance value. The variable inductors have a ferromagnetic shaft that can vary the flux linkage of the coil and change the inductance within a specified range. Inductor specifications will include an inductance value in µH, mH, or Henries and sometimes a test frequency for which the value was determined. There will also be a tolerance rating, a minimum Q value, working voltage rating, operating temperature range, and construction details such as dimensions and lead and core materials.

Inductors, also known as *chokes*, are not found in many passive guitar circuits. They can be utilized in tone controls, but there are disadvantages to using them. Being a coil of wire, it is susceptible to electromagnetic interferences and can make the instrument sound different in varying background conditions. It can also serve as a pathway for unwanted electromagnetic fields, or noise, to be introduced into the circuit. Used as a filter device, they are not price competitive with capacitors either.

CONNECTORS

Connectors are the electro-mechanical structures that allow electronic devices to communicate. They are made in hundreds of varieties, but there are only a few versions that are used commonly on musical instruments.

The jack is the guitar's electronic portal to the world. It is typically mounted on a pickguard, the body, or through the tail block of an acoustic or archtop guitar. The industry standard is known as the ¼" jack, in reference to the inside diameter of the device.

There are two, three, and multi-terminal jacks, but the most common are called mono and stereo jacks. The mono jacks usually have only two terminals, but some have more. The stereo jacks have three or more terminals, which may also serve as a mechanical switching de-

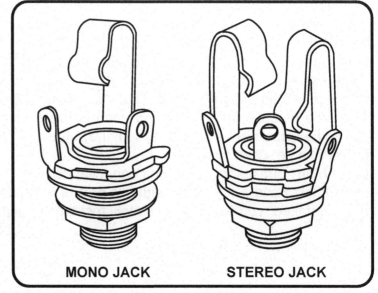

Figure 7.10 Jacks

AWG	Diameter (in)	Diameter (mm)	Turns of wire, without insulation (per in)	Turns of wire, without insulation (per cm)	Area (kcmil)	Area (mm²)	Resistance per unit length (mΩ/m)	Resistance per unit length (mΩ/ft)	Max I at 4 A/mm² current density	Copper wire Ampacity at temperature rating 60 °C (A)	75 °C (A)	90 °C (A)
0000 (4/0)	0.4600	11.684	2.17	0.856	212	107	0.1608	0.04901	—	195	230	260
000 (3/0)	0.4096	10.405	2.44	0.961	168	85.0	0.2028	0.06180	—	165	200	225
00 (2/0)	0.3648	9.266	2.74	1.08	133	67.4	0.2557	0.07793	—	145	175	195
0 (1/0)	0.3249	8.251	3.08	1.21	106	53.5	0.3224	0.09827	—	125	150	170
1	0.2893	7.348	3.46	1.36	83.7	42.4	0.4066	0.1239	—	110	130	145
2	0.2576	6.544	3.88	1.53	66.4	33.6	0.5127	0.1563	—	95	115	130
3	0.2294	5.827	4.36	1.72	52.6	26.7	0.6465	0.1970	—	85	100	115
4	0.2043	5.189	4.89	1.93	41.7	21.2	0.8152	0.2485	—	70	85	95
5	0.1819	4.621	5.50	2.16	33.1	16.8	1.028	0.3133	—	—	—	—
6	0.1620	4.115	6.17	2.43	26.3	13.3	1.296	0.3951	53.2	55	65	75
7	0.1443	3.665	6.93	2.73	20.8	10.5	1.634	0.4982	42.2	—	—	—
8	0.1285	3.264	7.78	3.06	16.5	8.37	2.061	0.6282	33.5	40	50	55
9	0.1144	2.906	8.74	3.44	13.1	6.63	2.599	0.7921	26.5	—	—	—
10	0.1019	2.588	9.81	3.86	10.4	5.26	3.277	0.9989	21.0	30	35	40
11	0.0907	2.305	11.0	4.34	8.23	4.17	4.132	1.260	16.7	—	—	—
12	0.0808	2.053	12.4	4.87	6.53	3.31	5.211	1.588	13.2	20	25	30
13	0.0720	1.828	13.9	5.47	5.18	2.62	6.571	2.003	10.5	—	—	—
14	0.0641	1.628	15.6	6.14	4.11	2.08	8.286	2.525	8.3	15	20	25
15	0.0571	1.450	17.5	6.90	3.26	1.65	10.45	3.184	6.6	—	—	—
16	0.0508	1.291	19.7	7.75	2.58	1.31	13.17	4.016	5.2	—	—	18
17	0.0453	1.150	22.1	8.70	2.05	1.04	16.61	5.064	4.2	—	—	—
18	0.0403	1.024	24.8	9.77	1.62	0.823	20.95	6.385	3.3	10	14	16
19	0.0359	0.912	27.9	11.0	1.29	0.653	26.42	8.051	2.6	—	—	—
20	0.0320	0.812	31.3	12.3	1.02	0.518	33.31	10.15	2.1	5	11	—
21	0.0285	0.723	35.1	13.8	0.810	0.410	42.00	12.80	1.6	—	—	—
22	0.0253	0.644	39.5	15.5	0.642	0.326	52.96	16.14	1.3	3	7	—
23	0.0226	0.573	44.3	17.4	0.509	0.258	66.79	20.36	1.0	—	—	—
24	0.0201	0.511	49.7	19.6	0.404	0.205	84.22	25.67	0.8	2.1	3.5	—
25	0.0179	0.455	55.9	22.0	0.320	0.162	106.2	32.37	0.7	—	—	—
26	0.0159	0.405	62.7	24.7	0.254	0.129	133.9	40.81	0.5	1.3	2.2	—
27	0.0142	0.361	70.4	27.7	0.202	0.102	168.9	51.47	0.4	—	—	—
28	0.0126	0.321	79.1	31.1	0.160	0.0810	212.9	64.90	0.3	0.83	1.4	—
29	0.0113	0.286	88.8	35.0	0.127	0.0642	268.5	81.84	0.26	—	—	—
30	0.0100	0.255	99.7	39.3	0.101	0.0509	338.6	103.2	0.20	0.52	0.86	—
31	0.00893	0.227	112	44.1	0.0797	0.0404	426.9	130.1	0.16	—	—	—
32	0.00795	0.202	126	49.5	0.0632	0.0320	538.3	164.1	0.13	0.32	0.53	—
33	0.00708	0.180	141	55.6	0.0501	0.0254	678.8	206.9	0.10	—	—	—
34	0.00630	0.160	159	62.4	0.0398	0.0201	856.0	260.9	0.08	0.18	0.3	—
35	0.00561	0.143	178	70.1	0.0315	0.0160	1079	329.0	0.06	—	—	—
36	0.00500[i]	0.127[i]	200	78.7	0.0250	0.0127	1361	414.8	0.05	—	—	—
37	0.00445	0.113	225	88.4	0.0198	0.0100	1716	523.1	0.04	—	—	—
38	0.00397	0.101	252	99.3	0.0157	0.00797	2164	659.6	0.032	—	—	—
39	0.00353	0.0897	283	111	0.0125	0.00632	2729	831.8	0.025	—	—	—
40	0.00314	0.0799	318	125	0.00989	0.00501	3441	1049	0.020	—	—	—

Figure 7.11

vice. The basic two terminal mono jack is called an *open-tip* jack. This means the circuit is open until the instrument cable's plug is fully inserted.

A popular three-terminal, stereo jack that is used in many active, or battery powered, circuits is the *open-tip, open-ring* model. The secondary terminal and the ring are connected when the plug is inserted, which activates the battery. This jack is also used for stereo and/or dual output applications.

Both versions of these jacks are manufactured in two varieties: (1) jack plate mounting, and (2) direct body mounting. The jack plate mounting models are more commonly used due to their durability and pricing. The direct body mounting versions offer a shielding advantage, but at a higher cost and a shorter working life.

Jacks don't have the plethora of specifications that a lot of the other electronic components have. Besides the terminal descriptions, the physical dimensions and mounting considerations are the specs most often provided.

WIRE

All these components have to be connected somehow before the signal goes anywhere. Although a few instruments have their pots loaded onto circuit boards, which have traces for connectors, the overwhelming majority of guitars and basses have their pickups and switches and pots connected by wire.

There are many different kinds of wire. The type that is used in instrument circuits is called hook-up, or equipment, wire and is classified according to its kind of insulation. The insulation used will determine the wire's safe voltage rating and temperature operating range.

Single-strand wire sizes have been standardized according to wire thickness, which is commonly measured in circular mils. The *circular mil, CM*, is a measure of the cross-sectional area of the conductor and is a factor in the calculation of a conductor's resistance.

A circular mil is simply the diameter of the wire in mils squared. One mil is equal to one thousandth of an inch. A wire measuring .009" in diameter would be 9 mils across, and would be $(9 mils)^2$, or 81 circular mils, in cross-sectional area.

Every conductive material has a resistivity, ρ, value. This is a measure of the resistance of a piece of the material measuring one foot in length by one mil in diameter at room temperature, or 20 °C.

Thus,

$$R = \rho(l/A) \tag{7.1}$$

Where R is resistance in ohms, ρ is resistivity, l is length in feet, and A is area in circular mils.

Resistivity units thus become

$$\rho = (cm\text{-}\Omega)/ft \tag{7.2}$$

Wire sizes have been standardized by thicknesses into a series of numbers called gauges. Each number is prefaced by AWG, which stands for American Wire Gauge. The lower the number, the thicker the wire; the higher the number, the thinner the wire.

AWG #0, for example, is 105, 530 cm in cross sectional area. AWG #14, a common size for speaker cable wire, is 4,106.8 cm. AWG #22, which is used in guitar circuits, is 642.4 cm, which works out to a diameter of .025 inches. AWG #40, with an area of 9.89 cm, is about the thickest wire used for the windings of a pickup coil.

The wire used in guitars can be grouped into three major categories: (1) solid conductor, (2) stranded conductor, and (3) shielded conductor.

The solid conductor wire is the least dependable of the group. It is used sometimes because it is inexpensive, but guitars wired with it have a higher circuit failure rate. Switches, pots, and jacks work loose from mechanical stressing from day-to-day usage and sometimes wood shrinkage due to low humidity. This results in solder joint deterioration and breakage as well as breakage of the wire itself.

The stranded conductor wire will flex much longer before solder joint failure or wire breakage and is the most common choice for guitar circuits. AWG #20, 22, and 24 are the top choices. The thicker #20 is the sturdiest but may be a bit noisier. I see more #22 in guitars than anything else, but I prefer #24.

The shielded conductor is found with foil or a braided shield wrapped around the insulated stranding. Many pickups have their output wiring encased in some sort of shielding to help reduce unwanted interference signals. Occasionally shielded conductor is used in the circuit itself, but if not used carefully, this type of conductor can also introduce noise into the signal as well as bleed off some high frequencies due to capacitive loss. If the shielding, which is grounded, moves inside the guitar and touches a hot connection, the signal drops. I only use it when restoring some vintage circuits to their original specifications.

Wire specifications are pretty basic compared to the rest of the circuit components. The typical features will include the conductor's operating temperature range, voltage rating, conductor material—such as stranded tinned copper—and insulation details such as color coding, flammability, solder iron resistance, and moisture and chemical resistance.

There are two considerations to keep in mind when doing guitar circuit wiring. The primary concern is for the function and survivability of the circuit. Make good solder joints. Never trust a previously soldered piece of wire; sometimes there can be a break inside the insulation, invisible to the eye. Always trim the old work away and solder fresh, unoxidized wire. Use lock washers between the components and their anchor points and tighten the securing nuts firmly. Make sure there is no conductive residue left in the control cavity. Clear out residual buffing compound out of the control cavities; it will break loose and find its way into a component and interrupt the connection. Test your wiring regularly as you progress through the job and test it thoroughly upon completion. Treat each job as though it will be played in front of fifty thousand people every night for the next month, and remember, you are only as good as your last job. The secondary concern involves the next person who will work on that circuit. Make it user-friendly. Use a consistent color code throughout the guitar; one color for the hot connections and a contrasting color for the grounds. I use primarily white and black, but also red and green and sometimes yellow and blue on new circuits. I try to match the manufacturer's original color codes, if possible, on repair circuits.

Chapter Eight
Circuit Diagrams and Organization

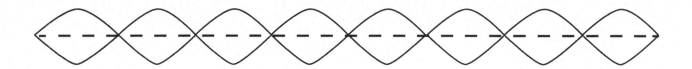

At this point in the guitar system, the energy from the string motion has washed through the instrument, collected an assemblage of consonant and dissonant harmonic information, and been transposed by the pickup into an electrical signal.

A reading of the pickup design chapter shows that each pickup design will transcribe the instrument's inherent voicing with the pickup's own dialect, so to speak. This information is then ready to be amplified and can be sent as is straight to processing or amplification at the player's discretion. But some fun can be had with it first.

The overwhelming majority of electric instruments have controls for modifying the pickup's signal before it is sent downstream. This is accomplished with switches and pots primarily, which can be passive; or without a power supply; or active, which requires a power supply.

The network of controls along the path that the signal follows is commonly known as the circuit, and the map illustrating the pathway is called a schematic. It is also known as a circuit diagram. The schematic is drawn with schematic symbols and shows what is happening electrically at each stage of the circuit; the circuit diagram is drawn with component representation pictorials and shows the connective path of the components.

The family of components in a circuit diagram usually consists of the following: (1) pickups, (2) switches, (3) pots, and (4) one or more output jacks. It is convenient, then, to organize this group by types of components and the number of each component. If you look at a guitar and see it has three pickups, one switch, three pots, and one output jack, you could describe it as a three-pickup, one-switch, three-pots, one-jack circuit, or simply a 3-1-3-1 circuit. On closer examination, when it is determined that it is a passive circuit, it could be called a 3-1-3-p circuit. If it is powered, or active, it would be a 3-1-3-a circuit.

Using this perspective and a familiarity with the most common pickups, switches, pots, and jacks will greatly reduce your dependance on schematics and circuit diagrams.

Most pickups will have either two, three, four, or five conductors to allow for full output or modified output. The cabling is color-coded and often has shielding and may have a bare drain wire. Some active pickups may have six or eight conductors. Most of these have plug-in terminals, but some don't.

There is no standard color code. Builders typically select a group of colors and assign that color code to all their models. It is important, then, to first identify the manufacturer of the pickup, then do an online lookup for the color coding. The manufacturers usually have pictorials showing sample wiring combinations illustrating full output, series/parallel, single coil, and phasing options as well as the ground and/or drain wire.

There are many pickups in circulation with no trade dress marks. A resistance tester will show the dc resistance of a coil when the starting and ending conductors of that coil are connected. When I have a mystery double coil pickup, I'll make sample connections after the initial resistance tests and listen to them through an amplifier. With the loudest combination established, I'll rewire the pickup in parallel mode and test the resistance. If it's about half the series output, then the combination is usually correct. The phasing with any other pickup won't be known until they are both in a guitar and sound checked.

Some mystery double coil pickups with three conductors will have one wire carrying full output; a second wire carrying single coil, or half output; and a third wire acting as ground. Other three wire double coil pickups will be full output only with a phasing option and the ground wire. Dc resistance testing as well as sound checking will determine the functions.

Switches are simple mechanical devices that open and close paths for the signal. The most commonly used switches in guitars and basses are these: (1) toggle; (2) lever, more commonly called three-way and five-way, according to the number of stops; (3) mini toggle; and (4) slider. Most of the toggle switches are three position, or stops, and are used for pickup selection. They can also be used for tone control and standby. The most used lever types are three-, four- and five-way models, but a six way is also built. The mini toggle are simply miniature toggle switches, usually found in two and three position varieties. They are typically used for pickup mode selection, such as series/parallel, series/split/parallel, and phasing, but are regularly used as pickup selector switches. Slider switches are found in two and three position varieties, mostly on older instruments. Like mini toggle switches, they're a little harder to change on the fly, so they are not used on many newer builds.

Potentiometers, or pots, are used for volume adjustment; treble, mid, and bass tone controls; and blend, or pan, functions. They are most commonly single function but are made in combination with a double pole/double throw switch called a push-pull pot. The spline switches up and down to change the switch setting, and the pot works in both modes. This is also made in a push-push version. Some pots have détentes, or stops, in the midpoint, and can be found in single and ganged versions. The ganged models have a secondary pot build beneath the top pot. These are commonly used for pickup selection or tone control.

Output jacks serve either passive or active circuits but come in a variety of builds. Taking the most mechanical stressing of any of the circuit components, they need to be sturdy. The most common of all will have only a hot and a ground terminal, and the three terminal versions used in active circuits will have a hot, a ground, and a battery ground connection. There are four connector versions for stereo active circuits as well as three connector versions with one ground and double-latching hot terminals.

All the circuits components, from the pickups to the jack and even the strings, with most pickup systems need to be grounded. The ground path connecting everything should be very streamlined; that is, there should be only one, simple route to the jack, and no duplicate paths anywhere.

Shielding, a ground surrounding the circuitry, is found in many guitars. It is used to help reduce noise from interfering fields, but it has friendly fire issues. When the components work loose, if any hot terminal touches the shield, the signal grounds. This can be intermittent or shut the component or circuit off completely. Some of the painted shielding can act as a resistance and drop the output level if a hot connection touches it. Many times, duplicate ground paths occur and induce noise. The adhesive holding shielding foils in place against the control cavity and/or pickguard can fail as well as it ages, and the foil can drop onto a hot terminal and shut off the signal.

When it is installed securely and efficiently, shielding will help cut down field interference in the control cavity, but it will not eliminate the field interference induced in the coil of a single coil pickup. Hum cancelling pickups can do that very effectively.

In conclusion, in guitar circuitry, it's not where the wire goes, but what goes through the wire. It's important to understand how all the circuit components function as the circuit is being built or repaired. A circuit diagram is a map of the signal path, but there is room on that map for experimentation and creativity. You can decide what combinations might be the most fun on a switch. It doesn't have to be exactly how the original manufacturer thought best when you are working on something for yourself. It's fun to experiment with pot values, too. Volume pots are available in 100k, 250k, 300k, 500k, and 1 meg for use with passive pickups. Sometimes using an unorthodox value with a pickup will have a surprisingly interesting tone. You won't know until you experiment. The same goes for tone controls; there are a lot of ways to bleed frequencies selectively to ground.

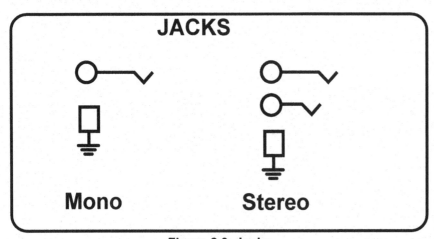

Figure 8.0 Jacks

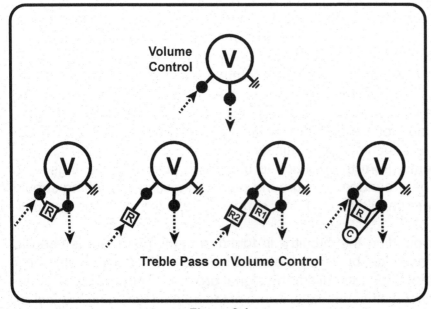

Figure 8.1

Volume Control
V = 25k up to 1M. Common values are 25k, 50k, 100k, 250k, 300k, 500k and 1M. Most common with passive pickups are 250k and 500k.

Treble Pass on Volume Control
R= 100k, 150k
C= .001 µf, .002 µf, or .003 µf

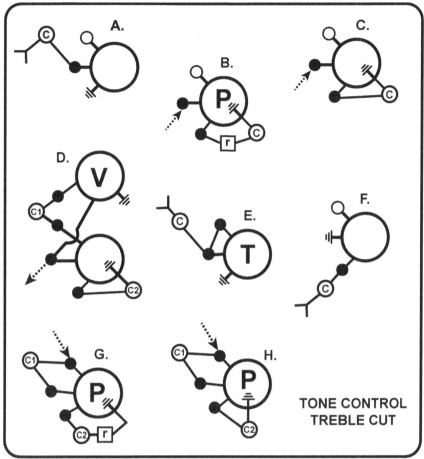

Figure 8.2

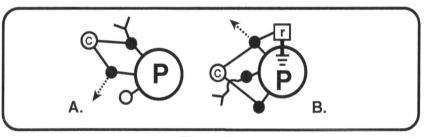

Figure 8.3

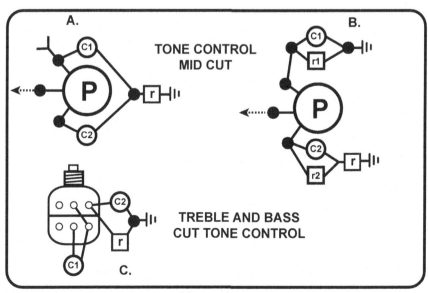

Figure 8.4

Treble Cut Tone Control 8.2
A.
P = 250k, 500k, or 1M
C = .02 µf, .047 µf, or .1 µf
C.
P = 250k, 500k, or 1M
C = .02 µf, .047 µf, or .1 µf
B.
P = 250k
R = 100k
C = .047 µf
E.
P = 250k, 500k, or 1M
C = .02 µf, .047 µf, or .1 µf
D.
C1 = .001 µf
C2 = .02 µf
F.
T = 100k, 150k, or 250k
C = .047 µf
G.
P = 250k or 1M
C1 = .1 µf
C2 = .02 µf
R = 4.7k or 5.6 k
H.
P = 500k
C1 = .02 µf
C2 = .01 µf

Bass Cut Tone Control 8.3
A.
P = 1M
C = .002 µf, .003 µf, or .0047 µf
B.
P = 500k
C = .002µf
R = 1M

Mid Cut Tone Control 8.4
A.
P = 1M
C1 = .001 µf
C2 = .001 µf
R = 100k
B.
P = 1M
C1 = .001 µf
R1 = 1.1 M
C2 = .039 µf
R2 = 270 k
I = 1.5 H
Treble and Bass Cut Tone Control
C.
P = Ganged, Center Détente, Upper = 1M, Lower = 250k
C1 = .001 µf
C2 = .02 µf
R = 1M

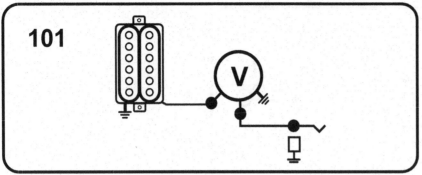

Figure 8.5

Circuit Diagram 8.5
101
V = 500k

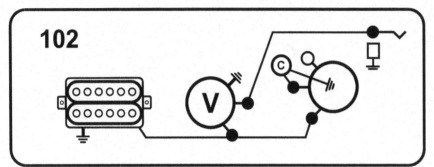

Figure 8.6

Circuit Diagram 8.6
102
V = 500k
T = 250k
C = .02µf

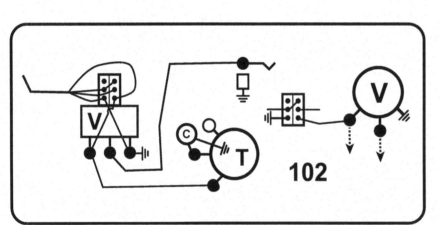

Figure 8.7

Circuit Diagram 8.7
102
V = 500k Push Pull Pot
T = 250k
C = .02µf

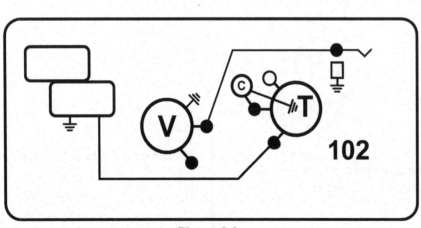

Figure 8.8

Circuit Diagram 8.8
103
V = 250k
T = 250k
C = .047µf

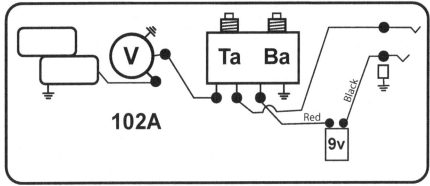

Figure 8.9

Circuit Diagram 8.9
102A
II
Refer to manufacturers' recommendations for active circuits' pot values.
25k are common. Active circuits will have a signal input, an output, a power input And a ground. A tip/ring jack is commonly used to switch on the power.

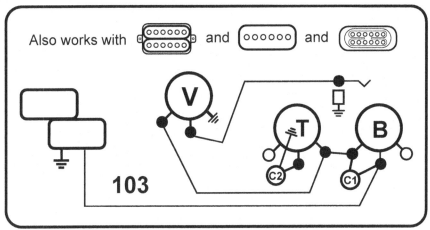

Figure 8.10

Circuit Diagram 8.10
103
V = 250k or 500k
T (treble cut) = 250k
B (bass cut) = 1M
C1 = .002µf
C2 = .047µf

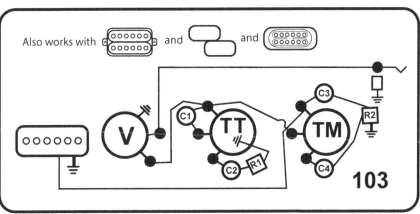

Figure 8.11

Circuit Diagram 8.11
103
V = 500k
TT (treble cut) = 1M
C1 = .02µf
C2 = .047µf
R1 = 5.6k
TM (mid cut) = 1M
C3 = .001µf
C4 = .001µf
R2 = 100k

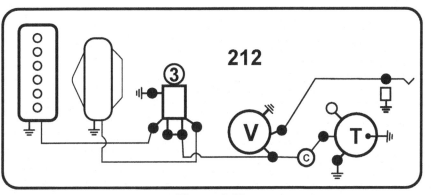

Figure 8.12

Circuit Diagram 8.12
212
V = 250k or 500k
T = 250k or 500k
C = .02µf or .047µf

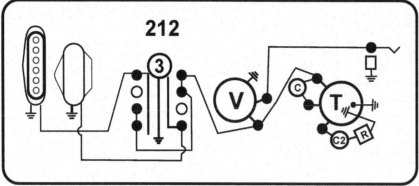

Figure 8.13

Circuit Diagram 8.13
212
V = 250k
T = 1M
C1 = .02µf
C2 = .047µf
R = 5.6k

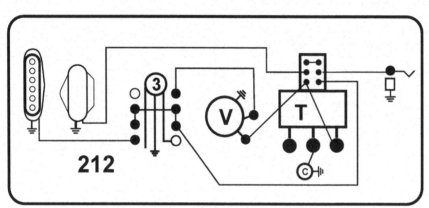

Figure 8.14 Control Bypass Bridge Pickup Only

Circuit Diagram 8.14
212
V = 500k
T = 250 Push Pull Pot
C1 = .02µf
C2 = .047µf

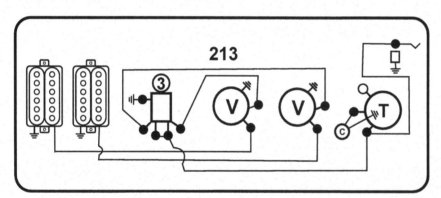

Figure 8.15

Circuit Diagram 8.15
213
V = 500k
T = 250k or 500k
C = .02µf or .047µf

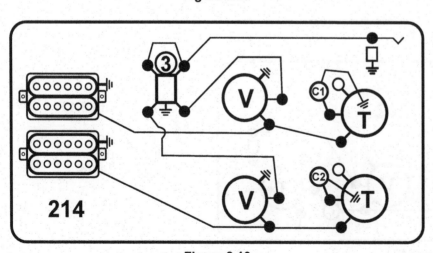

Figure 8.16

Circuit Diagram 8.16
213
V = 500k
T = 250k or 500k
C = .02µf or .047µf

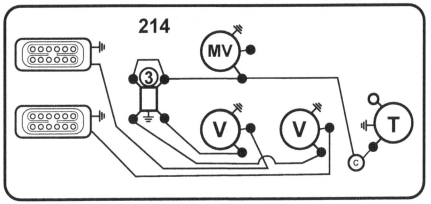

Figure 8.17 Master Volume

Circuit Diagram 8.17
214
MV = 500k
V = 500k
T = 250k
C = .047µf

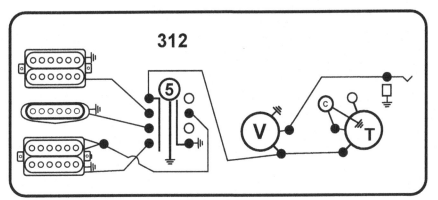

Figure 8.18

Circuit Diagram 8.18
312
V = 500k
T = 250k
C = .047µf

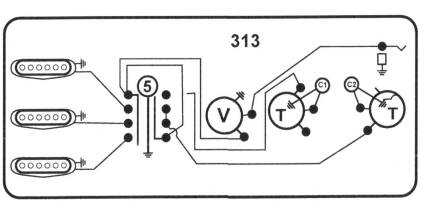

Figure 8.19

Circuit Diagram 8.19
313
V = 250k
T = 250k
C1 = .047µf
C2 = .02µf

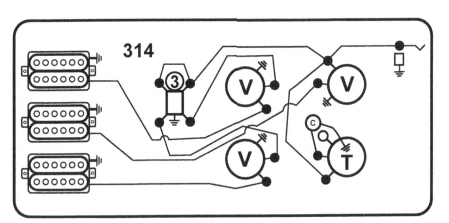

Figure 8.20

Circuit Diagram 8.20
314
V = 500k
T = 250k
C = .02µf

Epilogue

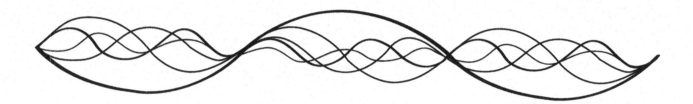

Now we have a challenge. If we are going to advance our body of knowledge, we must collaborate with each other. The Internet makes this easy enough. All we have to do is the hard work part. Let's review the basic scientific method for our field of music instrument science.

The scientific method for any endeavor simply tries to objectively explain phenomena in a reproducible way. This can begin with an observation like "guitars with bone nuts sound better." Why do they sound better, though? The next step is research. What's so special about bone? One of the points research reveals is parts of our ears are made of bone. Hmm. A hypothesis can be made that bone is the ideal transmitter of sound energy and therefore allows the maximum tonal information to move out of the instrument and into the strings, thus producing the most interesting tone.

An experiment has to be created to test the hypothesis. Maybe connecting an audio signal generator to various common nut plastics and bone samples and reading the outputs with an audio spectrum analyzer would provide clues. After the data is analyzed, and it appears to verify the hypothesis, then that information needs to be shared with your peer group, hich in our case is everyone who works on and builds musical string instruments. At this stage, we must ask for peer review and criticism. This is an opportunity for the initial findings to be questioned and tested on a much wider scale. Additional widespread testing may provide more accurate, improved data. When the results are verifiable, then there is a piece of knowledge that is scientifically established, useful for everyone in the field, and faithful to the original Latin root word for knowledge, scientia. Also key to the scientific method is the willingness to accept new ideas as new evidence presents itself. Perhaps you had thought one type of plastic was the best nut material until you examined the test results and heard the difference. Then the stronger argument prevailed.

But in science, the argument is never settled. Maybe a new bone and synthetic hybrid material may be developed that outperforms organic bone. If the data indicates that, and it sounds better than bone, then that argument wins. But we must not assume it is settled.

We, then, must look critically at everything we think we know about string instruments and evaluate this body of knowledge scientifically. There's a lot of testing and reevaluation and discussion to be done, and, just like playing the guitar, I'd start with whatever looks like the most fun!

Like I stated earlier, this is a great nonfiction adventure. You are the protagonist tasked with improving the numberless horde of string instruments created during the dark ages of music history, as well as those yet to be built in, hopefully, better times. They all need love; some much more than others. The universe, your antagonist, will do everything in its random, chaotic ability to slow you down and stop you, but you must meet adversity's every challenge.

Each instrument is a unique microcosm of predominately random resonant conditions which answer only to matching incoming energies. Utilizing a science-based understanding of this chaos of parts we can begin to identify and reassemble these structures so that they become more music friendly. This challenge will require your study, ideas, initiative and skilled methodology to create consonant order out of dissonant disorder. This is the way we will ultimately outsmart this tiny universe known as the guitar.

Then on to bigger things, right?

"What we do now echoes in eternity." -- Marcus Aurelius, 121–180 CE, Meditations

Appendix
Math Review

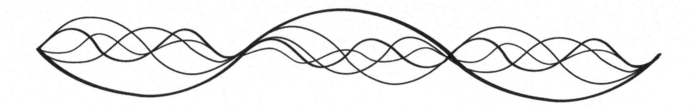

I've always viewed mathematical functions as fun puzzles. Every mathematical operation is governed by a set of rules, and like playing a game, you have to learn the rules before you can play. The first rule: stay calm. There's no need to panic when you encounter unfamiliar letters and symbols in an equation. They all have a function, and learning their functions is how you learn to solve the puzzles. Once you learn the rules, you just plug in the numbers and arrive at the solution. Be patient, have fun with the process, and the intellectual spider that many make it out to be will go away.

A working knowledge of algebra, trigonometry, and calculus is recommended. Get this in school if you can and review it periodically (I read a calculus workbook sometimes at bedtime to clear my thoughts). If you haven't studied these subjects at the school level, there are many self-instruction books and online classes you can opt for now.

Let's review the basic conventions used in scientific and engineering calculations so the symbols and formats you encounter will be more familiar.

Systems of Units

In the description of units of measurement such as lengths, weights, forces, etc., there were traditionally two systems: English and metric. English terminology included terms such as feet, slugs, and pounds; metric terminology included terms such as meters, kilograms, and newtons.

The metric system was further divided into two subsystems: the MKS, which is an acronym for meters, kilograms, and seconds; and the CGS, which is an acronym for centimeters, grams, and seconds.

In an effort to get everyone speaking a common language, the International Bureau of Weights and Measures adopted the International System of Units, or SI, from the French for Le Système International d'Unités, in 1960. The SI format, which shares a lot of conventions with the MKS system, has become the universal standard for scientific and engineering applications.

Calculations, however, regarding string movement, magnetism, electronics, and any music instrument science topic can be solved in any format: English, metric, or SI. Work in whichever system you find most convenient, but you should be comfortable in all variations and become fluent in systems conversions.

Here are three guidelines:
1.) Be sure each quantity has the proper unit and magnitude of measurement as required by the equation.
2.) Be sure each quantity is in the same system of units.
3.) Be sure the result is described by the proper unit of measurement in the same system as the rest of the equation.

Sometimes there may be units of measurement from two different systems that need to fit into an equation. A manufacturer's specification for string tension may be in pounds, for example, but your length measurements may be in centimeters. You will have to either convert the pounds to newtons or the centimeters to inches, depending on the context you prefer. Moral of the story: make sure all the units of measurement agree throughout the equation.

Scientific Notation

Very frequently when making string, magnetic, and electronic computations, very tiny and very large numbers are encountered. To help make information faster and easier to write and comprehend, it is more practical to use scientific notation.

Using this method, any cumbersome group of digits can be converted to a compact number between one and ten, followed by the appropriate power of ten.
Thus:

$$83,000,000 = 8.3 \times 10^7$$

This reads, eighty-three million equals eight point three times ten to the seventh power.
A few points to remember when using scientific notation:
1.) Numbers greater than one have a positive power of ten.
2.) Numbers less than one have a negative power of ten.
3.) $10^0 = 1$
4.) Count the number of places between the original decimal point and the new one. This will correspond to the appropriate power of ten.
    a. 83,000,000. ← original decimal point.
    b. 8ˆ3,000,000. Note the new decimal position between the eight and the 3three.
    c. 8ˆ3,000,000. There are seven places between the new decimal position and the original decimal point.
    d. $83,000,000 = 8.3 \times 10^7$

Also: $.000083 = 8.3 \times 10^{-5}$

Table A.1
Powers of 10 from 10^{-6} to 10^6

$10^{-6} = .000001$	$10^{-2} = .01$	$10^0 = 1.0$	$10^4 = 10,000.0$
$10^{-5} = .00001$	$10^{-1} = .1$	$10^1 = 10.0$	$10^5 = 100,000.0$
$10^{-4} = .0001$		$10^2 = 100.0$	$10^6 = 1,000,000.0$
$10^{-3} = .001$		$10^3 = 1,000.0$	

Note that the number of places the decimal point is transferred matches the value of the exponent of ten.

Engineering Notation

There are some values of the powers of ten that are used frequently in calculations and in component values. A special branch of scientific notation called engineering notation encompasses these value groups, which have their own names to help make them easier to use.

Engineering notation values are a select group of scientific notation values in multiples of three.

Table A. 2 shows engineering notation values along with their names and symbols.

Table A. 2
Engineering Notation

Value	Name	Symbol
$0.000\,000\,000\,001 = 10^{-12}$	pico	p
$0.000\,000\,001 = 10^{-9}$	nano	n
$0.000\,001 = 10^{-6}$	micro	µ
$0.001 = 10^{-3}$	milli	m
$1,000 = 10^{3}$	kilo	k
$1,000,000 = 10^{6}$	mega	M
$1,000,000,000 = 10^{9}$	giga	G
$1,000,000,000,000 = 10^{12}$	tera	T

For example, a frequency of 2,000 Hz would be expressed as

$$2000\ Hz = 2 \times 10^3\ Hz$$
$$10^3 = kilo = k$$
$$2000\ Hz = 2 \times 10^3\ Hz = 2\ kHz$$

Even with scientific and engineering notation, testing and the subsequent data preparation result in some enormous-sized numbers. Meaningful streamlining of this information becomes necessary to speed up the calculation process. There are three basic streamlining procedures.

The first step is to weed out questionable numbers. This is known as determining significant figures. A number is considered significant if it is a digit between one and nine. Zeroes are only significant if they are sandwiched between two non-zero digits. A zero can be made significant if its host number is greater than one and the zero is used as a place holder between a non-zero number and a decimal point.

The second step is to round off the number. If it can be trimmed down to three significant digits, it will be much more manageable. In the processes involved in music instrument science, three to four digits is enough.

In rounding, if the digit after the last significant figure to the right is less than five, drop it and replace it and all the digits after it with place-holding zeroes. If the digit after the last significant number is five or greater, increase the value of the last significant figure by one unit. Replace all the digits after the increased figure with place-holding zeroes.

The third step is sub calculation or getting all the entries ready for insertion into the equation. There are four basic math processes with positive and negative numbers in engineering notation. I will list those after a review of the basic math processes with signed (positive and negative) numbers.

Basic Math Processes for Positive and Negative Numbers

1.) For addition, if the signs of the numbers being added are the same, add the numbers and keep the same sign.

$$3 + 8 = 11 \qquad\qquad .5 + .25 = .75 \text{, or}$$
$$-6 + (-2) = -8 \qquad\qquad -.5 + (-.25) = -.75$$

2.) For addition, if the signs of the numbers being added are unlike, subtract the numbers and take the sign of the largest number.
$$+8 + (-6) = +2 \qquad -10 + (+2) = -8$$
3.) For subtraction, reverse the sign of the number being subtracted, reverse the subtraction sign, and follow the rules for addition. It's convoluted, but it works.
$$8 - 2 = 8 + (-2) = 6 \qquad -8 - 2 = -8 + (-2) = -10$$
4.) For multiplication, multiply the numbers. If the signs are alike, the product is positive.
$$8 \times 6 = 48 \qquad -8 \times -6 = 48$$
If the signs are opposite, the product is negative.
$$8 \times -6 = -48 \qquad -8 \times 6 = -48$$
5.) For division, the rules are the same as for multiplication. Thus, for same signs,
$$20 = 4 \qquad -20 \; -5 = 4$$
For opposite signs,
$$20 \; -5 = -4 \qquad -20 \; 5 = -4$$

Basic Math Processes in Engineering Notation

For addition and subtraction, when the powers of ten are the same, add or subtract the numbers and keep the same power of ten.
$$250k + 250k = 500k$$
Thus:
$$A \times 10^a \pm B \times 10^a = (A \pm B) \times 10^a$$

- For addition and subtraction, if the powers of ten are not the same, convert to basic units and add or subtract, then change the answer back to engineering notation. $50k + 1M = 50{,}000 + 1{,}000{,}000 = 1{,}050{,}000 = 1.05M$
- For multiplication, multiply the numbers and add the exponents of the powers of ten.
$$20k \times 3k = (20 \times 10^3) \times (3 \times 10^3) = 60 \times 10^6 = 60 \times 1{,}000{,}000 = 60{,}000{,}000$$
$$3k \times 5m = (3 \times 10^3) \times (5 \times 10^{-3}) = 15 \times 10^0 = 15 \times 1 = 15$$

Thus:
$$(A \times 10^a)(B \times 10^b) = AB \times 10^{a+b}$$

- For division, divide the numbers and subtract the powers of ten.
500k 100 m
So, $500 \; 100 = 5$
And, $(k = 10^3) - (m = 10^{-3}) = 10^0 = 1$
Then $5 \times 10^0 = 5 \times 1 = 5$

Thus:
$$(A \times 10^a) / (B \times 10^b) = (A/B) \times 10^{a-b}$$

- For division, whenever a power of ten is moved from numerator to denominator, or from denominator to numerator, the sign of the exponent is reversed.
$$1/10^{-3} \text{ becomes } 10^3/1$$

Thus:
$$1/10^a = 10^{-a} \text{ and } 1/10^{-a} = 10^a$$

- For powers of ten, the product of the powers of ten may be expressed by
$$10^a \times 10^b = 10^{(a+b)}$$
The division of powers of ten may be expressed by:
$$10^a / 10^b = 10^{(a-b)}$$

And the power of powers of ten may be expressed by:
$$(10^a)^b = 10^{(ab)}$$

When your numbers are in a manageable, working format, then you can plug them into your equation and solve.

TABLE A.3
Commonly Used Symbols and Abbreviations

Tables A3 and A4 both show symbols having more than one designation. With the evolution of disciplines such as mechanics, magnetics, mathematics, etc., multiple uses of the same symbols have become unavoidable, since there are only two alphabets available for use for abbreviations. When the field gets crowded to the point of confusion, tagging a subscript onto a symbol can help refine an identity or at least put it into an appropriate context.

Symbol	Meaning	Symbol	Meaning
a	area, number of paths	A	area, ampere
α	angle, temperature coefficient	ac	alternating current
Al	aluminum	AWG	American Wire Gauge
β	flux density, magnetic induction	β_d	remanence
β_g	flux density in air gap	β_i	intrinsic magnetism
β_m	flux density on normal magnetization curve	β_r	residual magnetism
β_s	saturation induction	β_{is}	intrinsic saturation magnetization
$(B/H)_{max}$	maximum energy product	B/H	load line, unit permeance
C	capacitance, coulomb	°C	Celsius
cm	centimeter	CGS	centimeter, gram, second
CM	circular mils	Cu	copper
Δ	change, delta	δ	density
d	diameter, dc, direct current	E	voltage source ϵ electron charge °F Fahrenheit ft foot F force G air gap, gauss, conductance G Giga, 10^9 H magnetic field strength, magnetizing force
H_c	normal coercive force	H_{ci}	intrinsic coercive force
H_d	demagnetizing force	H_g	magnetizing in air gap
H_s	saturating magnetizing force	h	Plank's constant
I	current	in	inch
J	magnetization intensity,	K	Kelvin, anisotropy current density, joule constant
k	Boltzmann's constant, leakage and reluctance factors	k	kilo, 10^3
kg	kilogram	L	inductance length L_g length of air gap
L_m	magnet length	M	mass
M	Mega, 10^6	MGO_e	million gauss-oersted
MKS	meter, kilogram, second	m	unit magnetic pole
m	milli, 10^{-3}	mmf	magnetomotive force
μ	micro, 10^{-6}	μ_o	magnetic constant
μ_d	differential permeability	μ_i	initial permeability
μ_r	recoil permeability	n	number of turns
N	north pole, demagnetization factor, Newton	Ni	nickel
NI	ampere turns	n	nano, 10^{-9}
O_e	oersteds	P	power, permeance
P_g	gap permeance	P_t	total permeance
P_i	power input	P_o	power output
p	packing factor, number of poles	ρ	pico, 10^{-12}
ϕ	magnetic flux	Q	charge
R	resistance	r	radius
R_{dc}	direct current resistance	ρ	resistivity
S	siemens, south pole, speed,		second
SI	International System of Units	T	tera, 10^{12}
T_c	Curie temperature	V	volume, voltage, velocity
W	watts	X	reactance
X_c	capacitive reactance	X_l	inductive reactance
Z	impedance	Z_t	total impedance

TABLE A.4
Greek Alphabet Designations

Greek alphabet letters are used to represent functions and relationships in fields ranging from physics, mathematics, magnetics, and electronics and just about anywhere a symbol is needed for an equation. Sometimes a letter will have more than one designation, but it is easy to identify the proper one from the context of its application. Here is a list of the most common designations.

Uppercase	Lowercase	Pronunciation	Designation
A	α	alpha	area, angle, coefficient
B	β	beta	angle, coefficient, flux density
Γ	γ	gamma	specific gravity, conductivity
Δ	δ	delta	density, change
E	ε or ϵ	epsilon	base of natural logarithms
Z	ζ	zeta	coefficients, coordinates, Impedance
H	η	eta	efficiency, hysteresis coefficient
Θ	θ or ϑ	theta	phase angle, temperature
I	ι	iota	variable
K	κ	kappa	dielectric constant, susceptibility
Λ	λ	lambda	wavelength
M	μ	mu	linear mass density, micro, amplification factor, permeability
N	ν	nu	reluctivity
Ξ	ξ	xi	variable
O	o	omicron	variable
Π	π	pi	3.1416...
P	ρ	rho	resistivity
Σ	σ	sigma	summation
T	τ	tau	time
Υ	υ	upsilon	variable
Φ	φ, ϕ	phi	angle, magnetic flux
X	χ	chi	variable
Ψ	ψ	psi	dielectric flux, phase difference
Ω	ω	omega	snippetohms, angular velocity

TABLE A.5
Math Symbols

Symbol	Meaning	Example
$\gg$	Much greater than	$100 \gg 2$
$>$	Greater than	$100 > 98$
$\geq$	Greater than or equal to	$x \geq 100$, x is equal to 100 or more
$=$	Equal to	$10^0 = 1$
$\leq$	Less than or equal to	$y \leq 100$, y is equal 100 and less
$\ll$	Much less than	$2 \ll 100$
$\cong$	Approximately equal to	$99.9 \cong 100$
$\neq$	Not equal to	$2 \neq 100$
$\mp$	Positive or negative value	± 100, plus or minus 100
$\sqrt{}$	Square root of	$\sqrt{9}$, square root of 9
$\sqrt[x]{}$	x root of	$\sqrt[x]{}$, x = 3, cube root
$|\ |$	Absolute magnitude of	$|x| = 100$, x = -100
$\sum$	Sum of	$\sum 100 + 2 + 3 = 105$
$\therefore$	Therefore	$x = (100+2+3) \therefore x = 105$
$+$	Plus	adds scalar quantities 2+2
$-$	Minus	subtracts scalar quantities 2-2
$\times$	Multiply	multiplies scalar quantities 2X2
$\div , /$	Divide	divides scalar quantities $2 \div 2$, 2/2
X^n	Powers	raises x to the nth power

TABLE A.6
Equivalencies

cycles per second	=	hertz
lines	=	maxwells
lines per square centimeter	=	gauss
ergs	=	dyne-centimeters
gauss	=	maxwells per square centimeter
oersteds	=	gilberts per square centimeter

STRING TESTS

The following graphs are the results from tests I conducted on GHS manufactured plain steel strings, nickel plated steel wound strings, and nickel wound strings.

This data can be used for bridge and saddle force load calculations, friction calculations, and comparative instrument force load calculations using different gauged strings.

Note: The areas shaded in light grey are theoretical, as the tension was too great for the equipment used.

UNITS
v = Velocity
m = Mass
l = Length
λ = Wavelength(m)
μ = L. Density m/l (kg/m)
f = Frequency (Hz)
τ = Tension(N)

Plain Steel Strings

High E String (E4) f = 329.628

String Gauge (in/mm)	Length (cm)	Mass (g)	μ Average (g/cm)	μ Average (kg/m)	τ (kg)	τ (N)	Scale Length (i)	Scale Length (cm)	v (m/s)	λ (m) via v/f	λ (m) via 2*l	f via v/λ
.008/.203	20	0.05	0.0025	0.00025	4.5	44.1315	25.07874016	63.7	420.15	1.27461858	1.274	329.788
.008/.203	82	0.209	0.00254878	0.000254878	4.5	44.1315	24.84251969	63.1	416.11	1.26236235	1.262	329.723
.008/.203	43	0.108	0.002511628	0.000251163	4.5	44.1315	25.03937008	63.6	419.1763	1.27166465	1.272	329.541
SUM	145	0.367	0.002531034	0.000253103	4.5	44.1315	24.98687664	63.46666667	417.5662	1.26954853	1.2693333	329.684
.009/.229	20	0.065	0.00325	0.000325	5.7	55.8999	24.76377953	62.9	414.7285	1.2581712	1.258	329.673
.009/.229	41	0.131	0.003195122	0.000319512	5.8	56.8806	25.19685039	64	421.928	1.28001267	1.28	329.631
.009/.229	29	0.093	0.003206897	0.00032069	5.5	53.9385	24.48818898	62.2	410.1162	1.24417899	1.244	329.675
SUM	90	0.289	0.003211111	0.000321111	5.66667	55.573	24.81627297	63.03333333	416.0105	1.26078762	1.2606667	329.66
.010/.254	20	0.08	0.004	0.0004	6.6	64.7262	24.21259843	61.5	402.263	1.22035438	1.23	327.043
.010/.254	49.9	0.197	0.003947896	0.00039479	6.9	67.6683	24.68503937	62.7	414.009	1.2559886	1.254	330.151
.010/.254	33.5	0.132	0.003940299	0.00039403	7.2	70.6104	25.23622047	64.1	423.321	1.28423848	1.282	330.204
SUM	103.4	0.409	0.003955513	0.000395551	6.9	67.6683	24.71128609	62.76666667	413.6102	1.25352715	1.2553333	329.132
.011/.279	20	0.097	0.00485	0.000485	8.6	84.3402	24.88188976	63.2	417.01	1.2650927	1.264	329.913
.011/.279	48.5	0.234	0.004824742	0.000482474	8.6	84.3402	25	63.5	418.1001	1.26839978	1.27	329.213
.011/.279	34.6	0.166	0.004797688	0.000479769	8.7	85.3209	25.15748031	63.9	421.7079	1.27934485	1.278	329.975
SUM	103.1	0.497	0.004820563	0.000482056	8.63333	84.6671	25.01312336	63.53333333	419.0911	1.27094577	1.2706667	329.7
.012/.305	21	0.113	0.005380952	0.000538095	9.7	95.1279	25.11811024	63.8	420.4597	1.27555822	1.276	329.514
.012/.305	38.8	0.218	0.005618557	0.000561856	10	98.07	24.88188976	63.2	417.7878	1.26745225	1.264	330.528
.012/.305	44.5	0.25	0.005617978	0.000561798	9.7	95.1279	24.52755906	62.3	411.4944	1.24836005	1.246	330.252
SUM	104.3	0.581	0.00557047	0.000557047	9.8	96.1086	24.84251969	63.1	415.3701	1.26379017	1.262	330.098
.013/.330	20	0.05	0.0025	0.00025	4.46745	43.8123	25	63.5	418.6276	1.27	1.27	329.628
.013/.330	82	0.209	0.00254878	0.000254878	4.55462	44.6671	25	63.5	418.6276	1.27	1.27	329.628
.013/.330	43	0.108	0.002511628	0.000251163	4.48823	44.016	25	63.5	418.6276	1.27	1.27	329.628
SUM	145	0.367	0.002531034	0.000253103	4.50343	44.1651	25	63.5	417.7253	1.27	1.27	329.628
.014/.356	20	0.155	0.00775	0.000775	13.8491	135.818	25	63.5	418.6276	1.27	1.27	329.628
.014/.356	38.4	0.299	0.007786458	0.000778646	13.9142	136.457	25	63.5	418.6276	1.27	1.27	329.628
.014/.356	44.6	0.346	0.007757848	0.000775785	13.8631	135.956	25	63.5	418.6276	1.27	1.27	329.628
SUM	103	0.8	0.00776699	0.000776699	13.8755	136.077	25	63.5	418.5677	1.27	1.27	329.628

Table A.7   High E String   **Plain Steel String**

Plain Steel Strings

B String (B3) f = 246.942

String Gauge (in/mm)	Length (cm)	Mass (g)	µ Average (g/cm)	µ Average (kg/m)	τ (kg)	τ (N)	Scale Length (in)	Scale Length (cm)	v (m/s)	λ (m) via v/f	λ (m) via 2*ℓ	f via v/λ
.011/.279	20	0.097	0.00485	0.000485	4.7	46.0929	24.60629921	62.5	308.281	1.2483926	1.25	246.6245
.011/.279	48.5	0.234	0.004824742	0.000482474	4.8	47.0736	24.92125984	63.3	312.357	1.26490144	1.266	246.7277
.011/.279	34.6	0.166	0.004797688	0.000479769	4.9	48.0543	25.35433071	64.4	316.483	1.28160789	1.288	245.7165
SUM	103.1	0.497	0.004820563	0.000482056	4.8	47.0736	24.96062992	63.4	312.493	1.26496731	1.268	246.3562
.012/.305	21	0.113	0.005380952	0.000538095	5.7	55.8999	25.66929134	65.2	322.312	1.30521177	1.304	247.1715
.012/.305	38.8	0.218	0.005618557	0.000561856	5.7	55.8999	25.15748031	63.9	315.423	1.27731546	1.278	246.8097
.012/.305	44.5	0.25	0.005617978	0.000561798	5.7	55.8999	25.11811024	63.8	315.439	1.2773813	1.276	247.2093
SUM	104.3	0.581	0.00557047	0.000557047	5.7	55.8999	25.31496063	64.3	316.781	1.28663618	1.286	247.0635
.013/.330	20	0.133	0.00665	0.000665	6.5	63.7455	24.68503937	62.7	309.609	1.2537732	1.254	246.8973
.013/.330	37.1	0.246	0.006630728	0.000663073	6.5	63.7455	24.68503937	62.7	310.059	1.25559393	1.254	247.2559
.013/.330	45.7	0.304	0.006652079	0.000665208	6.5	63.7455	24.68503937	62.7	309.561	1.25357728	1.254	246.8588
SUM	102.8	0.683	0.006643969	0.000664397	6.5	63.7455	24.68503937	62.7	309.75	1.2543148	1.254	247.004
.014/.356	20	0.155	0.00775	0.000775	7.6	74.5332	24.80314961	63	310.116	1.25582485	1.26	246.1237
.014/.356	38.4	0.299	0.007786458	0.000778646	7.7	75.5139	24.84251969	63.1	311.418	1.26109704	1.262	246.7653
.014/.356	44.6	0.346	0.007757848	0.000775785	7.7	75.5139	24.80314961	63	311.992	1.26342035	1.26	247.6123
SUM	103	0.8	0.00776699	0.000776699	7.667	75.187	24.81627297	63.03333333	311.132	1.26011408	1.26066667	246.8338
.015/.381	20	0.174	0.0087	0.00087	8.7	85.3209	25	63.5	313.161	1.2681573	1.27	246.5837
.015/.381	38.9	0.34	0.00874036	0.000874036	8.8	86.3016	25.03937008	63.6	314.228	1.2724766	1.272	247.0345
.015/.381	43.7	0.384	0.008787185	0.000878719	8.7	85.3209	24.84251969	63.1	311.604	1.26185037	1.262	246.9127
SUM	102.6	0.898	0.008752437	0.000875244	8.733	85.6478	24.96062992	63.4	312.819	1.26749476	1.268	246.8436
.016/.406	22.4	0.225	0.010044643	0.001004464	9.7	95.1279	24.52755906	62.3	307.742	1.24621147	1.246	246.9839
.016/.406	34.5	0.349	0.010115942	0.001011594	9.8	96.1086	24.94094488	62.4	308.232	1.24819661	1.248	246.9809
.016/.406	44.4	0.447	0.010067568	0.001006757	9.8	96.1086	24.64566929	62.6	308.972	1.2511918	1.252	247.7826
SUM	101.3	1.021	0.010078973	0.001007897	9.767	95.7817	24.58005249	62.43333333	308.271	1.24853329	1.24866667	246.9158
.017/.432	20	0.224	0.0112	0.00112	11.23	110.158	25	63.5	313.616	1.27	1.27	246.942
.017/.432	35.6	0.4	0.011235955	0.001123596	11.27	110.511	25	63.5	313.616	1.27	1.27	246.942
.017/.432	46.7	0.525	0.01124197	0.001124197	11.27	110.571	25	63.5	313.616	1.27	1.27	246.942
SUM	102.3	1.149	0.011231672	0.001123167	11.26	110.413	25	63.5	313.537	1.27	1.27	246.942
.018/.457	19	0.238	0.012526316	0.001252632	12.56	123.203	25	63.5	313.616	1.27	1.27	246.942
.018/.457	39.8	0.507	0.012738693	0.001273869	12.78	125.292	25	63.5	313.616	1.27	1.27	246.942
.018/.457	44.3	0.564	0.012731377	0.001273138	12.77	125.22	25	63.5	313.616	1.27	1.27	246.942
SUM	103.1	1.309	0.012696411	0.001269641	12.7	124.571	25	63.5	313.234	1.27	1.27	246.942

Table A.8   B String   **Plain Steel String**

G String (G3) f = 195.998

String Gauge (in/mm)	Length (cm)	Mass (g)	µ Average (g/cm)	µ Average (kg/m)	τ (kg)	τ (N)	Scale Length (in)	Scale Length (cm)	v (m/s)	λ (m) via v/f	λ (m) via 2*ℓ	f via v/λ
.014/.356	20	0.155	0.00775	0.000775	5	49.04	25.27559055	64.2	251.5372	1.28336621	1.284	195.9013
.014/.356	38.4	0.299	0.007786458	0.000778646	4.9	48.05	24.96062992	63.4	248.4255	1.2674899	1.268	195.9192
.014/.356	44.6	0.346	0.007757848	0.000775785	4.9	48.05	25	63.5	248.8832	1.26982498	1.27	195.971
SUM	103	0.8	0.00776699	0.000776699	4.93333	48.38	25.07874016	63.7	249.5812	1.27356036	1.274	195.9305
.015/.381	20	0.174	0.0087	0.00087	5.6	54.92	25.23622047	64.1	250.2479	1.28189022	1.282	195.9812
.015/.381	38.9	0.34	0.00874036	0.000874036	5.4	52.96	24.72440945	62.8	246.1503	1.25588152	1.256	195.9795
.015/.381	43.7	0.384	0.008787185	0.000878719	5.5	53.94	24.88188976	63.2	247.7562	1.26407517	1.264	196.0097
SUM	102.6	0.898	0.008752437	0.000875244	5.5	53.94	24.94750656	63.36666667	248.2475	1.2672823	1.26733333	195.9901
.016/.406	22.4	0.225	0.010044643	0.001004464	6.4	62.76	25.11811024	63.8	249.9717	1.27537877	1.276	195.9026
.016/.406	34.5	0.349	0.010115942	0.001011594	6.5	63.75	25.19685039	64	251.0277	1.2807665	1.28	196.1154
.016/.406	44.4	0.447	0.010067568	0.001006757	6.4	62.76	25.11811024	63.8	249.6869	1.27392587	1.276	195.6794
SUM	101.3	1.021	0.010078973	0.001007897	6.43333	63.09	25.14435696	63.86666667	250.1946	1.27669038	1.27733333	195.8991
.017/.432	20	0.224	0.0112	0.00112	7.1	69.63	25.11811024	63.8	249.3379	1.27214499	1.276	195.4059
.017/.432	35.6	0.4	0.011235955	0.001123596	7.1	69.63	25.11811024	63.8	249.8386	1.27010792	1.276	195.093
.017/.432	46.7	0.525	0.01124197	0.001124197	7.2	70.61	25.11811024	63.8	250.6185	1.27867886	1.276	196.4095
SUM	102.3	1.149	0.011231672	0.001123167	7.13333	69.96	25.11811024	63.8	249.5699	1.27364392	1.276	195.6361
.018/.457	19	0.238	0.012526316	0.001252632	8	78.46	25.11811024	63.8	250.2657	1.27687906	1.276	196.133
.018/.457	39.8	0.507	0.012738693	0.001273869	8.1	79.44	25.07874016	63.7	249.717	1.27407946	1.274	196.0102
.018/.457	44.3	0.564	0.012731377	0.001273138	8.1	79.44	25.07874016	63.7	249.7888	1.2744455	1.274	196.0665
SUM	103.1	1.309	0.012696411	0.001269641	8.06667	79.11	25.09186352	63.73333333	249.6173	1.27513467	1.27466667	196.0699
.019/.483	22.1	0.313	0.014162896	0.00141629	9	88.26	25.07874016	63.7	249.6395	1.27368393	1.274	195.9494
.019/.483	30.5	0.431	0.014131148	0.001413115	8.9	87.28	25	63.5	248.5275	1.26801017	1.27	195.6909
.019/.483	50.1	0.71	0.014171657	0.001417166	9	88.26	25.07874016	63.7	249.5623	1.27329018	1.274	195.8888
SUM	102.7	1.454	0.014157741	0.001415774	8.96667	87.94	25.05249344	63.63333333	249.2221	1.27166143	1.27266667	195.843
.020/.508	19.7	0.308	0.015634518	0.001563452	9.87777	96.87	25	63.5	248.9175	1.27	1.27	195.998
.020/.508	32.6	0.512	0.015705521	0.001570552	9.92263	97.31	25	63.5	248.9175	1.27	1.27	195.998
.020/.508	51.9	0.818	0.015761079	0.001576108	9.95773	97.66	25	63.5	248.9175	1.27	1.27	195.998
SUM	104.2	1.638	0.01571977	0.001571977	9.91938	97.28	25	63.5	248.7638	1.27	1.27	195.998
.021/.533	23	0.403	0.017521739	0.001752174	11.0701	108.6	25	63.5	248.9175	1.27	1.27	195.998
.021/.533	33.5	0.588	0.017552239	0.001755224	11.0894	108.8	25	63.5	248.9175	1.27	1.27	195.998
.021/.533	46.2	0.808	0.017489177	0.001748918	11.0495	108.4	25	63.5	248.9175	1.27	1.27	195.998
SUM	102.7	1.799	0.01751704	0.001751704	11.0697	108.6	25	63.5	248.946	1.27	1.27	195.998
.022/.559	23.8	0.447	0.018781513	0.001878151	11.866	116.4	25	63.5	248.9175	1.27	1.27	195.998
.022/.559	33.2	0.625	0.018825301	0.00188253	11.8937	116.6	25	63.5	248.9175	1.27	1.27	195.998
.022/.559	45.2	0.853	0.018871681	0.001887168	11.923	116.9	25	63.5	248.9175	1.27	1.27	195.998
SUM	102.2	1.925	0.018835616	0.001883562	11.8942	116.6	25	63.5	248.855	1.27	1.27	195.998
.024/.610	26.3	0.607	0.023079848	0.002307985	14.5817	143	25	63.5	248.9175	1.27	1.27	195.998
.024/.610	36	0.832	0.023111111	0.002311111	14.6014	143.2	25	63.5	248.9175	1.27	1.27	195.998
.024/.610	41.2	0.955	0.023179612	0.002317961	14.6447	143.6	25	63.5	248.9175	1.27	1.27	195.998
SUM	103.5	2.394	0.023130435	0.002313043	14.6093	143.3	25	63.5	248.8803	1.27	1.27	195.998

Table A.9   G String   **Plain Steel String**

Nickel Plated Steel Wound Strings

G String (G3) f=195.998

String Gauge (in/mm)	Length (cm)	Mass (g)	μ Average (g/cm)	μ Average (kg/m)	T (kg)	T (N)	Scale Length (in)	Scale Length (cm)	v (m/s)	λ (m) via v/f	λ (m) via 2*L	f via v/λ
.020/.508	20.2	0.291	0.014405941	0.001440594	9	88.263	24.96062992	63.4	247.5247	1.262894	1.268	195.209
.020/.508	26.8	0.391	0.014589552	0.001458955	9.2	90.2244	24.96062992	63.4	248.6801	1.2687889	1.268	196.12
.020/.508	46.2	0.676	0.014632035	0.001463203	9.1	89.2437	25	63.5	246.9656	1.2600413	1.27	194.461
SUM	93.2	1.358	0.014570815	0.001457082	9.1	89.2437	24.97375328	63.43333333	247.4838	1.2639081	1.268666667	195.263
.022/.559	18.4	0.298	0.016195652	0.001619565	10.2323	100.3481	25	63.5	248.9175	1.27	1.27	195.998
.022/.559	24.6	0.401	0.016300813	0.001630081	10.2987	100.9997	25	63.5	248.9175	1.27	1.27	195.998
.022/.559	50.4	0.821	0.016289683	0.001628968	10.2917	100.9307	25	63.5	248.9175	1.27	1.27	195.998
SUM	93.4	1.52	0.01627409	0.001627409	10.2742	100.7595	25	63.5	248.8254	1.27	1.27	195.998
.024/.610	22.1	0.43	0.019457014	0.001945701	12.2928	120.5555	25	63.5	248.9175	1.27	1.27	195.998
.024/.610	29.9	0.584	0.019531773	0.001953177	12.34	121.0187	25	63.5	248.9175	1.27	1.27	195.998
.024/.610	40.6	0.795	0.019581281	0.001958128	12.3713	121.3254	25	63.5	248.9175	1.27	1.27	195.998
SUM	92.6	1.809	0.019535637	0.001953564	12.3347	120.9665	25	63.5	248.8392	1.27	1.27	195.998
.026/.660	20.3	0.457	0.022512315	0.002251232	14.2231	139.4861	25	63.5	248.9175	1.27	1.27	195.998
.026/.660	25	0.564	0.02256	0.002256	14.2532	139.7815	25	63.5	248.9175	1.27	1.27	195.998
.026/.660	48.3	1.087	0.022505176	0.002250518	14.2186	139.4418	25	63.5	248.9175	1.27	1.27	195.998
SUM	93.6	2.108	0.022521368	0.002252137	14.2317	139.5698	25	63.5	248.9421	1.27	1.27	195.998
.028/.711	20.4	0.535	0.02622549	0.002622549	16.5691	162.4929	25	63.5	248.9175	1.27	1.27	195.998
.028/.711	27.4	0.719	0.026240876	0.002624088	16.5788	162.5882	25	63.5	248.9175	1.27	1.27	195.998
.028/.711	44.7	1.174	0.026263982	0.002626398	16.5934	162.7314	25	63.5	248.9175	1.27	1.27	195.998
SUM	92.5	2.428	0.026248649	0.002624865	16.5804	162.6042	25	63.5	248.8928	1.27	1.27	195.998

Table A.10 G String Nickel Plated Steel Wound String

D String (D3) f = 146.832

String Gauge (in/mm)	Length (cm)	Mass (g)	μ Average (g/cm)	μ Average (kg/m)	T (kg)	T (N)	Scale Length (in)	Scale Length (cm)	v (m/s)	λ (m) via v/f	λ (m) via 2*L	f via v/λ
.022/.559	18.4	0.298	0.016195652	0.001619565	5.7	55.8999	25.03937008	63.6	185.7831	1.265276904	1.272	146.0559
.022/.559	24.6	0.401	0.016300813	0.001630081	5.8	56.8806	25.07874016	63.7	186.8002	1.272203943	1.274	146.625
.022/.559	50.4	0.821	0.016289683	0.001628968	5.8	56.8806	25	63.5	186.8641	1.272638507	1.27	147.1371
SUM	93.4	1.52	0.01627409	0.001627409	5.766667	56.5537	25.03937008	63.6	186.4156	1.270039785	1.272	146.606
.024/.610	22.1	0.43	0.019457014	0.001945701	6.9	67.6683	25	63.5	186.4896	1.270088044	1.27	146.8422
.024/.610	29.9	0.584	0.019531773	0.001953177	6.9	67.6683	25	63.5	186.1323	1.267655045	1.27	146.5609
.024/.610	40.6	0.795	0.019581281	0.001958128	7	68.649	25.07874016	63.7	187.2391	1.275192782	1.274	146.9695
SUM	92.6	1.809	0.019535637	0.001953564	6.933333	67.9952	25.02624672	63.56666667	186.5629	1.270978624	1.271333333	146.7908
.026/.660	20.3	0.457	0.022512315	0.002251232	8	78.456	25.11811024	63.8	186.6822	1.27140023	1.276	146.3027
.026/.660	25	0.564	0.02256	0.002256	8.1	79.4367	25.19685039	64	187.6468	1.277969047	1.28	146.599
.026/.660	48.3	1.087	0.022505176	0.002250518	8.15	79.9271	25.23622047	64.1	188.4541	1.283467781	1.282	147.0001
SUM	93.6	2.108	0.022521368	0.002252137	8.083333	79.2733	25.18372703	63.96666667	187.6143	1.277612353	1.279333333	146.6339
.028/.711	20.4	0.535	0.02622549	0.002622549	9.4	92.1858	25.19685039	64	187.4866	1.27687826	1.28	146.4739
.028/.711	27.4	0.719	0.026240876	0.002624088	9.6	94.1472	25.27559055	64.2	189.4151	1.290012225	1.284	147.5195
.028/.711	44.7	1.174	0.026263982	0.002626398	9.5	93.1665	25.19685039	64	188.3431	1.282711207	1.28	147.143
SUM	92.5	2.428	0.026248649	0.002624865	9.5	93.1665	25.22309711	64.06666667	188.3981	1.283200564	1.281333333	147.0455
.030/.762	22.7	0.694	0.030572687	0.003057269	10.84042	106.312	25	63.5	186.4766	1.27	1.27	146.832
.030/.762	30.9	0.945	0.030582524	0.003058252	10.84391	106.346	25	63.5	186.4766	1.27	1.27	146.832
.030/.762	40.2	1.23	0.030597015	0.003059701	10.84905	106.397	25	63.5	186.4766	1.27	1.27	146.832
SUM	93.8	2.869	0.030586354	0.003058635	10.84446	106.352	25	63.5	186.4697	1.27	1.27	146.832
.032/.813	21.5	0.76	0.035348837	0.003534884	12.53395	122.92	25	63.5	186.4766	1.27	1.27	146.832
.032/.813	26.7	0.941	0.035243446	0.003524345	12.49658	122.554	25	63.5	186.4766	1.27	1.27	146.832
.032/.813	45.5	1.607	0.035318681	0.003531868	12.52325	122.816	25	63.5	186.4766	1.27	1.27	146.832
SUM	93.7	3.308	0.035304162	0.003530416	12.51793	122.763	25	63.5	186.4753	1.27	1.27	146.832
.034/.864	21.1	0.803	0.038056872	0.003805687	13.49416	132.337	25	63.5	186.4766	1.27	1.27	146.832
.034/.864	26.8	1.019	0.038022388	0.003802239	13.48193	132.217	25	63.5	186.4766	1.27	1.27	146.832
.034/.864	45.4	1.732	0.03814978	0.003814978	13.5271	132.66	25	63.5	186.4766	1.27	1.27	146.832
SUM	93.3	3.554	0.038092176	0.003809218	13.50106	132.405	25	63.5	186.4379	1.27	1.27	146.832
.036/.914	24.3	1.035	0.042592593	0.004259259	15.10243	148.11	25	63.5	186.4766	1.27	1.27	146.832
.036/.914	29.9	1.274	0.042608696	0.00426087	15.10814	148.166	25	63.5	186.4766	1.27	1.27	146.832
.036/.914	39.5	1.681	0.042556962	0.004255696	15.08979	147.986	25	63.5	186.4766	1.27	1.27	146.832
SUM	93.7	3.99	0.042582711	0.004258271	15.10012	148.087	25	63.5	186.484	1.27	1.27	146.832
.038/.964	23.2	1.115	0.048060345	0.004806034	17.04118	167.123	25	63.5	186.4766	1.27	1.27	146.832
.038/.964	27	1.295	0.047962963	0.004796296	17.00665	166.784	25	63.5	186.4766	1.27	1.27	146.832
.038/.964	41.6	1.993	0.047908654	0.004790865	16.98739	166.595	25	63.5	186.4766	1.27	1.27	146.832
SUM	91.8	4.403	0.047962963	0.004796296	17.01174	166.834	25	63.5	186.5045	1.27	1.27	146.832

Table A.11 D String Nickel Plated Steel Wound String

Nickel Plated Steel Wound Strings

A String (A2) $f = 110$

String Gauge (in/mm)	Length (cm)	Mass (g)	μ Average (g/cm)	μ Average (kg/m)	τ (kg)	τ (N)	Scale Length (in)	Scale Length (cm)	v (m/s)	λ (m) via v/f	λ (m) via 2*L	f via v/λ
.030/.762	22.7	0.694	0.030572687	0.003057269	6.1	59.8227	25.07874016	63.7	139.883	1.27166733	1.274	109.7986
.030/.762	30.9	0.945	0.030582524	0.003058252	6.1	59.8227	25.07874016	63.7	139.861	1.27146279	1.274	109.7809
.030/.762	40.2	1.23	0.030597015	0.003059701	6.2	60.8034	25.11811024	63.8	140.969	1.28153868	1.276	110.4775
SUM	93.8	2.869	0.030586354	0.003058635	6.133333	60.1496	25.09186352	63.73333333	140.234	1.2748896	1.274666667	110.019
.032/.813	21.5	0.76	0.035348837	0.003534884	7.2	70.6104	25.07874016	63.7	141.334	1.2848549	1.274	110.9372
.032/.813	26.7	0.941	0.035243446	0.003524345	7.2	70.6104	25.11811024	63.8	141.545	1.28677457	1.276	110.9288
.032/.813	45.5	1.607	0.035318681	0.003531868	7.1	69.6297	25.15748031	63.9	140.409	1.27644568	1.278	109.8662
SUM	93.7	3.308	0.035304162	0.003530416	7.166667	70.2835	25.11811024	63.8	141.096	1.28269172	1.276	110.5774
.034/.864	21.1	0.803	0.038056872	0.003805687	7.8	76.4946	25.23622047	64.1	141.775	1.28886123	1.282	110.5887
.034/.864	26.8	1.019	0.038022388	0.003802239	7.7	75.5139	25.23622047	64.1	140.927	1.28115321	1.282	109.9273
.034/.864	45.4	1.732	0.03814978	0.003814978	7.7	75.5139	25.19685039	64	140.691	1.27901238	1.28	109.9151
SUM	93.3	3.554	0.038092176	0.003809218	7.733333	75.8408	25.22309711	64.06666667	141.102	1.28300894	1.281333333	110.1437
.036/.914	24.3	1.035	0.042592593	0.004259259	8.6	84.3402	25.15748031	63.9	140.718	1.27925638	1.278	110.1081
.036/.914	29.9	1.274	0.042608696	0.00426087	8.6	84.3402	25.15748031	63.9	140.692	1.27901462	1.278	110.0873
.036/.914	39.5	1.681	0.042556962	0.004255696	8.6	84.3402	25.19685039	64	140.777	1.27979179	1.28	109.9821
SUM	93.7	3.99	0.042582711	0.004258271	8.6	84.3402	25.17060367	63.93333333	140.735	1.27935426	1.278666667	110.0592
.038/.964	23.2	1.115	0.048060345	0.004806034	9.5	93.1665	25.11811024	63.8	139.231	1.26573784	1.276	109.1153
.038/.964	27	1.295	0.047962963	0.004796296	9.6	94.1472	25.15748031	63.9	140.104	1.27367322	1.278	109.6276
.038/.964	41.6	1.993	0.047908654	0.004790865	9.6	94.1472	25.19685039	64	140.183	1.27439493	1.278	109.6897
SUM	91.8	4.403	0.047962963	0.004796296	9.566667	93.8203	25.14435696	63.86666667	139.861	1.27126866	1.277333333	109.4775
.040/1.015	22.7	1.155	0.050881057	0.005088106	10.12541	99.29993	25	63.5	139.7	1.27	1.27	110
.040/1.015	26.9	1.366	0.050780669	0.005078067	10.10544	99.10401	25	63.5	139.7	1.27	1.27	110
.040/1.015	44.2	2.259	0.051108597	0.00511086	10.17069	99.744	25	63.5	139.7	1.27	1.27	110
SUM	93.8	4.78	0.050959488	0.005095949	10.13385	99.38265	25	63.5	139.651	1.27	1.27	110
.042/1.067	23.9	1.406	0.058828452	0.005882845	11.70696	114.8101	25	63.5	139.7	1.27	1.27	110
.042/1.067	28.7	1.684	0.058675958	0.005867596	11.67661	114.5125	25	63.5	139.7	1.27	1.27	110
.042/1.067	40.8	2.398	0.05877451	0.005877451	11.69622	114.7049	25	63.5	139.7	1.27	1.27	110
SUM	93.4	5.488	0.05875803	0.005875803	11.69326	114.6758	25	63.5	139.702	1.27	1.27	110
.044/1.12	24.2	1.55	0.064049587	0.006404959	12.74597	124.9998	25	63.5	139.7	1.27	1.27	110
.044/1.12	30.4	1.941	0.063848684	0.006384868	12.70599	124.6077	25	63.5	139.7	1.27	1.27	110
.044/1.12	38.5	2.459	0.06387013	0.006387013	12.71026	124.6495	25	63.5	139.7	1.27	1.27	110
SUM	93.1	5.95	0.063909774	0.006390977	12.72074	124.7523	25	63.5	139.714	1.27	1.27	110

Table A.12   A String   Nickel Plated Steel Wound String

Low E String (E2) $f = 82.407$

String Gauge (in/mm)	Length (cm)	Mass (g)	μ Average (g/cm)	μ Average (kg/m)	τ (kg)	τ (N)	Scale Length (in)	Scale Length (cm)	v (m/s)	λ (m) via v/f	λ (m) via 2*L	f via v/λ
.038/.964	23.2	1.115	0.048060345	0.004806034	5.5	53.939	25.19685039	64	105.939	1.2855586	1.28	82.76487
.038/.964	27	1.295	0.047962963	0.004796296	5.5	53.939	25.19685039	64	106.0465	1.286863	1.28	82.84885
.038/.964	41.6	1.993	0.047908654	0.004790865	5.4	52.958	25.23622047	64.1	105.1376	1.2758331	1.282	82.01059
SUM	91.8	4.403	0.047962963	0.004796296	5.46666667	53.612	25.20997375	64.03333333	105.7247	1.2827516	1.280666667	82.54144
.040/1.015	22.7	1.155	0.050881057	0.005088106	5.7	55.9	25.19685039	64	104.816	1.2719304	1.28	81.88748
.040/1.015	26.9	1.366	0.050780669	0.005078067	5.8	56.881	25.23622047	64.1	105.8359	1.2843068	1.282	82.55528
.040/1.015	44.2	2.259	0.051108597	0.00511086	5.9	57.861	25.23622047	64.1	106.4013	1.2911688	1.282	82.99637
SUM	93.8	4.78	0.050959488	0.005095949	5.8	56.881	25.22309711	64.06666667	105.65	1.2824686	1.281333333	82.47971
.042/1.067	23.9	1.406	0.058828452	0.005882845	6.7	65.707	25.19685039	64	105.6846	1.2824714	1.28	82.56611
.042/1.067	28.7	1.684	0.058675958	0.005867596	6.8	66.688	25.27559055	64.2	106.6087	1.2936844	1.284	83.02854
.042/1.067	40.8	2.398	0.05877451	0.005877451	6.8	66.688	25.19685039	64	106.5192	1.2925993	1.28	83.21815
SUM	93.4	5.488	0.05875803	0.005875803	6.76666667	66.361	25.22309711	64.06666667	106.2727	1.289585	1.281333333	82.9376
.044/1.12	24.2	1.55	0.064049587	0.006404959	7.5	73.553	25.11811024	63.8	107.1619	1.3003985	1.276	83.98271
.044/1.12	30.4	1.941	0.063848684	0.006384868	7.3	71.591	25.15748031	63.9	105.8897	1.2849595	1.278	82.85576
.044/1.12	38.5	2.459	0.06387013	0.006387013	7.2	70.61	25.19685039	64	105.1442	1.2759138	1.28	82.14393
SUM	93.1	5.95	0.063909774	0.006390977	7.33333333	71.918	25.15748031	63.9	106.0804	1.2870906	1.278	82.99413
.046/1.167	23.9	1.649	0.068995816	0.006899582	8	78.456	25.15748031	63.9	106.6355	1.2940099	1.278	83.43934
.046/1.167	29.2	2.018	0.069109589	0.006910959	7.9	77.475	25.19685039	64	105.8796	1.284838	1.28	82.71847
.046/1.167	40	2.766	0.06915	0.006915	8	78.456	25.11811024	63.8	106.5165	1.2925665	1.276	83.4769
SUM	93.1	6.433	0.069097744	0.006909774	7.96666667	78.129	25.15748031	63.9	106.3346	1.2904715	1.278	83.21157

Table A.13   Low E String   Nickel Plated Steel Wound String

Nickel Wound Strings

G String (G3) *f* = 195.998

String Gauge (in/mm)	Length (cm)	Mass (g)	μ Average (g/cm)	μ Average (kg/m)	τ (kg)	τ (N)	Scale Length (in)	Scale Length (cm)	v (m/s)	λ (m) via v/f	λ (m) via 2 * L	f via v/λ
.020/.508	26.1	0.4	0.01532567	0.001532567	9.7	95.1279	25.11811024	63.8	249.14043	1.27113762	1.276	195.251
.020/.508	31.3	0.482	0.015399361	0.001539936	9.7	95.1279	25.03937008	63.6	248.54361	1.26809259	1.272	195.396
.020/.508	35.3	0.542	0.015354108	0.001535411	9.7	95.1279	25.03937008	63.6	248.90961	1.26995995	1.272	195.684
SUM	92.7	1.424	0.015361381	0.001536138	9.7	95.1279	25.0656168	63.66666667	248.85068	1.26973005	1.27333333	195.444
.022/.559	23.5	0.471	0.020042553	0.002004255	12.6627	124.1835	25	63.5	248.91746	1.27	1.27	195.998
.022/.559	30.1	0.593	0.019700997	0.0019701	12.4469	122.0672	25	63.5	248.91746	1.27	1.27	195.998
.022/.559	39.2	0.78	0.019897959	0.001989796	12.5714	123.2876	25	63.5	248.91746	1.27	1.27	195.998
SUM	92.8	1.844	0.01987069	0.001987069	12.5604	123.1794	25	63.5	248.97892	1.27	1.27	195.998
.024/.610	22.7	0.512	0.022555066	0.002255507	14.2501	139.751	25	63.5	248.91746	1.27	1.27	195.998
.024/.610	27.3	0.614	0.022490842	0.002249084	14.2095	139.353	25	63.5	248.91746	1.27	1.27	195.998
.024/.610	42	0.949	0.022595238	0.002259524	14.2755	139.9999	25	63.5	248.91746	1.27	1.27	195.998
SUM	92	2.075	0.022554348	0.002255435	14.2451	139.7013	25	63.5	248.87718	1.27	1.27	195.998
.026/.660	21.8	0.562	0.025779817	0.002577982	16.2875	159.7315	25	63.5	248.91746	1.27	1.27	195.998
.026/.660	30.9	0.783	0.025339806	0.002533981	16.0095	157.0052	25	63.5	248.91746	1.27	1.27	195.998
.026/.660	40	1.018	0.02545	0.002545	16.0791	157.688	25	63.5	248.91746	1.27	1.27	195.998
SUM	92.7	2.363	0.025490831	0.002549083	16.1254	158.1415	25	63.5	249.07549	1.27	1.27	195.998
.028/.711	22.2	0.704	0.031711712	0.003171171	20.0352	196.4855	25	63.5	248.91746	1.27	1.27	195.998
.028/.711	31.3	0.989	0.031597444	0.003159744	19.963	195.7775	25	63.5	248.91746	1.27	1.27	195.998
.028/.711	38.7	1.227	0.031705426	0.003170543	20.0313	196.4465	25	63.5	248.91746	1.27	1.27	195.998
SUM	92.2	2.92	0.031670282	0.003167028	20.0098	196.2365	25	63.5	248.92235	1.27	1.27	195.998

Table A.14 G String   Nickel Wound String

D String (D3) *f* = 146.832

String Gauge (in/mm)	Length (cm)	Mass (g)	μ Average (g/cm)	μ Average (kg/m)	τ (kg)	τ (N)	Scale Length (in)	Scale Length (cm)	v (m/s)	λ (m) via v/f	λ (m) via 2 * L	f via v/λ
.022/.559	23.5	0.471	0.020042553	0.002004255	7.1	69.6297	25	63.5	186.389	1.269404476	1.27	146.7631
.022/.559	30.1	0.593	0.019700997	0.0019701	7.1	69.6297	25.07874016	63.7	187.998	1.280361035	1.274	147.5651
.022/.559	39.2	0.78	0.019897959	0.001989796	7	68.649	25	63.5	185.743	1.26500466	1.27	146.2545
SUM	92.8	1.844	0.01987069	0.001987069	7.066667	69.3028	25.02624672	63.56666667	186.754	1.271590057	1.271333333	146.8609
.024/.610	22.7	0.512	0.022555066	0.002255507	7.9	77.4753	25.03937008	63.6	185.336	1.262231072	1.272	145.7043
.024/.610	27.3	0.614	0.022490842	0.002249084	7.9	77.4753	25	63.5	185.6	1.264031966	1.27	146.142
.024/.610	42	0.949	0.022595238	0.002259524	8.1	79.4367	25.07874016	63.7	187.5	1.276972138	1.274	147.1745
SUM	92	2.075	0.022554348	0.002255435	7.966667	78.1291	25.03937008	63.6	186.119	1.267745059	1.272	146.3403
.026/.660	21.8	0.562	0.025779817	0.002577982	9	88.263	25.03937008	63.6	185.033	1.260168783	1.272	145.4663
.026/.660	30.9	0.783	0.025339806	0.002533981	9.1	89.2437	25.07874016	63.7	187.667	1.278104689	1.274	147.3051
.026/.660	40	1.018	0.02545	0.002545	9.1	89.2437	25.07874016	63.7	187.26	1.275334699	1.274	146.9858
SUM	92.7	2.363	0.025490831	0.002549083	9.066667	88.9168	25.0656168	63.66666667	186.767	1.271202724	1.273333333	146.5857
.028/.711	22.2	0.704	0.031711712	0.003171171	11.2443	110.273	25	63.5	186.477	1.27	1.27	146.832
.028/.711	31.3	0.989	0.031597444	0.003159744	11.20378	109.875	25	63.5	186.477	1.27	1.27	146.832
.028/.711	38.7	1.227	0.031705426	0.003170543	11.24207	110.251	25	63.5	186.477	1.27	1.27	146.832
SUM	92.2	2.92	0.031670282	0.003167028	11.23005	110.133	25	63.5	186.48	1.27	1.27	146.832
.030/.762	25.7	0.912	0.035486381	0.003548638	12.58272	123.399	25	63.5	186.477	1.27	1.27	146.832
.030/.762	29.4	1.042	0.035442177	0.003544218	12.56704	123.245	25	63.5	186.477	1.27	1.27	146.832
.030/.762	36.7	1.295	0.035286104	0.00352861	12.5117	122.702	25	63.5	186.477	1.27	1.27	146.832
SUM	91.8	3.249	0.035392157	0.003539216	12.55382	123.115	25	63.5	186.51	1.27	1.27	146.832
.032/.813	23.3	0.974	0.041802575	0.004180258	14.8223	145.362	25	63.5	186.477	1.27	1.27	146.832
.032/.813	28.5	1.187	0.041649123	0.004164912	14.76789	144.829	25	63.5	186.477	1.27	1.27	146.832
.032/.813	41.2	1.721	0.041771845	0.004177184	14.81141	145.255	25	63.5	186.477	1.27	1.27	146.832
SUM	93	3.882	0.041741935	0.004174194	14.80054	145.149	25	63.5	186.475	1.27	1.27	146.832
.034/.864	22.1	1.025	0.04638009	0.004638009	16.44539	161.28	25	63.5	186.477	1.27	1.27	146.832
.034/.864	28.6	1.325	0.046328671	0.004632867	16.42716	161.101	25	63.5	186.477	1.27	1.27	146.832
.034/.864	41.4	1.924	0.04647343	0.004647343	16.47849	161.605	25	63.5	186.477	1.27	1.27	146.832
SUM	92.1	4.274	0.04640608	0.004640608	16.45035	161.329	25	63.5	186.452	1.27	1.27	146.832
.036/.914	23	1.123	0.048826087	0.004882609	17.31269	169.786	25	63.5	186.477	1.27	1.27	146.832
.036/.914	32.5	1.589	0.048892308	0.004889231	17.33617	170.016	25	63.5	186.477	1.27	1.27	146.832
.036/.914	35.6	1.728	0.048539326	0.004853933	17.21101	168.788	25	63.5	186.477	1.27	1.27	146.832
SUM	91.1	4.44	0.048737651	0.004873765	17.28663	169.53	25	63.5	186.505	1.27	1.27	146.832
.038/.964	25.7	1.377	0.053579767	0.005357977	18.99825	186.316	25	63.5	186.477	1.27	1.27	146.832
.038/.964	30	1.633	0.054433333	0.005443333	19.3009	189.284	25	63.5	186.477	1.27	1.27	146.832
.038/.964	34.8	1.905	0.054741379	0.005474138	19.41013	190.355	25	63.5	186.477	1.27	1.27	146.832
SUM	90.5	4.915	0.054309392	0.005430939	19.23643	188.652	25	63.5	186.377	1.27	1.27	146.832

Table A.15 D String   Nickel Wound String

A String (A2) *f = 110*

String Guage (in/mm)	Length (cm)	Mass (g)	μ Average (g/cm)	μ Average (kg/m)	τ (kg)	τ (N)	Scale Length (in)	Scale Length (cm)	v (m/s)	λ (m) via v/f	λ (m) via 2 * L	f via v/λ
.030/.762	25.7	0.912	0.035486381	0.003548638	7.2	70.6104	25.23622047	64.1	141.06	1.28236245	1.282	110.0311
.030/.762	29.4	1.042	0.035442177	0.003544218	7.2	70.6104	25.19685039	64	141.148	1.2831619	1.28	110.2717
.030/.762	36.7	1.295	0.035286104	0.00352861	7.2	70.6104	25.19685039	64	141.46	1.28599654	1.28	110.5153
SUM	91.8	3.249	0.035392157	0.003539216	7.2	70.6104	25.20997375	64.03333333	141.248	1.2838403	1.280666667	110.2727
.032/.813	23.3	0.974	0.041802575	0.004180258	8.4	82.3788	25.23622047	64.1	140.38	1.27618468	1.282	109.501
.032/.813	28.5	1.187	0.041649123	0.004164912	8.5	83.3595	25.15748031	63.9	141.473	1.28612131	1.278	110.699
.032/.813	41.2	1.721	0.041771845	0.004177184	8.4	82.3788	25.19685039	64	140.432	1.27665402	1.28	109.7125
SUM	93	3.882	0.041741935	0.004174194	8.433333	82.7057	25.19685039	64	140.761	1.27965334	1.28	109.9708
.034/.864	22.1	1.025	0.04638009	0.004638009	9.4	92.1858	25.23622047	64.1	140.983	1.28166207	1.282	109.971
.034/.864	28.6	1.325	0.046328671	0.004632867	9.4	92.1858	25.23622047	64.1	141.061	1.28237312	1.282	110.032
.034/.864	41.4	1.924	0.04647343	0.004647343	9.4	92.1858	25.27559055	64.2	140.841	1.28037435	1.284	109.6894
SUM	92.1	4.274	0.04640608	0.004640608	9.4	92.1858	25.24934383	64.13333333	140.943	1.28146985	1.282666667	109.8975
.036/.914	23	1.123	0.048826087	0.004882609	10	98.07	25.23622047	64.1	141.724	3.86167805	1.282	110.5488
.036/.914	32.5	1.589	0.048892308	0.004889231	9.8	96.1086	25.15748031	63.9	140.204	3.82027647	1.278	109.7059
.036/.914	35.6	1.728	0.048539326	0.004853933	9.8	96.1086	25.19685039	64	140.713	3.83414198	1.28	109.932
SUM	91.1	4.44	0.048737651	0.004873765	9.866667	96.7624	25.19685039	64	140.903	3.83869883	1.28	110.0623
.038/.964	25.7	1.377	0.053579767	0.005357977	10.66246	104.5668	25	63.5	139.7	1.27	1.27	110
.038/.964	30	1.633	0.054433333	0.005443333	10.83232	106.2326	25	63.5	139.7	1.27	1.27	110
.038/.964	34.8	1.905	0.054741379	0.005474138	10.89362	106.8338	25	63.5	139.7	1.27	1.27	110
SUM	90.5	4.915	0.054309392	0.005430939	10.79614	105.8777	25	63.5	139.626	1.27	1.27	110
.040/1.015	22.4	1.347	0.060133929	0.006013393	11.96675	117.3579	25	63.5	139.7	1.27	1.27	110
.040/1.015	27.7	1.667	0.060180505	0.006018051	11.97602	117.4488	25	63.5	139.7	1.27	1.27	110
.040/1.015	39.6	2.384	0.06020202	0.006020202	11.9803	117.4908	25	63.5	139.7	1.27	1.27	110
SUM	89.7	5.398	0.060178372	0.006017837	11.97436	117.4325	25	63.5	139.693	1.27	1.27	110
.042/1.067	22.6	1.517	0.067123894	0.006712389	13.35776	130.9996	25	63.5	139.7	1.27	1.27	110
.042/1.067	27.4	1.836	0.067007299	0.00670073	13.33456	130.772	25	63.5	139.7	1.27	1.27	110
.042/1.067	40.2	2.686	0.06681592	0.006681592	13.29648	130.3986	25	63.5	139.7	1.27	1.27	110
SUM	90.2	6.039	0.06695122	0.006695122	13.3296	130.7234	25	63.5	139.732	1.27	1.27	110
.044/1.12	24	1.744	0.072666667	0.007266667	14.46079	141.8169	25	63.5	139.7	1.27	1.27	110
.044/1.12	30.7	2.222	0.07237785	0.007237785	14.40331	141.2533	25	63.5	139.7	1.27	1.27	110
.044/1.12	35.8	2.624	0.073296089	0.007329609	14.58604	143.0453	25	63.5	139.7	1.27	1.27	110

Table A.16   A String   Nickel Wound String

Low E String (E2) *f = 82.407*

String Gauge (in/mm)	Length (cm)	Mass (g)	μ Average (g/cm)	μ Average (kg/m)	τ (kg)	τ (N)	Scale Length (in)	Scale Length (cm)	v (m/s)	λ (m) via v/f	λ (m) via 2 * L	f via v/λ
.038/.964	25.7	1.377	0.053579767	0.005357977	6	58.842	25.23622047	64.1	104.7957	1.271684	1.282	81.74389
.038/.964	30	1.633	0.054433333	0.005443333	6.2	60.803	25.27559055	64.2	105.6894	1.2825295	1.284	82.31262
.038/.964	34.8	1.905	0.054741379	0.005474138	6.4	62.765	25.27559055	64.2	107.078	1.2993798	1.284	83.39407
SUM	90.5	4.915	0.054309392	0.005430939	6.2	60.803	25.26246719	64.16666667	105.8099	1.2845311	1.283333333	82.48353
.040/1.015	22.4	1.347	0.060133929	0.006013393	7	68.649	25.15748031	63.9	106.8458	1.2965618	1.278	83.60389
.040/1.015	27.7	1.667	0.060180505	0.006018051	7	68.649	25.19685039	64	106.8044	1.2960599	1.28	83.44095
.040/1.015	39.6	2.384	0.06020202	0.006020202	6.9	67.668	25.11811024	63.8	106.0198	1.2865391	1.276	83.08764
SUM	89.7	5.398	0.060178372	0.006017837	6.9666667	68.322	25.15748031	63.9	106.5517	1.2930536	1.278	83.37749
.042/1.067	22.6	1.517	0.067123894	0.006712389	7.8	76.495	25.19685039	64	106.7522	1.2954263	1.28	83.40015
.042/1.067	27.4	1.836	0.067007299	0.00670073	7.6	74.533	25.07874016	63.7	105.4663	1.2798224	1.274	82.78362
.042/1.067	40.2	2.686	0.06681592	0.006681592	7.5	73.553	25.15748031	63.9	104.9201	1.2731942	1.278	82.09711
SUM	90.2	6.039	0.06695122	0.006695122	7.6333333	74.86	25.14435696	63.86666667	105.7416	1.2828143	1.277333333	82.76029
.044/1.12	24	1.744	0.072666667	0.007266667	8.3	81.398	25.15748031	63.9	105.8375	1.2843264	1.278	82.81493
.044/1.12	30.7	2.222	0.07237785	0.007237785	8.2	80.417	25.15748031	63.9	105.4077	1.2791105	1.278	82.47861
.044/1.12	35.8	2.624	0.073296089	0.007329609	8.2	80.417	25.15748031	63.9	104.7453	1.271073	1.278	81.96034
SUM	90.5	6.59	0.07281768	0.007281768	8.2333333	80.744	25.15748031	63.9	105.3022	1.27817	1.278	82.41796
.046/1.167	22.1	1.714	0.077556561	0.007755656	8.9	87.282	25.19685039	64	106.085	1.2873295	1.28	82.87888
.046/1.167	30.4	2.371	0.077993421	0.007799342	8.9	87.282	25.19685039	64	105.7874	1.2837191	1.28	82.64644
.046/1.167	37.3	2.912	0.078069705	0.007806971	8.9	87.282	25.19685039	64	105.7357	1.2830918	1.28	82.60605
SUM	89.8	6.997	0.077917595	0.007791759	8.9	87.282	25.19685039	64	105.8389	1.2847134	1.28	82.71045

Table A.17   Low E String   Nickel Wound String

INDEX

A

Aaroe, Kenneth	107
Abu al-Salt	50
al'ud	18
ALE standard	4
alternating current	73
American Wire Gauge	120
ampere	70
Ampere, Andre Marie	52
amplitude	3
anode	68
antinodes	4
Arago, Dominique Francois	52
Aristoxenus	39, 41
Armstrong, Dan	106
asperities	228
attracting field condition	63
averaged density	5

B

bandwidth	81
barbitos	16
Baron Napier of Merchistoun	40
Bartolini, Bill	105
Beauchamp, George	87
Beller, Kevin	110
berimbau	15
Bloch wall	55
Blucher, Steve	108, 109
boundary points	3
bridge	18
Burns, James	99
Butts, J.R.	94

C

cambrium layer	43
Cantigas de Santa Maria	19
capacitance	75
capacitive current	77
capacitive reactance	78
capacitors	116
cathode	68
cents	41
Chandler, Gordon	99
chelys	15
Chobanian, Dennis	106
choke	79, 118
circuits	70
cithara	16
claims	84
Clevinger, Martin	108
coefficient of coupling	79
coefficient of friction	28
coercive force	56
compression	7
condenser	78
conductor	69
consonance	38
constructive interference	3
Cookerly, J. C.	103
Coulomb friction	30
coulomb	70
Coulomb, Charles Augustin de	52, 68
coupling surface	45
coupling	8
crest	5
Crooks, William	68
Curie point	59
current	70

D

damping	9
DeArmond, Harry	92
Democritus	53
destructive interference	3

dielectric constant	77
dielectric	75
Dimarzio, Larry	108
dipoles	76
direct current	73
discontinuities	11
dissonance	38
domains	55, 56
double-pole/double-throw	113
Du Fay, Charles Francois de Costernay	67
dual friction component headstock	31

E

Einstein, Albert	53
elastic boundary	11
electric	67
electromotive force	69
electron	68
elektron	67
Euclid	38

F

Faraday, Michael	52, 68
Fender, Clarence Leo	90, 92, 97, 98, 100, 102, 105, 109
filtering boundary	10
first condition of translational equilibrium	25
flux density	56
forces	2
forcing function	8
Franklin, Benjamin	68
free water	43
frequency	2
frets	17
friction	27
Fuller, Walter	89
ganged pots	114

G

Gauss	57
Geissler, Johann Heinrich Wilhelm	68
ghost waves	12, 63, 64
Gilbert, William	51, 67
gravitational constant	12
Grimshaw, Emile	91
growth ring	42
Guericke, Otto von	67

H

Hall, George	103
harmonic cancellation	11
harmonic	4
Har-mose	21
Hart, Guy	87
headstock	18
Helmholz, Hermann Ludwig Ferdinand van	68
hertz	2
hysteresis	56

I

inductance	79
inductive reactance	79
inductors	78, 118
insulator	70
intermediate interference	3

J

Jacobs, Charles T.	85
Joule, James Prescott	68

K

kanon	38
Keller, Ralph	92
Kelley Jr., Joseph J.	97
kerf joint	43
kinetic friction	31
Knoblaugh, Armand	88

L

Lace, Donald	109
law of inertia	1
Lesti, Arnold	86
libriform fibers	42
line of force	8
linear mass density	5
lodestone	51

longitudinal motion	7	permittivity	76
Lover, Seth	95, 102	Petrus Peregrinus	51
lute	17	phorminx	16
luthier	18	pickup	82
lyra	15	pith	43

M

		plain sawn	42
Maenads	38	Planck, Max Karl Ernst Ludwig	53
magnetic flux	57	Plato	38
magnetic moment	54	pot	113
magnetic viscosity	59	potential energy	8
Marin Mersenne	41	potentiometer	113
Marquis Yi of Zeng	38	power	70
mass	1	pre-stabilizing	60
matter model	9	Priestly, Joseph	68
maxwell	57	Principia	1
Maxwell, James Clerk	52	Ptolemy	38
Mccarty, Ted	102	push/pull pots	114
McNaughton, Alan	106	Pythagoras	38
Miessner, Benjamin F.	85	Pythagorean comma	39
Mitchell, John	52	Pythagorean theorem	32
momentum	1	Pythagoreans	38
musical bow	15		

Q

Musschenbroek, Peter van	68	qanun	38
mutual inductance	79	quality factor	80

N

		quarter sawn	42
neck	17	quitarra Latina	19

R

Newton, Isaac	12		
no field condition	63	rarefaction	7
nodes	4, 10	ravanastron	17
normal force	24, 30	relative permeability	57

O

		relative permittivity	77
Oersted, Christian	52	reluctance	58
Ohm's Law	71	repelling field condition	63
open-tip jack	120	resistance	69, 71
oscillation	2	resistors	114

P

		resonance	8, 80
parasitic capacitance	75	rift sawn	42
period	2	Root Mean Square	73
permeability	57	Rule of 18	39

S

Sappho	16
schematic	122
Schrodinger, Erwin	54
Schultz, Charles	96
Scientific method	39
single-pole/double-throw	112
single-pole/single-throw	112
sinusoidal wave	4
standing waves	4, 48
static friction	31
stationary point of contact	46
Stich, Willi Lorenz	103, 104
string boundary conditions	45, 46
Sturgeon, William	52
Sunshine, Herbert S.	88

T

tailpiece	18
taper	114
tension	5
Thales of Miletus	51, 67
Theophrastus	67
thermal after-effect	59
Thompson, Joseph John	68
Three Brothers' Cave	14
Tomb of Nakht	21
tracheids	42
transverse wave	2
traveling wave	3
trough	5
truss rod	20
tuners	18

U

unit crystal	55
unit pole	56
unobvious	84

V

vectors	24
velocity	1
voicing	6
Volta, Alessandro Guiseppe	68
voltage	69
volts	69

W

Warner, Lorenzo	101
wave equation	27
wave motion	1
wave path	47
wavelength	3, 4
weber	57
Webster, Jimmy	96
Weiss molecular field	59
wood vessels	42
working thickness	44

Y

Young's modulus	7

Z

Zhu Zaiyu	40
Zoller, Attila	102